Fallen Among Reformers

SYDNEY STUDIES IN AUSTRALIAN LITERATURE

Robert Dixon, Series Editor

The **Sydney Studies in Australian Literature** series publishes original, peer-reviewed research in the field of Australian literary studies. It offers engagingly written evaluations of the nature and importance of Australian literature, and aims to reinvigorate its study both locally and internationally.

Alex Miller: The Ruin of Time
Robert Dixon
Australian Books and Authors in the American Marketplace 1840s–1940s
David Carter and Roger Osborne
Christina Stead and the Matter of America
Fiona Morrison
Colonial Australian Fiction: Character Types, Social Formations and the Colonial Economy
Ken Gelder and Rachael Weaver
Contemporary Australian Literature: A World Not Yet Dead
Nicholas Birns
Elizabeth Harrower: Critical Essays
Ed. Elizabeth McMahon and Brigitta Olubas
Fallen Among Reformers: Miles Franklin, Modernity, and the New Woman
Janet Lee
The Fiction of Tim Winton: Earthed and Sacred
Lyn McCredden
Gail Jones: Word, Image, Ethics
Tanya Dalziell
Gerald Murnane: Another World in This One
Ed. Anthony Uhlmann
Richard Flanagan: Critical Essays
Ed. Robert Dixon
Shirley Hazzard: New Critical Essays
Ed. Brigitta Olubas

Fallen Among Reformers

Miles Franklin, Modernity, and the New Woman

Janet Lee

SYDNEY UNIVERSITY PRESS

First published by Sydney University Press

© Janet Lee 2020
© Sydney University Press 2020

Reproduction and communication for other purposes

Except as permitted under the Act, no part of this edition may be reproduced, stored in a retrieval system, or communicated in any form or by any means without prior written permission. All requests for reproduction or communication should be made to Sydney University Press at the address below:

Sydney University Press
Fisher Library F03
University of Sydney NSW 2006
AUSTRALIA
sup.info@sydney.edu.au
sydneyuniversitypress.com.au

A catalogue record for this book is available from the National Library of Australia.

ISBN 9781743326886 paperback
ISBN 9781743326893 epub
ISBN 9781743327074 mobi
ISBN 9781743326909 pdf

Cover image: Stella Miles Franklin, from the Papers of Miles Franklin (MS 681), National Library of Australia, http://nla.gov.au/nla.obj-229628581.

Contents

Acknowledgements	vii
Introduction	1
Part I: Work	33
1 A Picture of Contemporary Existence	35
2 Like a Thunderstorm	49
Part II: Marriage	65
3 That Vexatious Failure	67
4 Her Boldest Throw	83
5 The Chicago Spinsters	101
Part III: Men	117
6 Moral Squalor	119
7 Courage and Confession	137
Conclusion	151
Works Cited	169
Index	183

Acknowledgements

My thanks are due to the College of Liberal Arts at Oregon State University for research funding, leave, and support for this project, and especially to colleagues in the School of Language, Culture, and Society who helped sustain my commitment to it. Thanks are especially due to the Oregon State University Center for the Humanities for a fellowship that came at a crucial time at the initiation of this book and provided a community of colleagues who generously gave invaluable feedback. Thanks also to Leonora Rianda, Loretta Wardrip, and Jo Jensen for clerical support.

I express gratitude to Robert Dixon and Susan Murray at Sydney University Press and to anonymous reviewers along the way who helped shape this project and earlier versions of it. Portions of chapters in Part I are published as "Miles Franklin and 'The Survivors'", *Australian Literary Studies* 26.1 (2011): 83-93; and "'The Waiter Speaks': Stella Miles Franklin and the Chicago Garment Workers' Strike", *Women Studies International Forum* 34 (2011): 290-301. Earlier versions of chapters in Part II are published as "'Marriage Among the 'Murkans': Miles Franklin's Marriage Problem Stories", *Australian Feminist Studies* 26:70 (2011): 469-483; "Aunt Sophie Smashes a Triangle': Stella Miles Franklin and the 1913 Adultery Narratives", *Journal of Australian Studies* 37: 2 (2013): 225-242; "The Chicago Spinsters: Stella Miles Franklin and the New Woman Response to Marriage Inequality", *Women's Studies International Forum* 44 (May-June 2014): 1-9; and "How Miles Franklin Queered a Queer's Party", *Hecate: An Interdisciplinary Journal of Women's Liberation* 39: 1/2 (2014): 64-71. Portions of versions of chapters in Part III are published as "Miles Franklin on American Manhood and White Slavery: The Case of 'Red Cross Nurse'", *Australian Literary Studies* 23:1 (2007): 36-48; "'Living in Sin': Money and Morals in 'Virtue', a Play by Stella Miles Franklin", *Australian Literary Studies* 31: 5 (2016): 1-12; and "'Early Flower Meets Petted Lion': The New Woman and the Pro-Feminist

Man in Miles Franklin's 'Lost' Novel, *The Net of Circumstance*", *Women: A Cultural Review* 28: 3 (2017): 193–216.

    I would like to thank Leigh Dale for her guidance as well as Susan Shaw, Becky Warner, and Anita Helle for their insight and support. Thanks also to family and friends who have sustained me and to my mother, Leti Halvorsen, for providing me with a Sydney home away from home. A large debt of gratitude is due to the late Jill Roe, who helped me sort out some discrepancies and kindly answered numerous questions about the mass of documents in the Franklin archives. I am eternally grateful to her meticulously detailed biography, without which I could not have completed this project. I dedicate this book to her.

Introduction

Such Destiny

Stella Miles Franklin, known for her debut novel, *My Brilliant Career,* whose feminist rebellion against Australian culture and literary traditions caused both acclaim and consternation when it was published in 1901, describes the heroine of one of its sequels, *Cockatoos,* as "fallen among reformers", unable to pursue her art and suffering from a heart "frozen" by this secret tragedy. "Such destiny for an artist is more fatal than for a merchant to fall among bandits", she declares.[1] This quote reflects Franklin's own situation among reformers in the decade between 1906 and 1915 when, seeking adventure and new literary opportunities, she moved to Chicago, Illinois, in the heartland of the United States. For here she would also work tirelessly in social reform as National Secretary of the National Women's Trade Union League (NWTUL), the first national association dedicated to organise and advocate for women workers, and co-editor of its journal, *Life and Labor,* where she cultivated an extensive network of friends and colleagues, and indulged in the social pleasures of this dazzling and culturally diverse metropolis. It most likely felt like a secret tragedy because she led a double life in Chicago, sometimes typing her stories late into the night at the end of a long workday and spending weekends in bed writing and barely venturing out into the cold and dreary Chicago weather. And even though during this period Franklin produced the mass of New Woman novels, short stories, and plays that have received relatively scant attention and which comprise the focus of this book, she published very little. The New Woman literary tradition sought to write about the modern woman in new ways,

---

1 Miles Franklin (Brent of Bin Bin), *Cockatoos: A Story of Youth and Exodists* (Sydney: Angus & Robertson, 1954), 251.

representing redefinitions of gender and advocating women's desire and independence.² This passion for women's freedom, originally employed in *My Brilliant Career*, undergirds all Franklin's Chicago work, literary and otherwise. As Susan Magarey notes, Franklin was "so committedly a feminist" that it formed the focus of both her "causes" – writing and activism – such that "working for one fuelled the other".³

This decade in the United States highlights Franklin as a socially-engaged fictional polemicist who took the modern world of urban Chicago as her subject and employed the romance tradition to dramatise the effects of sexism and misogyny on women's lives. This tradition went beyond realism's focus on the known world to that of fantasy and desire, including visions for social and cultural freedoms originating in this tumultuous and transformative historical moment. Franklin's feminist realist approach nuanced the proximity to "truth" and employed fictional expressions of women's agency that articulated their own reality from their own experience and represented transformations of women's consciousness to realise and change these conditions. Such an aesthetic was motivated by political interest; it tested and subverted women's material conditions at the same time that it troubled a literary establishment bent on redefining fiction as a masculine project.⁴ Indeed, these Chicago works continue *My Brilliant Career*'s attempt to unsettle masculinist traditions as well as facilitate the "dismemberment of the female fictional world of the nineteenth century" through its propulsion into the twentieth – or what Stephen Garton called the "considerable gulf" between a sentimental literature of "an older 'woman movement'" and that of more modern feminist activism.⁵ My hope is to include Franklin's Chicago writing in this temporal location, again recognising this cusp as a site of struggle between differently structured oppositions where a feminised sentimentality was a "past to be outgrown [and] a present tendency to be despised", but also noting the ways its feminist representational strategies and innovations function as bridges in their inclusion of elements from both Victorian fiction and later twentieth-century

---

2 Ann Heilmann, *New Woman Fiction: Women Writing First-Wave Feminism* (New York: St. Martin's Press, 2000).
3 Susan Magarey, "*My Brilliant Career* and Feminism", *Australian Literary Studies* 20, no. 4 (2002): 389.
4 Molly Youngkin, *Feminist Realism at the Fin de Siècle: The Influence of the Late-Victorian Woman's Press on the Development of the Novel* (Columbus: The Ohio State University Press, 2007), 7.
5 Susan K. Martin, "Relative Correspondence: Franklin's *My Brilliant Career* and the Influence of Nineteenth-Century Australian Women's Writing", in *The Time to Write: Australian Women Writers, 1890-1930*, ed. Kay Ferres (New York: Penguin, 1993), 64; Stephen Garton, "Contesting Enslavement: Marriage, Manhood and *My Brilliant Career*", *Australian Literary Studies* 20, no. 4 (2002): 345.

writing.⁶ *Fallen Among Reformers* thus emphasises the ways these hybridised bridging strategies of Franklin's feminist realism, first displayed in *My Brilliant Career*, were shaped between 1906 and 1915 by a version of modernity arising from her experience of women's condition in this diverse American metropolis. In other words, Franklin's Chicago stories and plays reflect a specific narrative authority earned from living and working in this landscape and engaging with these particular cultural and political dimensions of modernity. As an expatriate, the transnational acted as a barometer for her encounter with modernity.⁷

In her consideration of "rebel writers", Jane Eldridge Miller also discusses these bridging strategies of New Woman literature and specifically refers to *My Brilliant Career* as "an early modernist novel" in its formal rebellion against Victorian literary traditions. A close reading of Miller's argument reveals that she is not claiming Franklin's novel as an example of the kind of literature we understand as conventionally modernist so much as representing a "modernism of content" that served as an antecedent to later approaches. Her case is that New Woman employment of subversive protagonists, disruptive plotting and innovative narrative strategies exerted pressure on traditional form and convention, foreshadowing future stylistic changes associated with modern literature.⁸ Modernism, at least how we understand it now as an experimental aesthetic, was not the New Woman's, and certainly not Franklin's, inclination. Along with contemporaries like Katherine Susannah Prichard, Vance and Nettie Palmer, and James Devaney, her goal was to articulate and promote an Australian national poetics that tended to oppose itself to experimental modernism and perpetuated a divide between Australian nationalism and stylistic innovations originating elsewhere (something she confirmed later in life in the collection of essays, Laughter, Not for a Cage).⁹ A rejection of stylised approaches of modernism was in this sense a rejection of global cosmopolitanism.

However, as Anouk Lang points out, Australian nationalist writers were more easily able to integrate international exposure to modern political thought than to modernist literary experimentation, and certainly this was true in Franklin's case.¹⁰ Her engagement with US modernity was precisely through the gender and

---

6   Suzanne Clark, *Sentimental Modernism: Women Writers and the Revolution of the Word* (Bloomington: University of Indiana Press, 1991), 2.
7   Paul Giles, *Antipodean America: Australasia and the Constitution of U.S. Literature* (New York: Oxford University Press, 2013), 331.
8   Jane Eldridge Miller, *Rebel Women: Feminism, Modernism and the Edwardian Novel* (London: Virago, 1984), 118, 7.
9   Robert Dixon, "Home or Away? The Trope of Place in Australian Literary Criticism and Literary History", *Westerly* 54, no.1 (2009): 16.
10 Anouk Lang, "Modernity in Practice: A Comparative View of the Cultural Dynamics of Modernist Literary Production in Australia and Canada", *Canadian Literature* 209 (2011): 59.

class politics of the city. It was these politics that helped produce representational innovations in her feminist realist approach with its bridging of the traditions between the centuries. In other words, despite Franklin's self-conscious response to the stylistic innovations of modernism, she did engage with cosmopolitanism as an expatriate, was energised by the new American realism in Chicago, and sought to integrate these into a romance tradition. As Lang insists in reference to both Franklin's *My Brilliant Career* and Katherine Susannah Prichard's *Coonardoo*, written almost two decades later, these approaches were vital in the emergence and expression of modern literature because they "rupture[ed] conventions in ways analogous to canonical Anglo-American modernists, albeit in ways not usually thought of as modernist by critics" (and I add in the case of Franklin specifically, also by the authors themselves).[11]

The Cosmopolitan Bushwoman[12]

Born on 14 October 1879 in Talbingo, New South Wales, Australia, Stella Maria Sarah Miles Franklin was destined to become a writer and would publish her first essay in the *Goulburn Evening Penny Post* on the topic of the school picnic. She spent her early years at the Brindabella sheep station in southeastern Australia in a valley west of what is now Canberra, the national capital, and later in a small dairy holding near Bangalore located at a railway stop on the line to Goulburn, south west of Sydney. Witnessing extreme hardships as a result of the 1890s economic Depression and its effects on working peoples' lives, including her own family who lost land and status during this period, Franklin was invigorated by the cultural moment and her place in it. She eagerly absorbed socio-economic analyses of these events in the pages of the *Post*, and especially its forum on class inequity that showcased sweeping proposals for land reform preventing occupation by a single privileged class. The *Post*'s editor, T.J. Hebblewhite, supported woman suffrage and routinely exposed injustice of all kinds.[13] In addition, Franklin's politics were shaped by the nationalist magazine, *The Bulletin*, despite its sexist bent.[14] This

---

11 Lang, "Modernity in Practice", 61.
12 Kerryn Higgs, "The Cosmopolitan Bushwoman", Review of *Her Brilliant Career: The Life of Stella Miles Franklin* by Jill Roe (Cambridge, MA: Harvard University Press, 2009), *Women's Review of Books* 27, no. 4 (July / August 2010): 10–12.
13 Bruce Scates, "*My Brilliant Career* and Radicalism", *Australian Literary Studies* 20, no. 4 (2002): 373.
14 Katie Holmes, "Spinster Indispensable: Feminists, Single Women and the Critique of Marriage, 1890–1920", *Australian Historical Studies* 29, no. 110 (1998): 68–90; Susan Sheridan, *Along the Fault Lines: Sex, Race and Nation in Australian Women's Writing* (St. Leonards, NSW: Allen and Unwin, 1995).

periodical self-consciously contributed to a new literary culture for the new nation. As a vociferous reader, Franklin was also influenced by interrogations of gender prompted by a literary heritage that included such writers as Ada Cambridge, Rosa Campbell Praed, Mary Gaunt, and Jessie Catherine Couvreur (Tasma).[15] These transformations in literary representations of gender mark the cultural and technological changes associated with modernity taking place in Australian society at the turn of the century when White women were becoming educated and enfranchised, were claiming their right to public space, and were increasingly unwilling to accept their traditional domestic destinies.[16]

Such influences would coalesce to form the production of Franklin's best known work: the manuscript originally titled "My Brilliant (?) Career", which was guided for publication by Australian nationalist writer Henry Lawson, and eventually published in 1901 by Blackwell without the question mark, much to Franklin's dismay, and with Lawson's introduction outing "Miles" as a woman, and a young one at that.[17] As a "federation" text published the same year the six Australian colonies became federated as an independent commonwealth, it employed literary expressions of nationalist politics in ways that would be hailed as original and definitively Australian. And, while its feminist protagonist, Sybylla Penelope Melvyn, sought freedom and refused to choose between love and ambition, she represented the "Australian Girl" or "Bush Girl" who openly criticised gender arrangements of late-Victorian society, but whose mixture of boldness, innocence, and common sense secured her participation in nationalist mythologies.[18]

The Australian Girl emerged in the domestic fiction of colonial Australia through the nineteenth century in, for example, Catherine Helen Spence's novel, *Clara Morison* (1854), Rosa Campbell Praed's *An Australian Heroine* (1880), and Ethel Turner's children's story, *Seven Little Australians* (1894). Alongside executing the work of colonial economics, the Australian Girl became integral to, and served as a contrast to, masculinist cultural icons like the Lone Hand and the Bushman.[19]

---

15 Susan Magarey, Sue Rowley, Susan Sheridan, eds., *Debutante Nation: Feminism Contests the 1890s* (St. Leonards, NSW: Allen and Unwin, 1993).

16 Martin, "Relative Correspondence", 54–70.

17 Ian Henderson, "Gender, Genre, and Sybylla's Performative Identity in Miles Franklin's *My Brilliant Career*", *Australian Literary Studies* 18, no. 2 (1997): 165; Magarey, "*My Brilliant Career* and Feminism", 389–398; Susan Sheridan, "*My Brilliant Career*: The Career of the Career", *Australian Literary Studies* 20, no. 4 (2002): 330–335; Elizabeth Webby, "Reading *My Brilliant Career*", *Australian Literary Studies* 20, no. 4 (2002): 350–358.

18 Susan Gardner, "My Brilliant Career: Portrait of the Artist as a Wild Colonial Girl", in *Gender, Politics and Fictions: Twentieth Century Australian Women's Novels*, ed. Carole Ferrier (St Lucia: University of Queensland Press, 1985), 22–43.

19 Tanya Dalziell, *Settler Romances and the Australian Girl* (Perth: University of Western Australia Press, 2004); Tanya Dalziell, "Colonial Displacements: Another Look at *My Brilliant Career*", *ARIEL* 35, nos. 3–4 (2004): 39–56; Angela Woollacott, *To Try Her Fortune*

The courage and innovation of *My Brilliant Career*, however, centred on its expression of this new literary nationalism alongside a feminist journey negotiating romance and independence. In essence, its narrative illustrated the exclusionary politics of the nationalism it sought to represent. As Susan Magarey points out, it was precisely the ways bush nationalism participated in the marginalisation of women's writing by privileging a realist, though thoroughly masculinist voice set against the feminised sentimentality and bourgeois excesses of colonialist discourse, which helped shape *My Brilliant Career*.[20] Ultimately however, the "bracing figure" of the Australian Girl could not be accommodated in this novel, poised as she was to critique her domestic and intellectual confinements, and she would morph instead into the "New Woman".[21] Free-spirited and independent, educated and critical of marriage, these new models of femininity disrupted conventional ideals about Victorian womanhood.[22] Although the Australian Girl had much in common with the New Woman in this resistance to conventional femininity, and Magarey for one has dubbed her a "specifically Australian" manifestation of the New Woman, the Australian Girl's association with national identity reflected a distinct set of cultural and discursive conditions that set her apart.[23] She also tended to be seen as less radical than the more improper New Woman, was more closely associated with pastoral than urban contexts, and was more preoccupied with issues of girlhood rather than womanhood and sexual desire.[24] Sybylla Penelope Melvyn functioned as the Australian Girl who bridges these feminist types, emerging as a "'new woman' for a new century" who sought freedom, including sexual agency, and refused to choose between marriage and ambition.[25] Franklin thus arrived in Chicago with these New Woman insights and achievements already under her belt.

---

    in London: *Australian Women, Colonialism, and Modernity* (Oxford: Oxford University Press, 2001).
20 Magarey, "*My Brilliant Career* and Feminism", 391.
21 Michelle J. Smith, "The 'Australian Girl' and the Domestic Ideal in Colonial Women's Fiction", in *Domestic Fiction in Colonial Australia and New Zealand*, ed. Tamara Wagner (London: Routledge, 2014), 83.
22 Ann Ardis, *New Woman, New Novels: Feminism and Early Modernism* (New Brunswick: Rutgers University Press, 1990).
23 Gillian E. Sykes, "The New Woman in the New World: *Fin de Siècle* Writing and Feminism in Australia". Ph.D. thesis, School of English, Art History, Film and Media, University of Sydney, 2002, 132.
24 Susan Magarey, "History, Cultural Studies, and Another Look at First-Wave Feminism in Australia", *Australian Literary Studies* 106 (1996): 108; Leonie N. Prime, "The New Woman and the Australian Girl". MPhil thesis, Department of English, 1998, University of Western Australia, 15; Sykes, "The New Woman in the New World", 125.
25 Delys Bird, "Miles Franklin" in *Dictionary of Literary Biography: Australian Literature* (Volume 230), ed. Selina Samuels (Farmington Hills, MI: Gale, 2001), 120.

Introduction

However, in the years between *My Brilliant Career* and arrival in the US, Franklin would continue to create sassy feminist protagonists even more audacious than the first. The "emphatically feminist" "The End of My Career", written between 1902 and 1904, was soundly rejected fearing "the spectre of libel actions", but formed the basis for *My Career Goes Bung*, published in 1946.[26] Franklin also worked on a novel, "On the Outside Track", similarly rejected and reworked into *Cockatoos* and published in 1954, which again according to Leigh Dale, "clearly and provocatively" signalled its relationship to Sybylla Melvyn.[27] A third novel about marriage equality and Australian woman suffrage, *Some Everyday Folk and Dawn*, was also written during this period and met the same fate, although it would be revised in 1909 when Franklin was working in Chicago and published with indifferent reviews that same year by Blackwood.

These manuscripts were all initiated during Franklin's propulsion into the feminist circles of Rose Scott and Vida Goldstein of Sydney and Melbourne, respectively, who helped lead the Australian women's movement and its struggle for social, political, and economic rights. Scott was an ardent suffragist, who in 1902 founded the Women's Political Education League, and was known for her evening salons in Woollahra that attracted a diverse group of writers and activists. She befriended Franklin and took her under her wing. Similarly, Goldstein was also influential, running for political office in 1903 as one of the first four women to stand for federal parliament.[28] With Scott and Goldstein as mentors, Franklin participated in the "first wave" of the Australian women's movement, as demonstrated in an interview she gave for *The Vote*, the British Women's Freedom League (WFL) magazine in 1911 about her work for Australian women's social and political equality. "Suffrage", she explained, was "the one great question which possessed me; you see, I was fresh from keen work for the cause . . . I could not quench my burning enthusiasm for the political equality of men and women".[29]

During this period Franklin was reading the feminist periodical, *Woman's Voice*, as well as Louisa Lawson's *The Dawn* magazine.[30] This was the "great age of newspaper journalism", and women like Lawson had a distinct "voice of their own": a voice that was shaped by the instrumental role of New Woman writers in

---

26 Verna Coleman, "Foreword" to Miles Franklin, *The End of My Career* (New York: St. Martin's Press, 1981), 2.
27 Leigh Dale,"'Only Scratch the Surface': Reading Franklin's Cockatoos", *Southerly* 67, no. 1–2 (2007): 337.
28 Marilyn Lake, *Getting Equal: The History of Australian Feminism* (St Leonards, NSW: Allen and Unwin, 1999).
29 Stella Miles Franklin, quoted by A.A. Smith, "Organising Women Workers in America", *The Vote*, (16 September 1911): 256.
30 Jill Roe, *Stella Miles Franklin: A Biography* (Sydney: Fourth Estate/Harper Collins, 2008), 141.

the development of the transnational popular periodical press.[31] Franklin was also developing her own voice and published thirty-one feature articles for the *Sydney Morning Herald* and the *Daily Telegraph* under the pen name "Vernacular" between April 1905 and January 1906.

These feminist networks and the experiences fostered within them launched Franklin's expatriate adventures. Initiated by literary disappointments and in anticipation of new opportunities (including hopes for a singing career and motivation to disengage from a lovelorn suitor and second cousin, Edwin Bridle of Wilga Vale, who continued to write that "love would overcome all obstacles"), Franklin's travel to the United States was ultimately complicated by the catastrophic earthquake that hit San Francisco in May 1906.[32] Disembarking in its aftermath following a long sea voyage, Franklin mobilised feminist contacts procured by these Australian mentors, left California, and travelled east. Goldstein had secured Franklin with an introduction to Carrie Whelan, friend of suffragist Carrie Chapman Catt, whom she met in 1902 after attending the International Council of Women and testifying before Congress for US women's suffrage.[33] Similarly, as International Secretary of the National Council of Women in New South Wales, Scott mobilised US contacts for Franklin.[34] Women expatriates played a "unique role" in Australian history as feminist ambassadors, revered in part because of the early date of woman suffrage compared to elsewhere. It was because they were Australian and not in spite of it that Franklin and her compatriots were especially welcomed in the United States.[35] And, as Susan Pfisterer and Carolyn Pickett remind us, the Australian women's movement during this period was an early challenge to British colonialism, suggesting that feminists like Franklin who actively resisted authority in collective social movements as well as in literary canons "had a post-colonial maturity well ahead" of their time.[36]

---

31 Susan Sheridan, "Louisa Lawson, Miles Franklin and Feminist Writing, 1888–1902", *Australian Feminist Studies* 3, no. 7–8 (1988): 31; Ann Heilmann and Margaret Beetham, eds., *New Women Hybridities: Femininity, Feminism, and International Consumer Culture 1880–1930* (New York: Routledge, 2004), 2–3.
32 Roe, *Stella Miles Franklin*, 207; Coleman, *Her Unknown Brilliant Career*, 74.
33 Janice N. Brownfoot, "Vida Jane Goldstein", *Australian Dictionary of Biography* at http://adb.anu.edu.au/biography/goldstein-vida-jane-6418.
34 Judith Allen, *Rose Scott: Vision and Revision in Feminism* (Oxford: Oxford University Press, 1994).
35 Marilyn Lake, "Between Old Worlds and New: Feminist Citizenship, Nation, and Race, the Destabilisation of Identity" in *Suffrage and Beyond: International Feminist Perspectives*, edited by Caroline Daley and Melanie Nolan (Auckland: University of Auckland Press, 1994), 278.
36 Susan Pfisterer and Carolyn Pickett, *Playing with Ideas: Australian Women Playwrights From the Suffragettes to the Sixties* (Sydney: Currency Press, 1999), 11; Brigitta Olubas, "'Infinite Rehearsal' in the Work of Miles Franklin", *New Literature Review* 18 (1989): 37-47.

Unfortunately knowledge about Franklin's early months in the United States is relatively scant, in part because the pocket diary entries that survive do not begin until 1909, but it appears that she worked briefly in hotels in Utah and Colorado during a cross-country journey from California to Chicago.[37] Franklin eventually arrived in the city in October 1906 when snow was already on the ground, armed with letters of introduction to one of the most famous of all US Progressive-era reformers, Jane Addams. Addams was founder of the Hull House settlement and its array of facilities that included a theatre and art gallery, gymnasiums, kindergarten, libraries, and a cooperative residence for working women, all aimed at enriching the experience of new immigrants and providing them with education and support.[38] Hull House was attended by a wide array of reformers and labour leaders, who would form the new feminist networks invigorating Franklin's work and life in Chicago.

It was at Hull House where Franklin met compatriot Alice Henry, who was engaged in secretarial work for the Chicago branch of the National Women's Trade Union League (NWTUL), an organisation dedicated to improving the working lives of Chicago women. Over twenty years Franklin's senior, Henry would become a life-long friend and the two at first took lodgings together. It seems Franklin worked as a domestic servant on first arriving in the city, and may have been employed in a department store and most likely as a clerk having taken a short course in stenography. We know from a cheery article in the *Book Lover*, written by Franklin "lost in the wilds of America", that she was undertaking a sociological study of "the terrifying work dens of Chicago". Reflecting on such insights and her experiences of the annual US Independence Day celebrations, she would also cheekily tell her Australian readers that "it would be healthier for America to make less noise on the 4th, and more effort on the other 364 days to free herself from far worse things than Old England".[39]

Franklin's mood would shift, however, in late 1907 on hearing that her beloved sister Linda, with whom she was particularly close, had died of pneumonia, and her parents had lost their home at Penrith. Franklin responded with a nervous collapse, was hospitalised, and would eventually be rescued by Henry, who took Franklin to recuperate at Wayside, the family home of writer and reformer Henry Demarest Lloyd, which often served as a gathering place of "repose and stimulus for like-minded people". She had already met the son, William (Bill) Bross Lloyd,

---

37 Eleanor Flexner, *Century of Struggle: The Woman's Rights Movement in the United States* (New York: Atheneum, 1974), 244-5. Jill Roe corroborates in *Stella Miles Franklin*, 125.
38 Jane Addams, *Twenty Years at Hull House* (New York: Macmillan), 191.
39 S.M. Franklin, *Book Lover*, 1 September 1907: 97-98, reprinted as "Letter from Chicago", in *A Gregarious Culture: Topical Writings of Miles Franklin*, ed. Jill Roe and Margaret Bettison (St Lucia: University of Queensland Press, 2001), 31, 33.

lawyer and real estate agent, and may have been familiar with his younger brother, Demarest, employed at that time at the American Automobile Company. Both were Harvard-educated and wealthy, and both would go on to feature prominently in Franklin's romantic life.[40]

After this episode in 1907, it was again Henry who stepped in and helped Franklin get her first job in Progressive reform. She introduced Franklin to the influential Margaret Dreier Robins, an outspoken and wealthy philanthropist and advocate for working women, and the newly elected President of the NWTUL. Franklin started work on 1 January 1908 as Dreier Robins' personal secretary, employed to undertake labour research and clerical tasks at a salary of twelve dollars a week. At this time she was living in the Harvard Hotel on Washington Street on the West Side of the city, but would move to 12 East Indiana Street in late 1909. By 1910 the executive board of the NWTUL put Franklin on the payroll as unofficial National Secretary and invested her with the everyday administrative responsibilities of the League, raising her salary to twenty-five dollars a week, and making the position official the following year at the biennial convention. At this time Franklin was living in an airy fourth floor room in a residential hotel on 200 East Superior Street within walking distance to the NWTUL offices on Dearborn Street in downtown Chicago.[41]

Franklin also began co-editing the League's journal, *Life and Labor,* with Henry in 1911.[42] This magazine, which sold for 10 cents a copy, sought to mobilise working women, but appealed mostly to the feminist reformers who worked for the cause.[43] Such opportunities sustained Franklin for nine years in Chicago, supported the literary endeavours undertaken there, and provided impressive work experience and personal connections with some of the most famous feminist and labour activists, and writers of the day. Franklin also enjoyed a very full social life, singing in the League chorus, visiting and dining out with friends on an almost daily basis (apartments at the time tended to lack kitchen facilities), and attending the theatre, opera, concerts, and the cinema. Alongside fighting off the attentions of Edwin Bridle, Franklin was also seriously courted by a number of suitors in Chicago, including the Lloyd brothers and her friend and colleague Emma Pischel's older brother, Fred, who worked in his father's lumber and estate business in north-west Chicago.

---

40 Roe, *Stella Miles Franklin*, 126, 127.
41 Roe, *Stella Miles Franklin*, 130, 151.
42 Roe, *Stella Miles Franklin*, 128, 147, 141; Susan Amsterdam, "The National Women's Trade Union League", *Social Service Review* 56, no. 2 (1982): 259–272.
43 Diane Kirkby, "Miles Franklin on Dearborn Street, 1906–15", *Australian Literary Studies* 10, no. 3 (1982): 347.

Introduction

In late 1915 Franklin left Chicago for London. Although there is "no clear record of her decision" to move, she again had hopes for fresh publishing venues. A visit to London some years previously had also "assuaged her homesickness" and given new opportunities for community with friends and expatriates. In addition, these opportunities were set against conflict within the leadership of the NWTUL and overwork associated with the journal, which she had taken over as lone editor in 1915. Perhaps there was also a surge of patriotism for the Allies as war raged in Europe. In London she worked for the National Housing and Town Planning Council and served briefly in Macedonia with the Scottish Women's Hospital for Foreign Service as an assistant cook during World War I.[44]

In London Franklin wrote the unpublished novel, "Sam Price from Chicago" (1921) and began a series of novels under the pseudonym Brent of Bin Bin that resulted in six books in a series that were published out of order of their chronology, and which spanned her time there and her return to Australia in 1932: *Up the Country* (1928); *Ten Creeks Run* (1930); *Back to Bool Bool* (1931); *Prelude to Waking* (1950); *Cockatoos* (1954); and *Gentlemen at Gyang Gyang* (1956). These novels chronicle the history of families who settled in the high Monaro country of Australia where Franklin spent her early childhood. The book *All That Swagger* (1936) also deals with this region, and like the other stories is what Delys Bird describes as "full of surprising and sometimes infuriating detail, fresh and invigorating, lapsing into extravagant self-indulgence, sometimes embarrassingly artificial and clichéd, often opinionated, but always eccentric and individual". Such writing, declares Bird, went against "the marketing and critical reception of her work that for so long sought to conventionalize it".[45] Finally, along with the novels *Bring the Monkey* (1931), *Old Blastus of Bandicoot* (1931), *Pioneers on Parade* (1939) (with Dymphna Cusack), and an array of plays, essays, and commentary, Franklin would also write a series of essays published as *Laughter, Not for a Cage* posthumously in 1956. These works reflect her love of place, her support for liberal values of individual political rights and free speech, and would consolidate her contributions to Australian nationalist literature. This *oeuvre* would form the basis for Franklin's notoriety as an iconic Australian author and mentor of young Australian writers that included Dymphna Cusack, who wrote *Come in Spinner* in 1951, Eleanor Dark, known for her novel *The Timeless Land* (1941), and Katharine Susannah Prichard, who wrote *Coonardoo* (1929). She also supported author Jean Devanney and poet and peace-activist Ian Mudie. Franklin died on 19 September 1954 at the age of almost 75 years, following heart problems and subsequent illnesses. Her ashes were spread in Jounama Creek, Talbingo, near the homestead

---

44 Roe, *Stella Miles Franklin*, 150, 189, 193–4.
45 Bird, "Miles Franklin", 126.

where she was born and raised. After her death it was revealed that Franklin, in "a generous act of personal philanthropy for Australian literature, unequalled in its time", established the Miles Franklin Literary Award for the year's best novel or play that presents "Australian life in any of its phases".[46]

Despite her nationalist bent, as Nicholas Birns has noted, Franklin did not "wish to be bound by Australia" – and certainly, as *Fallen Among Reformers* attests, she was not bound in this way. Like Christina Stead, Franklin perceived the world "more astute[ly]" precisely because she was Australian. Although Franklin did not share with Stead her caution about feminism, the fact of being a woman (a condition that Birns in reference to Stead describes as Stead's "other country") produced a "natality" – or general condition of existence – that was shared by both.[47] Also shared by both was their profound engagement with American culture and politics, which energised these authors to write about gender, politics, and modernity.[48] With this in mind I offer Franklin's transnational credentials and make the case for the incorporation of such expatriate cultural production into our cultural histories and memories. As Elizabeth Webby notes, not only have Franklin's "Australian" books defined her literary reputation, but critics have contributed to this short-sightedness by overlooking the transnational context of Franklin's work and forgetting that national literatures are always globally produced.[49] I hope to contribute to her legacy by resurrecting this expatriate writing from the Chicago years.

The Book

Fallen Among Reformers aims to amend this little-understood record of Franklin's Chicago years (1906-1915) by focusing on a series of manuscripts (short stories, plays, and novels) included within three thematic sections. Part I, "Work", explores Franklin's immersion in the opportunities and challenges of Progressive-era social reform, especially her socialist feminist critique of capitalism and class relations in Chicago. The broad theme, "Marriage", comprises the focus of Part II. A key aspect

---

46 Paul Brunton, *Miles Franklin: A Brilliant Career?* State Library of New South Wales (March 2004), 20.
47 Nicholas Birns, *Contemporary Australian Literature: A World Not Yet Dead* (Sydney: Sydney University Press, 2015), 26, 28.
48 Fiona Morrison, *Christina Stead and the Matter of America* (Sydney: Sydney University Press, 2019).
49 Elizabeth Webby, "Miles Franklin Revealed in Her Letters", *Sydney Morning Herald* ("*Spectrum*"), 2 October 1993, 11; Robert Dixon and Brigid Rooney, eds., *Scenes of Reading: Is Australian Literature a World Literature?* (Melbourne: Australian Scholarly Publishing, 2013).

in debates about gender relations, anxieties about the status and transformation of marriage in the new century reflected ways women were claiming the necessity of work and education while resisting the compulsory nature of matrimony. Part III, "Men", addresses masculinity and the state of American manhood. In particular, Franklin was concerned with men's sexual behaviours and the consequences of "male vice" on women and wives, and was especially intrigued by the promises of companionate relationships with the egalitarian New Man, the caring and compassionate feminist suitor.[50] Each of these thematic sections tangles with overlapping aspects of Franklin's personal and political passions. My exploration of these themes focuses especially – although not exclusively – on Franklin's Chicago writing that was unpublished during her lifetime, and which resides in the Franklin archive in the Mitchell Library of the State Library of New South Wales. My hope is that these less-accessible manuscripts may be brought to light and recognised as examples of a continuity of earlier (and better-known) concerns for gender and economic justice.

Part I: Work in the Windy City

Chicago, located in the upper-Midwest state of Illinois and known facetiously as "the Windy City" for its icy gales, was a rowdy metropolis with a long history of poverty, crime, and worker rights as well as their suppression, in part a result of the growing rage of a newly politicised immigrant population. Here "robber barons" with conspicuous wealth gained from exploited immigrant labour faced off against union agitators on a daily basis. Remembered for its infamous Haymarket riots of 1886, when workers and police clashed with deadly results, the Pullman strike of 1894, spearheaded by labour leader Eugene Debs, and the Teamsters' strike and the Stockyard strike of 1905, Chicago was rapidly becoming one of the most radical and violent US cities.[51] With this as its challenge, the NWTUL certainly had its work cut out for it, as did Franklin as she sought to serve the working women and labour leaders of the city.

On her arrival, Franklin was welcomed into networks of dedicated Chicago reformers, who were active in local and state-wide campaigns establishing new public schools, playgrounds, and parks, and improving urban housing and sanitation. In particular, Hull House reformers initiated and lobbied for suffrage reform, protective labour legislation, occupational health and safety provisions, and unemployment and workers' compensation. They also helped establish the US

---

50 Tara MacDonald, *The New Man, Masculinity and Marriage in the Victorian Novel*. (New York: Routledge, 2016).
51 Richard Lindberg, *Chicago by Gaslight: A History of Chicago's Netherworld, 1880–1920* (Chicago: Academy Chicago Publishers, 1996).

Children's Bureau. They sought tax reform and the regulation of corporations and monopolies through anti-trust laws, and they supported the goals of organised labour and the rights of working people.[52] The feminists Franklin met as she began to participate in this work included University of Chicago academics Edith Abbott (who wrote the influential Women in Industry [1910]) and Sophonisba Breckinridge (who co-founded the Chicago School of Civics and Philanthropy), as well as Edith's sister Grace Abbott, who directed the Immigrants' Protective League, and Mary McDowell, known for her anti-sweatshop crusades and work with the Women's International League for Peace and Freedom. These reformers sought to respond to the vast changes brought about by industrialisation, urbanisation, and the consequences of unbridled capitalist expansion: a momentum energised by the foundation of the Progressive Party in Chicago in 1912.[53] Reform was aided by investigative journalism and also by critical academics at the University of Chicago whose political frameworks were shared in public talks and lectures that helped shape the reform goals of the period.[54]

This was the community into whose company Franklin was thrown and with whom she would find meaningful employment. Her work with the NWTUL involved administering the work of the League, including preparing for and running meetings, attending rallies, lobbying at the state capital for the eight-hour bill for working women, helping organise and attending NWTUL conventions, as well as supporting strikers and helping hold their picket lines.[55] She laboured alongside such notable labour and socialist leaders as Agnes Nestor, Rose Schneiderman, Mary Kenney O'Sullivan, Leonora O'Reilly, and Elizabeth Maloney: officers and activists within women's unions and various branches of the working women's movement. She also worked closely with the male union leaders of the Chicago Federation of Labor, who included a section for the League in their monthly *Union Labor Advocate*. Through these alliances and affiliations, Franklin met the Pankhursts, was introduced to the redoubtable Emma Goldman, whom she heard speak several times, and came to know the writer and feminist economist Charlotte Perkins Gilman as a friend and colleague.[56] The NWTUL also sponsored

---

52 Eleanor J. Stebner, *The Women of Hull House: A Study in Spirituality, Vocation, and Friendship* (Albany: State University of New York Press, 1997).
53 Arthur S. Link and Richard L. McCormick, *Progressivism* (Arlington Heights, IL: Harlan, Davidson, 1983).
54 Andrew Feffer, *The Chicago Pragmatists and American Progressivism* (Ithaca: Cornell University Press, 1993); Maureen Flanagan, *Seeing With Their Hearts: Chicago Women and the Vision of the Good City, 1871–1933* (Princeton, NJ: Princeton University Press, 2002).
55 Allen F. Davis, "The Women's Trade Union League: Origins and Organization." *Labor History* 5, no.1 (1964): 3–17.
56 Coleman, *Her Unknown Brilliant Career*, 88; Kirkby, "Miles Franklin on Dearborn Street", 198.

Franklin's travel to London in 1911, where she was not only introduced to feminists in the WFL, but enjoyed a brief fling with several beaus.[57] Chicago, and the NWTUL in particular, thus offered Franklin opportunities to expand her personal and political life and participate more fully in broad cross-class feminist networks that invariably invigorated her writing.

A key point discussed in this first section of *Fallen Among Reformers* is that reform work gave Franklin first-hand experience of the deep injustices associated with the excesses of capitalism that consolidated her understanding of class relations. She was exposed to the terrible working conditions of working women and children in factories around the city, saw police brutality against the most vulnerable of its citizens, and witnessed strikes and the starvation that resulted from them. Although these experiences were new in the sense they were uniquely about the injustices of US modernity in this particular turbulent city, as already mentioned Franklin was exposed to economic injustice through her keen interest in Australian progressive political movements of the day. Such budding political zeal is amply demonstrated in *My Brilliant Career* as Sybylla decries the system that subordinates the poor as an outrageous and immoral act. Rather, Franklin's motivation for social activism blossomed and matured in the United States. Franklin biographer Jill Roe insisted Chicago was Franklin's "university", complete with friendship and passionate idealism.[58] "I love my work very much", Franklin wrote in a letter to her aunt in 1913, "as it brings me in to close friendship with everyone in the world who is making thought and history".[59]

Alongside the specific material conditions of working against injustice in Chicago, it is also important to note that Franklin's Chicago was widely recognised for being what critics have dubbed "the literary capital of the United States".[60] This "Chicago literary renaissance" critiqued corporate expansion and saw theatre, literature, and the arts as vehicles for enlightenment and transformation.[61] Writers and poets like Carl Sandburg and Sherwood Anderson propagated realist and naturalist approaches combining nostalgia for rural and small-town living alongside the violence and poverty of urban life. This was a growth of a literary culture that coincided with the advent of modernism and helped orchestrate its encounter, especially through the "little movement" as evidenced by Margaret

---

57 Roe, *Stella Miles Franklin,* 131, 150.
58 Jill Roe, "The World of Miles Franklin", *Southerly* 54, no. 4 (1995): 86.
59 Quoted in Brunton, *Miles Franklin: A Brilliant Career?* 10.
60 Henry Louis Mencken, "The Literary Capital of the United States" in *Our American Books*, Francis Hackett ed., (New York: W.B. Huebsch, 1920).
61 Jan Pinkerton and Randolph H. Hudson. eds., *Encyclopaedia of the Chicago Literary Renaissance* (New York: Fact on File Inc., 2004); Carl Smith, *Chicago and the American Literary Imagination, 1880–1920* (Chicago: University of Chicago Press, 1984).

Anderson's *Little Review* magazine and Maurice Browne's Little Theatre movement.[62] Although Franklin actively consumed these artistic opportunities through attendance at the theatre and lectures and so forth, she did not actively participate in their literary circles, and remained relatively secretive and elusive about her writing. Perhaps this was prompted by a lack of self-confidence associated with earlier literary rejections as well as by certain aspects of this movement itself. For example, invigorated by the gritty realism depicted by these Chicago writers and poets, Franklin was most likely less enthusiastic about emerging experimental and stylistically innovative forms. She had inherited a framework that held Australian nationalist and European literature as opposed and "mutually exclusive possibilities", which would let modernism "fall inevitably on the non-nationalist side".[63] In addition, masculinist and somewhat misogynous, the Chicago literary scene was known for its male leadership by such artists as Floyd Dell and Theodore Dreiser, whom Franklin did not like.[64] Women writers, poets, and dramatists such as Anna Morgan, Alice Gerstenberg, Harriet Monroe, and Margaret Anderson were also involved in the movement, but peripherally. Still, despite her reticence and the reasons for it, Franklin referred to members of this literary movement as "our crowd" nonetheless.[65] Certainly having this venue for artistic representation and critique right on her doorstep proved energising. Innovative drama at Hull House and the variety of progressive plays performed through Chicago's Little Theatre movement were especially formative for Franklin's aspirations as a playwright. As Roe emphasises, Chicago "created some of the most powerful works of contemporary literature . . . [as well as] poetry and the theatre. Dull would she be of soul to remain unaffected, and whatever Miles Franklin may have been, dull she was not".[66]

These first-hand working experiences among the excesses and deprivations of capitalism, and their interpretations shaped by the lenses established by Chicago's literary elite, were readily utilised in Franklin's New Woman manuscripts discussed in Part I of *Fallen Among Reformers*. Chapter 1, "A Picture of Contemporary Existence", discusses the effects of Franklin's work and political endeavours for class equality and gender justice as represented in her 1908 protest play, "The Survivors", which she wrote when working as Margaret Dreier Robins' personal secretary. It employs the radical sociology of Chicago and its impressive exploration

---

62 Liesl Olson, *Chicago Renaissance: Literature and Visual Art in the Midwest Metropolis* (New Haven, CT: Yale University Press, 2017).
63 Lang, "Modernity in Practice", 58.
64 Miles Franklin to Frank Ryland, 21 April 1943, quoted in Jill Roe, *My Congenials: Miles Franklin and Friends in Letters*, vol. 1: 1879–1938 (Sydney: Angus & Robertson, 1993), 91.
65 Quoted in Roe, *Stella Miles Franklin*, 161.
66 Roe, *Stella Miles Franklin*, 143.

of industrial capitalism, especially the analysis of evolutionary theories shaping debates on gender and poverty. Through the mouthpiece of the New Woman negotiating the urban social conditions of modernity, Franklin critiques the Spencerian notion of the "survival of the fittest" as an ethical explanation for injustice. She also employs a New Woman actress, who not only secures a romantic relationship of equals, but uses her passion for socially responsible theatre to educate about its role in the pursuit of social justice.

Typed on the back of NWTUL stationery, "The Survivors" is marked "Shawondasee, August," in Franklin's handwriting. Located in the small, historic, seaside town of Stonington in the state of Connecticut, Shawondasee was the family estate of Margaret Dreier Robins and her sister Mary E. Dreier, President of the New York chapter of the Women's Trade Union League (WTUL). Franklin was on holiday and had been staying with suffragist Jessie H. Childs in New York, and then had taken a trip out to Shawondasee with Mary Dreier when she wrote – or at least got the inspiration for -- this play.[67] Almost nothing is known about its progress as producible drama, although Franklin would have faced the "formidable barrier" erected during this period against feminist protest plays in traditional venues. Despite critics often finding Franklin's plays "lacking in artistry",[68] like those of her feminist contemporaries, these plays often came across as didactic precisely because they came out of a feminist tradition providing women with a vehicle and an alternative to public speaking. "The Survivors" was eventually performed in 2008 to celebrate its centenary year.[69]

By 1911 Franklin was working as National Secretary for the NWTUL and beginning her co-editorship of *Life and Labor* with Alice Henry. Chapter 2, "Like a Thunderstorm", focuses on Franklin's writing about this period and particularly the infamous Chicago Garment Workers' Strike, which began in September 1910 and lasted until early 1911, when Franklin was in charge of publicity. Along with local socialists, religious leaders, and concerned citizens, the Chicago chapter of the WTUL responded to the strike both in terms of movement organisation and humanitarian assistance. Led by Margaret Dreier Robins, it provided fundraising, education, publicity, and relief distribution, as well as the documentation of grievances and participation in a Joint Strike Conference Board with labour

---

67   Roe, *Stella Miles Franklin*, 129.
68   Katherine E. Kelly, ed. *Modern Drama by Women, 1880s–1930s: An International Anthology* (London: Routledge, 1996), 5; Robyn R. Warhol. *Gendered Interventions: Narrative Discourse in the Victorian Novel* (New Brunswick, NJ: Rutgers University Press, 1989), xii–xv.
69   "The Survivors" was performed at the State Library of New South Wales on September 11, 2008, produced by Jocelyn Hedley with support from Macquarie University. See also, Jocelyn Hedley, "The Unpublished Plays of Miles Franklin". Master's Thesis, School of English, Media and Performing Arts, UNSW, 2007, 18.

representatives and union leaders. Profoundly affected by this injustice and the extreme hardships experienced by women workers and their families during the cold winter months, Franklin wrote a series of articles in *Life and Labor* about the strike ("Chicago at the Front: A Condensed History of the Garment Workers' Strike"; "Holding the Fort"; and "The End of the Struggle") published in *Life and Labor* in January, February, and March 1911, respectively. They employ advocacy journalism, an approach challenging traditional dichotomies of news culture on the one hand and literature on the other. As Ann Heilmann points out, such hybridity of form and narrative structure was central to New Woman writing hoping to reach a broad audience, and, as a result, opened up a "gynocentric space for the discussion and dissemination of feminist thought".[70] Although Franklin's pre-Chicago journalism produced engaging and lyrical discussion of topics ranging from weather, place, flora, and cultural issues like women's dress, and could not be characterised as advocacy journalism, Roe suggests this writing "strengthens the hypothesis that Miles Franklin was really cut out to be a journalist, a possibility sustained during her American years".[71] Such efforts certainly gave Franklin voice and experience vital for her editorship with *Life and Labor*, as well as resources to help pay for her fare to Chicago.

Chapter 2 also discusses "The Waiter Speaks", a dramatic sketch about the strike, which addresses relationships between reformers and working people and makes connections across classes of workers. The play is undated, but evidence exists for its completion in early 1913 rather than at the time of the strike. This is based upon the fact that one of the waiters in the play announces that "little Bessie Mahoney", of the Waitresses' Union spoke at the Waiters' Union meeting. "Mahoney" represents Elizabeth Maloney who organised the Chicago Waitresses' Union, Local 484, and sat on the executive board of the Chicago WTUL. In February 1913 Franklin published an article about Elizabeth Maloney in *Life and Labor*, writing that Maloney had "the previous evening" addressed the Chicago Waiters' Union: "the first woman who has ever done so".[72] Along with Chapter 1, "Like a Thunderstorm" explores Franklin's focus on class politics, underscoring Bruce Scates' argument for understanding Franklin's legacy as a "powerful political testament: a relentless critique of the inequalities of class as well as gender, [and] a passion for social justice".[73]

---

70 Ann Heilmann, *New Woman Strategies: Sarah Grand, Olive Schreiner, Mona Caird* (Manchester: Manchester University Press, 2004), 2.
71 Roe, *Stella Miles Franklin*, 11.
72 S.M. Franklin, "Elizabeth Maloney and the High-Calling of the Waitress", *Life and Labor* (February 1913): 40.
73 Scates, "Miles Franklin and Radicalism", 370.

Introduction

Part II: The Promise and Peril of Marriage

Resistance to domesticity and compulsory matrimony was invigorated by social and legal changes of the new century that enabled some women in Australia and the US to pursue careers and higher education, own property and their own wages, and in some cases divorce spouses and retain custody of children. An increasing age at marriage, a declining birth-rate among white populations, and increasing proportions of middle-class women never marrying all fuelled these emerging cultural anxieties.[74] These instabilities, and the literary responses to them, were widely perceived as threats to the stability of the family and to society in general, especially since the indissolubility of marriage was strongly enforced at this time and both sexual morality and romantic traditions preached the inevitability and infallibility of marriage. Chicago, like many urban centres during this period, was preoccupied with these issues of gender and modernity, and especially by impulses energised by the mobility of women in its public urban spaces.[75] As Liz Conor explains, the technologies and practices of modernity created specific spatial formations, producing the metropolis as a form of "human geography" configuring urban femininity and diminishing woman's "natural" role as wife and mother.[76] A central trope thus emerged with the female subject representing a disruption of traditional gender performances generally and marriage roles specifically, illustrating what Wendy Parkins has described as the "instabilities of modern subjectivity" aroused by the gendered conditions of city life.[77]

It was exactly these material and discursive responses to the potential demise of such institutions as marriage that established the New Woman as both target and panacea for the problems and questions associated with gender.[78] A term coined by Irish feminist Sarah Grand in 1894, there was actually no rigid definition of the New Woman, and, ironically, it evolved as a term used against those very women who were outspoken enough to disavow it.[79] Described as "complex and contradictory", the New Woman signature was thus embraced by a diversity of

---

74 Sally Ledger, *The New Woman: Fiction and Feminism at the Fin de Siècle* (College Station: Penn State University Press, 1999), Carol L. Bacchi, "The Woman Question in South Australia", in E. Richards, ed., *The Flinders History of South Australia: Social History* (Adelaide: Wakefield Press, 1986), 405; Ann Summers, *Damned Whores and God's Police: The Colonization of Women in Australia* (London: Allen Lane, 1975), 305.
75 Carla Cappetti, *Writing Chicago: Modernism, Ethnography, and the Novel* (New York: Columbia University Press, 1993).
76 Liz Conor, *The Spectacular Modern Woman: Feminine Visibility in the 1920s* (Bloomington: Indiana University Press, 2004), 46–7.
77 Wendy Parkins, "Moving Dangerously; Mobility and the Modern Woman", *Tulsa Studies in Women's Literature* 20, no. 1 (2001): 77.
78 Ann Heilmann, *The Late-Victorian Marriage Question: Volume 1: Marriage and Motherhood* (New York: Routledge, 1998).

characters, including Australian author and suffragist Catherine Helen Spence, who announced in 1905 on her 80th birthday, "I am a New Woman, and I know it".[80] Basically employed to describe any woman who resisted templates of traditional femininity and by extension marriage, this label could be said to represent such diverse identities as free love advocates, outspoken women critiquing the free love advocates, educated spinsters and wives who deemed to prioritise a career over domesticity, or merely independent working and middle-class women trying to make a living.[81] In terms of these wage-earning women in early-twentieth-century US society, their bodies were read through the categories of employment they inhabited: a practice that distinguished class differences and set up certain expectations of public and private behaviours. The working-class "shop girls" and "office girls", employed as Franklin's New Woman heroines, provided a vehicle of urban fantasy that precipitated different responses than the bookish, educated, middle-class spinster. The former were more likely to be implicated in anxieties about new sexual performances while the latter precipitated worries about hetero/sexual repression: both of course potentially disrupting traditional courtship and marriage practices. Franklin portrays both versions of the New Woman in her stories and plays explored in Part II, but especially the former version. An "office girl" herself, she was surrounded in Chicago by what Kate Krueger describes as the "male projection of the new urban everywoman".[82]

Literature depicting the New Woman's response to marriage was especially effective in appropriating and transforming a feminised romance tradition. This tradition bound authors to literary conventions encouraging sentimental discourses that appealed to the sympathy of the reader and inevitably ended in marriage (or else madness or death).[83] However, as cultural changes in modernising societies of the early-twentieth century prompted new kinds of literature, New Woman writers of the period across the continents, still bound by literary conventions, responded by blending feminised discourses of romance with a politicised rhetoric of realism that transformed marriage as women's literary

---

79 Sarah Grand, quoted by Martha H. Patterson, "The New Aspect of the Woman Question" in *The American New Woman Revisited*, ed. by Martha H. Patterson (New Brunswick, NJ: Rutgers University Press, 2008), 29.

80 Susan Magarey, *Passions of First Wave Feminists* (Sydney: University of New South Wales Press, 2001), 43.

81 Ann Heilmann, ed., *Feminist Forerunners: New Womanism and Feminism in the Early Twentieth Century* (London: Pandora, 2003); Charlotte J. Rich, *Transcending the New Woman: Multiethnic Narratives in the Progressive Era* (Columbia: University of Missouri Press, 2009).

82 Kate Krueger, "Evelyn Sharp's Working Women and the Dilemma of Urban Romance", *Women Writing* 19, no. 4 (2012): 564.

83 Rita S. Kranidis, *Subversive Discourse: The Cultural Production of Late Victorian Feminist Novels* (New York: St. Martin's Press, 1995).

destiny by writing "beyond the ending".[84] In Chicago Franklin continued this critique of marriage, creating narratives that centred the lives and needs of the modern urban American woman negotiating between love and vocation. Her purpose included what Sarah Grand called "books of good intention" that aimed to energise a broad feminine reading public to question gender injustice.[85]

Part II of *Fallen Among Reformers* includes three chapters that investigate Franklin's literary response to marriage and domesticity. Chapter 3, "That Vexatious Failure", discusses Franklin's courtship and marriage-problem narratives, which include four short stories. The first is "Teaching Him", one of Franklin's earliest Chicago works. Undated, it is mentioned in Franklin's diary in late 1909 when she was working as Margaret Dreier Robins' private secretary. Alongside leadership roles in her Stenographers and Typists' Union, that year Franklin also served as NWTUL biennial convention secretary, facilitating convention demands that included the 8-hour day for women, elimination of night work, and provision of minimum wage for the sweated trades.[86] As she wrote "Teaching Him", Franklin was providing clerical assistance for the New York Clothing Workers' Strike. Her spirits were up, *Some Everyday Folk and Dawn* was in press (she had yet to see the lukewarm reviews), and she had just published a piece on "American Working Women" for the *Sydney Morning Herald*.[87]

The second story is "Mrs. Mulvaney's Moccasins", also undated, but sent to a literary agent in April 1911.[88] The Chicago Garment Workers' Strike had just ended, and Franklin and colleagues were mobilised to the state capital in Springfield as part of a delegation led by Margaret Dreier Robins aboard a "suffrage special" to represent working women's issues in a woman suffrage debate. Upon her return she helped the Chicago League support a switchboard operators' strike.[89] The third story, "The Illogical Sex", also dates to 1911 and was published in the September issue of *Life and Labor*. By September Franklin had returned from the NWTUL conference and was focused on assisting striking mineworkers and their families in Pittsburgh, Pennsylvania, as well as preparing the new issue of *Life and Labor*.

---

84 Sally Ledger, "The New Woman and the Crisis of Victorianism" in *Cultural Politics at the Fin de Siècle*, ed. Sally Ledger and Scott McCracken (Cambridge: Cambridge University Press, 1995); Rachel Blau DuPlessis, *Writing Beyond the Ending: Narrative Strengths of Twentieth-Century Women Writers* (Bloomington: Indiana University Press, 1985), 4.
85 Sarah Grand (Frances McFall), *The Beth Book: Being a Study of the Life of Elizabeth Caldwell McClure, A Woman of Genius* (Introd. Elaine Showalter), (New York: Dial, 1980 [1897]), 460.
86 Miles Franklin, Pocket diary, 11 December 1909, ML MSS 364/2.
87 Roe, *Stella Miles Franklin*, 132, 133; Miles Franklin, Chicago, "American Working Women", *Sydney Morning Herald*, 15 December 1909: 5, reprinted in *A Gregarious Culture*, 34–37.
88 Franklin, Pocket diary, 15 April 1911.
89 Roe, *Stella Miles Franklin*, 143–4.

Franklin tended to do the "dogsbody" work of the magazine that included copyediting, preparing dummy, and negotiating with the printers.[90] "The Illogical Sex" is unsigned but almost definitely written by Franklin, containing as it does all her literary mannerisms and loquacious writing style, complete with folksy pseudonym, "Grandpa Griddle". The final story discussed in Chapter 3 is one of Franklin's later Chicago narratives, "A Business Emergency", written in 1915 under the obtuse pseudonym Mr. and Mrs. Ogniblat L'Artsau (Talbingo, Australia spelled backwards). "A Business Emergency" presents a decidedly frank critique of marriage that also reflects Franklin's more mature, and increasingly jaded, take on the institution as a "business", the acceptance of which might be a rational decision given the trade-offs against women's poorly paid wage labour.

These stories that trouble marriage and domesticity are also shaped by Franklin's romantic entanglements. These include several young men met during summer school at the University of Wisconsin in 1909 as well as Guido Mariotti, who gave Italian lessons to Franklin's friend, Editha Phelps, and whom Franklin accompanied on various dining and theatre outings during 1912, but who was eventually relegated to a line in her diary as "a most vacuous specimen of humanity".[91] More serious suitors throughout this period included the kindly Fred Pischel, and both Lloyd brothers. Correspondence with Demarest started in earnest in 1912 when he was working as a journalist, but by 1913 it is his brother Bill who appears in Franklin's diary on an almost daily basis. Demarest or "Demi" is featured again in 1914 and her relationship with Bill would continue to 1915. A key factor affecting Franklin at this time that shaped her disinclination for marriage was the war now raging in Europe. Franklin understood militarism to be a manifestation of male aggression and vice, which soured her thoughts about intimacy and prompted her to recognise mothering as rearing cannon fodder in a world gone mad.

A central justification for marriage reform in both Australia and the US was its role in women's sexual degradation, confining them to involuntary childbearing, requiring them to bear the brutality of men's bad behaviours, and exposing them to disease as a consequence of husbands' sexual practices.[92] Louisa Lawson, for example, described the marital chamber as one of "horrors", and Bessie Harrison Lee, the Australian temperance evangelist, dubbed it the "most unholy gratification of man's worst desires". Rose Scott, also privately advised mothers to "warn" their daughters about avoiding the "disgusting desire" associated with matrimony generally and male lust in particular, citing "its dangers, its pains, its perils".[93] These

---

90 Roe, *Stella Miles Franklin*, 147, 152.
91 Quoted in Roe, *Stella Miles Franklin*, 131; Franklin, Pocket diary, 12 and 19 September 1912; 13 November 1912.
92 Marilyn Lake, "Sexuality and Feminism: Some Notes on their Australian History", *Lilith* 7 (1991): 33–5.

Introduction

critics advocated social purity feminism, a particular brand of nineteenth- and early-twentieth-century feminism also subscribed to by Franklin, which made the case that men's sexual and social freedom protected their sexual transgressions, enslaved women emotionally and economically, and posed a threat to the stability of the family and society.[94]

Despite this problem with male lust, or perhaps in the face of it, Franklin was also interested in women's sexual desire: the focus of Chapter 4, "Her Boldest Throw", which discusses Franklin's novel, *On Dearborn Street* (undated, *circa*. 1913). It presents a modern version of Sybylla Melvyn in the form of the more mature and urban, although equally frank and independent, New Woman heroine, Sybyl Penelo, who demands autonomy and expresses sexual agency through negotiations of love and independence with two suitors: the supportive feminist New Man and the arrogant playboy, who mirror Fred Pischel and Demarest Lloyd, respectively. These negotiations are overshadowed in the novel by the spectre of war, as they also were in Franklin's personal life. Started in 1913, *On Dearborn Street* was revised as late as 1918 and eventually published posthumously in 1981.[95] At its inception Franklin noted reading *The Freewoman* magazine, which advocated sexual agency and encouraged women to remain unmarried. Although it published articles on women's issues generally, the notoriety of *The Freewoman* rested on its frank discussions of sexual morality. Like many of her contemporaries (and this is one reason why *The Freewoman* was relatively short-lived), it is known that Franklin was at odds with the politics of its editors.[96] Still, issues of sexual politics were in the air, and shaped Franklin's world.[97] These politics also produced two extraordinary unpublished chapters or outtakes from *On Dearborn Street* that include "When Bobby Got Religion", providing insights on the story's playboy, and the "Miss Toby's Party: How I Queered a Queer's Party", presenting an alternative picture of the New Man.

A key feature of such sexual politics was the role of the spinster, and especially the spinster feminist, who functioned as an easy target for those wishing to promote

---

93 Louisa Lawson, quoted in Judith Allen, *Rose Scott: Vision and Revision in Feminism* (Melbourne: Oxford University Press, 1994), 89; Bessie Harrison Lee, quoted in Patricia Grimshaw, "Bessie Harrison Lee and the Fight for Voluntary Motherhood" in *Double Time: Women in Victoria–150 Years*, ed. Marilyn Lake and Farley Kelly (Melbourne: Penguin, 1985), 139–47; Rose Scott, quoted in Allen, *Rose Scott*, 89.

94 Lucy Bland, *Banishing the Beast: Sexuality and the Early Feminists* (New York: New Press, 1995); Angelique Richardson, *Love and Eugenics in the Late-Nineteenth Century: Rational Reproduction and the New Woman* (Oxford: Oxford University Press, 2003); and Beryl Satter, *Each Mind a Kingdom: American Women, Sexual Purity and the New Thought Movement, 1875–1920* (Berkeley: University of California Press, 2001).

95 Roe, *Stella Miles Franklin*, 209, 223.

96 Grimshaw, "Bessie Harrison Lee and the Fight for Voluntary Motherhood", 139–47.

97 Franklin, Pocket diary, 30 January 1913; Roe, *Stella Miles Franklin*, 173.

marriage, nationhood, and the importance of reproduction. In the nineteenth century, for example, spinsters were pitied and ridiculed and held up as a warning to women who dared to shirk their domestic destinies.[98] By the first decades of the twentieth century, however, and without giving up on attempts to reform marriage, feminists began to represent singleness as a desirable state, enabled by social and economic changes that allowed some women to live more independent lives outside the confines of matrimony.[99] The subversive trope of the unmarried woman, central in New Woman literature, is addressed in Chapter 5, "The Chicago Spinsters", which declares the spinster a worthy and attractive figure. It explores several manuscripts in order to make this claim.

First is Franklin's short story "Uncle Robert's Wedding Present", written in 1908 at the same time and location as "The Survivors".[100] Franklin was hard at work as Robins' personal secretary, but starting to enjoy the amusements of the city. This story portrays a clever and spirited spinster, who helps a young couple get married by intervening on their behalf with the bride's benefactor and then looks forward to her own marriage with him. The second narrative, "When Cupid Tarried", is a lengthy, almost three hundred page manuscript that also presents the assets and potential marriageability of self-empowered spinsters. Started in 1909 as "The Business of Being Cupid" and described in Franklin's diary as the "Cupid Story", it was adapted in late 1909 into the four-act play, "The Love Machine". Franklin sent the novel to a series of UK publishers including Blackwood and Lothian, and it is known that in 1914 she was preparing the manuscript to be sent to H.H. Champion in Melbourne with the hopes of it appearing in the *Book Lover* magazine, although to no avail.[101]

The third manuscript discussed in Chapter 5 is the play, "Aunt Sophie Smashes a Triangle", again unpublished and never performed, which presents the self-actualised spinster who, unlike the spinsters from the other stories, happily rejects matrimony and claims her independence. Franklin first mentions the play on a cold Sunday in early January 1913 and its last mention is noted later in the spring that year, with no correspondence surviving regarding any potential stage productions.[102] Like *On Dearborn Street*, it was written when Franklin was particularly consumed with the trade-offs between the distinctly opposed productivities of writing and domesticity, which might result in books or children,

---

98 Martha Vicinus, *Independent Women: Work and Community for Single Women, 1850–1920* (Chicago: University of Chicago Press, 1985).
99 Holmes, "Spinster Indispensable".
100 Roe, *Stella Miles Franklin*, 129.
101 Roe, *Stella Miles Franklin*, 179.
102 Franklin, Pocket diary, 15 and 17 January 1913; 22 May 1913.

respectively. The oppressively binary nature of these choices is explored and subverted in the manuscripts that comprise Part II.

Part III: Male Vice and the New Man

Like femininity, which was in flux in the early twentieth century, notions of contemporary US masculinity were also changing. The growth of consumer culture and demise of small-scale competitive capitalism, along with other social and economic changes, resulted in the decline of nineteenth-century ideals of middle-class manliness like discipline, mastery, and self-restraint, and challenged its supremacy.[103] Such challenges resided in the social forces and practices of modernity, especially mass immigration, labour unrest, and the visibility of immigrant, non-white working-class men in urban politics and sport and entertainment, all of which were particularly disruptive because patriarchy relied on notions of white supremacy to produce a racially based ideology of male power.[104] In other words, fears about mass immigration and "race suicide", while interpreted as attacks on white supremacy, were also seen to disrupt normative notions of manhood and complicated the gender politics of the period.[105] Such ideals and their decline invigorated the social purity critique of masculinity and are evident in Franklin's depiction of the moral flaws associated with American manhood in these New Woman manuscripts.

Part III addresses these flaws along with the promise of gender reform. This focus on the failure of masculinity again represents a continuity of concern for Franklin, who portrayed colonial manhood in *My Brilliant Career* as "fatally lacking", and a "sham" that enslaved women and impoverished men.[106] In these Chicago stories husbands and suitors are often portrayed as less clever and articulate and lacking in moral fibre compared to the more highly evolved New Woman heroine, whose brains and good looks, along with hard work and integrity, elevate her. These men, especially frequent in Franklin's marriage and courtship stories presented in Part II, are not usually portrayed as malicious, and instead are relatively well-intentioned, if somewhat hapless interpersonally and clueless

---

103 Michael Kimmel, *Manhood in America: A Cultural History* (New York: Free Press, 1996); John Tosh, *A Man's Place: Masculinity and the Middle-Class Home in Victorian England* (New Haven, CT: Yale University Press, 1995); and Martin Crotty, *Making the Australian Male: Middle-Class Masculinity, 1870-1925* (Melbourne: Melbourne University Press, 2001).
104 Gail Bederman, *Manliness and Civilization: A Cultural History of Gender and Race in the US, 1880–1914* (Chicago: University of Chicago Press, 1995), 5.
105 Marilyn Lake and Henry Reynolds, *Drawing the Global Colour Line: White Men's Countries and the International Challenge of Racial Equality* (Cambridge: Cambridge University Press, 2008).
106 Garton, "Contesting Enslavement", 346.

regarding their masculine entitlements. Alongside serving as romantic interest, they tend to be used as contrast to the heroine and their behaviours function as examples of institutionalised sexism. Set against them is the New Man, who provides a promising, although not completely satisfactory, solution to the New Woman's trade-off between romance and vocation. He is poised to fulfil her need for egalitarian courtship and companionate marriage by modelling gentle and supportive masculine performances and offering a "progressive model of romantic partnership". For social purity feminists particularly, he also promised "a healthy" solution that replaced "passion with sexual selection", and offered a eugenic "boost" to the future of humankind.[107] His place in the New Woman novel, however, was notoriously precarious because the heroine's acceptance of him invariably detracted from her own quest for independence and self-actualisation. And as Franklin is quick to point out, he is not without his flaws, and his pro-feminist politics must be interrogated.

Despite these flaws, this idealised New Man offered visionary potential to quell the anxieties associated with changing notions of masculinity and provided a contrast to the manly Australian hero, the "Coming Man" who "evolved in the outposts of empire" and whose relationship to mateship was shaped by his opposition to racial and sexual others.[108] Harold Beecham of *My Brilliant Career* is in many respects "the quintessential" Coming Man.[109] In Franklin's US context this Coming Man has taken on the trappings of wealth and privilege and a playboy persona resulting from exposure to the decadence of American urban life. He drinks cocktails and champagne, dresses well, and indulges in the leisure activities the city has to offer. He is also enamoured with fast cars and aeroplanes, which again reflect the preoccupations of US modernity. Through the lens of feminist social purity politics he illustrates some of the flaws of American manhood perceived as weakening the "race" and contributing to cultural degeneration and women's impoverishment. Yet he is charming, attractive, and seductive, and able to satisfy at least some of the New Woman's desires. At base, however, he is a misogynist and ultimately ill-suited as a long-term solution for the New Woman's quest. In his worst form he practices various forms of male vice that controls women's lives. This is the feature of American manhood that comprises a focus of Part III.

As a key aspect of Franklin's social purity politics, men's bad behaviours posed dangers to women, families, and society through adultery, pregnancy, prostitution, sexually transmitted infections, and physical and sexual abuse. Although social purity feminism advocated for women's liberation as a way to

---

107 MacDonald, *The New Man, Masculinity and Marriage in the Victorian Novel*, 1, 14.
108 Dixon, "The New Woman and the Coming Man", in *Debutante Nation*, 167.
109 Garton, "Contesting Enslavement", 342.

counter men's proclivity for such vice, it is important to note that this movement was diverse and ambivalent in practice with tension between "policing and punishment" on the one hand, and "rescue and support" on the other".[110] Franklin erred on the side of rescue and support with policing employed to rein in male vice. However, just as Franklin and her contemporaries employed evolutionary sociology in the pursuit of economic justice, they also used scientific discourse to make the case that male vice might be tempered by women's advancement and would not only improve the future of families and society but also contribute to progressive evolution. Biology and its accomplice, the new science of eugenics, were thus forced into service to explain and potentially solve the problem of men's "moral squalor". If certain men were actively discouraged from sexual activity and women had control over mate selection through "rational reproduction", it would not only better women's lives but also improve the "race" itself (recognising that "race" was a flexible concept at this time and used to justify anxieties about immigration and other racial and class differences).[111] These anxieties were especially apparent in cities like Chicago where vice and corruption reigned.[112] In 1911 the Vice Commission published *The Social Evil in Chicago*, a 400 page report on what came to be known as the "white slave panic", featuring stories of coerced prostitution of chaste white women, that was followed the next year by Jane Addams' treatise on prostitution, *A New Conscience and an Ancient Evil*.[113] Science brought narrative authority to the struggle against male vice and bolstered the commitment of Progressive reformers. It was a seductive weapon in the fight for social justice, and like her contemporaries, Franklin was willing to accommodate such a tool to further her aims.

Specifically, Franklin's nuanced – and I argue strategic – take on evolutionary understandings of male vice was to prioritise women's economic and political freedom because only when women were economically self-sufficient and politically emancipated could they avoid prostitution and make the rational and civically responsible choices about matrimony that prevented "race suicide". In this she supported Addams' analysis and resisted perceptions that women were to

---

110 Leslie Hall, "Hauling Down the Double Standard: Feminism, Social Purity and Sexual Science in Late Nineteenth-Century Britain", *Gender and History* 16, no. 1 (2004): 36.
111 Richardson, *Love and Eugenics in the Late Nineteenth Century*, 2.
112 Brian Donovan, *White Slave Crusades* (Urbana: University of Illinois Press, 2006); Emma Liggins, "Prostitution and Social Purity in the 1880s and 1890s", *Critical Survey* 15, No. 3 (2003): 39–55.
113 Chicago Vice Commission, *The Social Evil in Chicago: A Study of Existing Conditions with Recommendations by the Vice Commission of Chicago: A Municipal Body Appointed by the Mayor and the City Council of the City of Chicago, and Submitted as its Report to the Mayor and City Council of Chicago*, 1911; Jane Addams, *A New Conscience and an Ancient Evil* (Urbana: University of Illinois Press, 2002 [1912]).

blame for their situation. For example, along with NWTUL colleague Ethel Mason, Franklin wrote an article in *Life and Labor* on the "Chicago Testimony" of the Vice Commission. Their title "Low Wages and Vice: Are They Related?" was rhetorical: they keenly believed that "the great evil of prostitution", and women's subsequent fall from what they perceived as virtue or high sexual moral standards, was related to a lack of economic self-sufficiency.[114] This insight illustrates the intersection of Franklin's socialist-informed economic politics, her suffrage commitments, and her social purity feminism. If women were freed from economic scarcity, the enslavements of marriage, and provided with political freedom, education, and a fuller range of employment choices that included a living wage, they would be in a position to be able to make choices other than those based upon economic survival. In this way, female sexual agency, underpinned by economic and political advancement and made legitimate by the scientific discourse of evolutionary sociology, was *the* solution for Franklin in its ability to avoid male vice. This solution undergirds all Franklin's New Woman writing in Part III.

Chapter 6, "Moral Squalor", discusses these problems of male vice and presents scenarios for both men's rehabilitation and women's survival. Its focus is two-fold. First, it examines male adultery and revisits the play, "Aunt Sophie Smashes a Triangle", and the short story, "A Business Emergency". Insight about Franklin's analysis of infidelity can be gleaned from her personal relationship with Bill Lloyd, who was married to her friend, Lola. As Roe explains, no correspondence remains to clarify the relationship with Lloyd, but by all accounts Franklin never became his mistress even though she found him attractive and appreciated his politics. In turn Lloyd was "entranced by Miles, once saying she was the most complex mortal he had ever known".[115] Other insights about adultery can be gleaned from Franklin's relationship to Floyd Dell, poet and leader in the Chicago literary renaissance as well as feminist and free love advocate, who espoused progressive politics about women's social and economic rights at the same time that he was well known for an impulsive adultery. Franklin was close friends with his wife, Margery Curry Dell, who served as Charlotte Perkins Gilman's US literary agent.[116] Franklin and Floyd Dell were not friends and she argued with him on several occasions around the time she was working on "Aunt Sophie Smashes a Triangle". She found his particular brand of masculinity, whereby his success relied on the talents of his wife, parasitical.[117]

---

114 Ethel Mason and S.M. Franklin, "Low Wages and Vice – Are They Related? Chicago Testimony", *Life and Labor* (April. 1913), 109.
115 Quoted in Roe, *Stella Miles Franklin*, 170.
116 John Hart, *Floyd Dell* (New York: Twayne, 1971).
117 Franklin, Pocket diary, 7 February 1913; 24 September 1912; 25 September 1912; Hart, *Floyd Dell*, 3; Roe, *Stella Miles Franklin*, 145.

Introduction

Chapter 6 also addresses sexual predation and prostitution through a focus on Franklin's play, "Virtue", possibly started in 1915 around the same time as "A Business Emergency" and under the same pseudonym Mr. and Mrs. Ogniblat L'Artsau, although worked on during Franklin's early years in London.[118] Virtue was influenced by cultural preoccupations with white slavery as well as by Franklin's unravelling relationship with Bill Lloyd and the fact that he was known to have visited prostitutes. Alongside war raging across Europe that proved an initial obstacle to Franklin's hopes of seeing "Virtue" on the stage, resistance also came from a London arts establishment, which tended to deride feminist drama.[119] After the play was rejected by "the redoubtable" Lilian Baylis, manager of London's Old Vic theatre, Franklin sent it to Annie Horniman, a leading provincial theatre producer, who also rejected it, explaining that the play was not "suitable" for the English stage because Franklin's attempt at writing American colloquial speech produced dialogue with a "different idiom and inflection".[120]

Chapter 7, "Courage and Confession", follows with attention to another aspect of male vice: men's violence against women. This chapter discusses the fragmented New Woman novel, "Red Cross Nurse and Armored Chauffeur", and analyses the frank and detailed accounting of physical and sexual violence against an anonymous nurse, who represents everywoman in her lack of specificity. Alongside heavy hand-written and often illegible corrections on multiple pages, the biggest challenge of this story is an incomplete manuscript with chapters fifteen through nineteen missing. Franklin also possibly imagined the story as a potential movie script, triggered after a "close call" with an intoxicated Demarest Lloyd on her thirty-fifth birthday in 1914.[121] As a critique of contemporary manhood written at the outset of war, "Red Cross Nurse" also explores global notions of male vice as demonstrated in men's responsibility for war. Although this story appropriates the traditional "white slave" narrative popular at the time, it also subverts it through unique racialised portrayals of the perpetrator and the characterisation of a strong and empowered survivor.

---

118 Franklin, Pocket diary, 14 January 1917.
119 Lyn Pykett, "Writing Around Modernism: May Sinclair and Rebecca West," in *Outside Modernism: In Pursuit of the English Novel, 1900–1930*, ed. Lynne Hapgood and Nancy L. Paxton (New York: St. Martin's Press, 2000), 111.
120 Quoted in Roe, *Stella Miles Franklin*, 209.
121 Franklin, Pocket diary, 17 October, 14 October 1914.

Her Delicate Wings

A huge question mark hovering over Franklin's writing of this period concerns why so little was ever published. I address this by referring to Franklin's biographies, especially Roe's invaluable, extensive, and meticulous *Stella Miles Franklin: A Biography* (2008) to supplement archival evidence wherever possible. An exhaustive accounting of Franklin's submissions and rejections concerning these manuscripts, however, is ultimately impossible because much of the evidence was either not retained or intentionally destroyed in the way that writers tend not to archive their rejections. Those of us who claim this identity can probably relate to this fact, although Franklin was especially sensitive, having "peaked" early with the publication of My Brilliant Career and then suffered a series of rejections immediately thereafter. She was also known for being elusive and secretive, and especially for obscuring her work as autobiography by declaring it so, then re-narrating stories and turning autobiography into fiction and back into autobiography again. This "complicated dance with truth and fiction"[122] and its accompanying "layers of secrecy and performance"[123] would complicate the publishing and marketing of her writing. In addition, the constraints of the marketplace and its masculinist control over certain literary genres shaped the production and reception of feminist writing in the first decades of the twentieth century, and caused Franklin and her contemporaries sometimes insurmountable obstacles. Lyn Pykett describes these obstacles as a time when "'virile' abstraction, lofty impersonality, and linguistic rigour were favoured over 'effeminate' affectiveness and preoccupation with extreme emotional states and the inner life (especially the inner lives of women)".[124]

One novel that was published is discussed in "A Rush and a Swing", the conclusion to *Fallen Among Reformers*. This is *The Net of Circumstance*, the "lost novel" that was published by Mills and Boon in 1915 under the Mr. and Mrs. Ogniblat L'Artsau penname, but only came to light some thirty years after Franklin's death. Started in 1911 and written during the height of Franklin's work with the NWTUL, it epitomises Franklin's preoccupation with the lot of the modern urban woman who beat her "delicate wings" against "the net of circumstance", or what Franklin understood as the institutionalised gender practices shaping her world ("her" implying both the New Woman and Franklin). I employ this novel to illustrate and bring closure to discussions about the ways Franklin's New Woman

---

122 Dale, "Only Scratch the Surface", 381.
123 Sandra Knowles, "'Oh, for Some Refuge – for Myself – to Be Myself': The Search for Gender Neutrality in the Diaries of Miles Franklin", *Australian Feminist Studies* 25, no. 63 (2010): 63.
124 Pykett, "Writing Around Modernism", 111.

writing and its hybrid strategies of realism and romance bridged nineteenth-century literary traditions and later forms. Almost all the disruptive practices of feminist new realism discussed in Parts I to III of *Fallen Among Reformers* are exemplified in various degrees in the novel, including an outspoken artistic challenge to masculinist productions appropriating the New Woman as literary object.

I attempt to tread lightly in *Fallen Among Reformers* between the tangled practices of historicising Franklin's writing and focusing on the author herself. My goal here is to follow Katherine Bode and Robert Dixon's call for a shift from textual criticism as the sole reason of literary studies and instead towards an analysis of "the political, economic, cultural and material contexts" in which texts are "produced, circulated, and received".[125] These sometimes difficult negotiations, which Elizabeth Webby attends to in her discussion of the relationship between life and literature, are not merely rhetorical or textual, but also further complicated by the subjectivities of writers, critics, and readers themselves.[126] As Tanya Dalziell notes, such efforts to historicise fictions are almost always "indebted to", if not "embedded in", the very practices we presume are the objects of our critique. Similarly, it becomes difficult to avoid the ways in which any author's work – and Franklin's writing in particular – re-inscribes her multifaceted nature as well as the practices of power that informed that work.[127]

Invariably, like all "truth", the "real scoop" about Franklin's middle years in Chicago and their relationship to the politics of her later life remains elusive: how she "felt" – or how she constructed the complex identity we have come to recognise – is ambiguous. Biographer Marjorie Barnard, for example, wrote about Franklin's impenetrable façade and persistent desire for anonymity when she declared that no one knew how Franklin really felt, "even when she told you".[128] In letters and diaries written while she was in Chicago, Franklin professed low self-esteem, chronic anxiety and depression, and multiple emotional and physical burdens. She shrouded herself through various denials and use of obtuse pseudonyms and kept a low profile as an author, even though she rubbed shoulders with some of the most influential artists of the Chicago literary and cultural establishments. Yet despite woeful self-proclamations sometimes bordering on the suicidal, there is ample

---

125 Katherine Bode and Robert Dixon, eds., *Resourceful Reading: The New Empiricism, eResearch and Australian Literary Culture* (Sydney: Sydney University Press, 2009), 15.
126 Elizabeth Webby, "Introduction", *My Brilliant Career and My Career Goes Bung* [1901, 1946] (Sydney: Harper Collins, 2004), xiii.
127 Tanya Dalziell, "No Place for a Book? Fiction in Australia to 1890", in *The Cambridge History of Australian Literature*, ed. Peter Pierce (Melbourne: Cambridge University Press, 2009), 96.
128 Marjorie Faith Barnard, *Miles Franklin* (New York: Twayne Publishers, 1967), 45.

and ongoing evidence of her social engagement and interpersonal confidence. This alternative portrait presents a successful professional woman, respected by a diverse array of influential reformers and labour leaders making up a venerable "Who's Who" of Progressive-era activism. And indeed, as her biographers amply attest, Franklin was a lively and sought-after companion. These relationships, and the negotiations they fostered about the possibilities of romance and vocation, matrimony and socially meaningful work, were part of the rich tapestry of Franklin's life during this period. And it is to this rich tapestry that we now turn.

Part I: Work

1
A Picture of Contemporary Existence

This chapter begins my exploration of Miles Franklin's literary response to social class: the great "struggle for survival" played out in Chicago's turbulent urban landscape. Franklin's work among reformers nuanced her understandings of economic privilege and inequality by immersing her in communities of immigrant women, who were isolated by custom and language, and who toiled in factory sweatshops and slaved as wives in dilapidated overcrowded tenement rooms without water, sanitation or light. This work exposed her to the privileges and entitlements of a Chicago elite and the gross differences among rich and poor. As Franklin biographer Verna Coleman suggests, Franklin was both exhilarated and challenged in witnessing the excesses and deprivation of "the struggle for survival, in this gilded, smoking, mid-west colossus".[1]

This chapter focuses on the ways Franklin's witness to the poverty of Chicago's underclass and the privileges of its elite produced "The Survivors", a four-act protest play written in 1908.[2] This play addresses class inequities through critique of the ways an emerging evolutionary science shaped debates on gender and poverty, especially the notion of the survival of the fittest as an explanation for economic injustice. Franklin resists the new science of Social Darwinism and its hereditarian argument by making the case for the role of environment and the potential of human agency in both class and gender relations. As a suffrage romance, the play also reflects Franklin's feminist passions through its New Woman heroine, poised to succeed professionally and secure a romantic relationship of equals. Because it

---

1 Verna Coleman, *Her Unknown Brilliant Career: Miles Franklin in America* (Sydney: Angus & Robertson, 1981), 79.
2 Miles Franklin, "The Survivors", ML MSS 445/25, 1. Subsequent references appear in parentheses in the text.

presents a play within a play, "The Survivors" also addresses the future of art and its role in the pursuit of social justice.

Susan Pfisterer and Carolyn Pickett label "The Survivors" a suffrage play because of its feminist content, New Woman lead character, and a small sub-plot that includes a suffrage speaker, but it might more accurately be termed a feminist-inspired workers' protest play that focuses on the material conditions of modernity and its consequences for urban life.[3] As such it gestures towards what has come to be known as "proletarian literature": propagandist short stories, social drama, and political poetry precipitated by the social turmoil of early twentieth-century life.[4] As one aspect of progressive politics, and central to the Chicago literary renaissance, such realist protest drama encouraged understandings of the relationship between personal struggles and wider social injustice. The Hull House Settlement, Franklin's first introduction to Chicago, was especially formative for this approach in its seamless integrations of political and artistic protest in the form of dramatic readings and theatre workshops. The Hull House Players, whom Franklin enthusiastically enjoyed, were especially popular in this regard.[5]

Although there is "no question" of Franklin's commitment as a playwright, since she wrote for the stage all her life, believed passionately in the transformative power of the dramatic arts, and understood theatre as the "supreme weapon for feminist activism", she was mostly unsuccessful as a playwright.[6] Certainly as Jill Roe explains in her biography, Franklin attempted time and again to write the drama that might educate the masses through commercial success, and the failure to do so must be understood as product of the conservatism and resistance that women and feminist playwrights of her era faced.[7] Franklin's expatriate plays were "classic examples of feminist dramaturgical non-closure" that provided evocative representations of

---

3   Susan Pfisterer and Carolyn Pickett, *Playing With Ideas: Australian Women Playwrights From the Suffragettes to the Sixties* (Sydney: Currency Press, 1999), 55.
4   Nicholas Coles and Janet Zandy, *American Working-Class Literature: An Anthology* (New York: Oxford University Press, 2007); Charlotte Nekola and Paula Rabinowitz, eds., *Writing Red: An Anthology of American Women Writers, 1930–1940* (New York: Feminist Press at the City University of New York, 1987).
5   Shannon Jackson, *Lines of Activity: Performance, Historiography, Hull-House Domesticity* (Ann Arbor: University of Michigan Press, 2000); Melanie N. Blood, "Theatre in Settlement Houses: Hull-House Players, Neighborhood Playhouse, and Karamu Theatre", *Theatre History Studies* 16 (1996): 45–69.
6   Jocelyn Hedley, "The Unpublished Plays of Miles Franklin". Master's thesis, School of English, Media and Performing Arts, University of New South Wales, 2007, 17; Pfisterer and Pickett, *Playing With Ideas*, 243.
7   Jill Roe, *Stella Miles Franklin: A Biography* (Sydney: Fourth Estate/Harper Collins, 2008), 248–9; Vivian Gardner and Susan Rutherford, ed., *The New Woman and Her Sisters: Feminism and Theatre, 1850–1914* (Ann Arbor, MI: University of Michigan Press, 1992); and Maggie B. Gale and Vivian Gardner, eds., *Women, Theatre and Performance: New Histories, New Historiographies* (Manchester: Manchester University Press, 2000).

pertinent social issues of the day, but which were often met with disapproval by a more conservative public and arts establishment.[8] Such denigration of women's place in theatre history arose also as a result of lack of performance possibilities and the "formidable barrier" of repertory selection that women playwrights faced.[9] Because theatre moved outside the domestic realm associated with women, its public aspects of production and performance were especially transgressive. As Michelene Wandor suggests, "the public control of an imaginative world (the action on the stage) . . . [makes them] a far greater threat than the female novelist to the carefully maintained dominance of men as the custodians of cultural creation".[10] Franklin would not have disagreed. Indeed, to flaunt her wit and perhaps in anticipation of such rejection, "The Survivors" includes instructions to the "Stage Manager" of what Franklin described as "The Society of Unplayed Plays" and lists her "nom-de-plume" as "Tomphooll" (as in tomfoolery). She also describes her characters as "Necessary to Discharge the Mouthing and Strutting Incidental in Stage Presentation", and describes the play's "motif" as "[a] picture of contemporary existence pulled into theatrical shape and necessarily conventional conclusion by having right or wrong – possibly the wrong psychological insight, and more or less – probably less, sociological experience and experiment" (1).

"The Survivors" is self-described as "a modern play" set in "a great American city" (1). It features the accomplished and socially aware New Woman actress, Avis Gaylord, niece of a wealthy industrialist, who befriends, and eventually hires as political advisors, a working-class duo: Billy, who lost his legs in an industrial accident, and Ginger, a newsboy who helps run a newspaper stand. A consumptive working-man-turned-writer Richard (Dick) Dallas, who functions as a mouthpiece for dialogue about the premise of the survival of the fittest as well as a suitor for the New Woman, also befriends this duo. When Avis announces her decision to leave commercial theatre unless she can act in a socially just play, her manager, Lincoln Freeman, who epitomises the ambitious businessman motivated only by financial interest, approaches Dick. He agrees to write the play despite the double toil of factory work ruining his health. Dick's play is called "The Survivors", encapsulating the play within a play, which like Franklin's attempt, employs social realism with a focus on "real LIFE" (61). Avis chooses to change the ending of his play, however,

---

8 Susan Pfisterer, ed., *Tremendous Worlds: Australian Women's Drama 1890–1960* (Sydney: Currency Press, 1999), 81.
9 Katherine E. Kelly, ed., *Modern Drama by Women, 1880s–1930s: An International Anthology* (London: Routledge, 1996), 5; Keith Newlin, *American Plays of the New Woman* (Chicago: Ivan R. Dee, 2000).
10 Michelene Wandor, "The Impact of Feminism on the Theatre", *Feminist Review* 18 (1984): 86. See also Susan Bennett, "Theatre History, Historiography and Women's Dramatic Writing", in *Women, Theatre and Performance*, 46–59.

disrupting the plot of the consumptive artist unable to profess his love to the actress and instead reworking it to include his articulation of desire and the actress' agency in recognising and reciprocating that desire. The play (and the play within the play) end happily as Dick accepts the revision, declares his love for Avis, and they go out hand in hand as equals to greet the audience's thunderous applause.

In the sections below I first discuss the ways "The Survivors" provides Franklin with a stage, literally, for the portrayal of urban poverty and the opportunity to employ a socialist critique that makes the case for collective bargaining. This was the mission of the NWTUL in its relationship to women workers. Second I explore Franklin's understanding of contemporary debates about the application of the new science of evolution to human populations as represented in the play. Its recurring motif, "the survival of the fittest", is examined and rejected by the play's protagonists as an explanation for social inequality. The third section addresses another issue close to home for Franklin: the role of liberal reform generally and the practices of philanthropy in particular, which are demonstrated in the play as inadequate for remedying social inequities. Finally, "The Survivors" addresses the topic of art as social protest by politicising the role of theatre and its potential for social transformation. Not surprisingly Franklin's affirmation of social protest drama through the mouthpiece of the socially responsible actress, Avis Gaylord, also includes a critique of the misogynous practices of contemporary theatre and their constraints on women in the arts.

"Lungs and Legs of Strong Men"

"The Survivors" opens with a frank reminder of class inequality in the modern city through the character of Billy, who had his legs "cut away by machinery" in the factory where he worked (1). He is squatting on the pavement outside a saloon "with his hat in readiness to receive alms" and talking with the saloon keeper about the injustices of a class system that uses people for others' conspicuous gain. Throughout the play Franklin critiques industrial capitalism through the repeated motif about wealth accumulated at the "expense of lungs and legs of strong men" (40) and accompanies this refrain with the spectacle of the amputee. Although Pfisterer and Pickett suggest the legless Billy serves primarily as a "dramatic symbol of the oppression of un-enfranchised women", this amputee represents the disenfranchisement of the working class as a result of the institutionalised violence of industrial capitalism.[11] Billy's plight thus serves as a powerful metaphor for the loss of dignity and destruction of lives caused by corporate greed.

---

11 Pfisterer and Pickett, *Playing with Ideas*, 55.

Adjacent on a cold windy street corner is Billy's friend, Ginger, "a thin, bright boy insufficiently clothed against the rigors of the climate" (1), who is shown eagerly accepting the overcoat that the starlet, Avis, brings him. He works to help a sick mother who dies during the play. On seeing Avis featured in Ginger's newspaper, Billy professes his disdain for Avis' uncle, "the old skin-flint Gaylord", describing him as one of "them as has everything … silks an' satins, automobiles an' half a dozen palaces to live in at once, with no danger of havin' their legs cut off of 'em". Gaylord is someone who "ground his help down to the dust and opposed every protective machinery bill" (3). This is precisely the factory machinery that maimed Billy and forced him to beg on the street.

This opening act with its dramatic rendering of urban inequality illustrates Franklin's budding worker rights politics, developed through her experiences working for the NWTUL and living in Chicago, where monopolies, trusts, and organised crime controlled much of the economy. This consolidation of power in the hands of too few individuals, the ways owners and investors grew rich at the expense of the very workers who produced their wealth, and the ways inherited wealth perpetuated the miseries of ordinary working people, were a central focus of the NWTUL. This was also a concern of academics at the University of Chicago, from whom Franklin recalled receiving "a great bag of words".[12] Despite her socialist critique and association with labour leaders who espoused these politics, Franklin did not identify as a socialist and certainly never joined the Socialist Party. At this time socialism was broadly accepted as a legitimate populist politics in the US and represented wide-ranging networks of relatively diverse and loosely affiliated movements coming together in their advocacy for worker rights. When the Socialist Party of America was founded in 1901, for example, it emerged as part of a larger socialist movement (with a small "s") hoping to transform US economic life. These politics included a variety of positions explaining class inequality that were broadly and popularly received.[13] Franklin's socialist populism drew from this and was always located in strong moral responses to injustice. She addresses this class-based immorality when the wealthy Avis questions the ethics of her inheritance: "I am heiress to a large fortune which I cannot use, because I have not earned it and therefore am not entitled to it, and also I do not approve of the methods of its accumulation" (40).

Labour organisations like the NWTUL attempted to resist the abuses of corporations through collective bargaining. Franklin illustrates this spirit of collectivism in the first act of the play when a union worker, Charlie, enters the

---

12 Martin Bulmer, *The Chicago School of Sociology: Institutionalization, Diversity, and the Rise of Sociological Research* (Chicago: University of Chicago Press, 1984); Roe, *Stella Miles Franklin*, 127.
13 Jack Ross, *The Socialist Party of America: A Complete History* (Lincoln, NE: Potomac, 2015).

scene looking for Dick Dallas in the hopes of encouraging him to help start a local union. The most prominent US unions of the time included the American Federation of Labor, the Knights of Labor, and the Industrial Workers of the World. The NWTUL worked closely with the former in particular, whose offices were next door to those of the NWTUL on Dearborn Street. Coughing (a gesture Franklin's potential audience would recognise as an indication of tuberculosis), Charlie hopes to save Dick, who is "workin' all day and book learnin' all night" (4), from a similar life of suffering by initiating a process of collective bargaining. Along with Ginger's situation as a destitute street boy and Billy's injury and loss of physical and economic livelihood, Charlie's monologue – and the breaks in that monologue from his coughing fits – helps set up the play's focus on the selfishness of the bourgeoisie and the misery of the working class. Charlie tries to convince Dick and educate a potential audience about the need for labour regulation: "If you were organized and worked eight hours a day instead of ten and twelve and overtime on top of that, you'd have more time for improving yourself ... [We are] entitled to a decent living for ourselves and our families" (5–6). Dick's response to Charlie at this point in the play is to decry wage labour as an equal bargain and to insist that problems are personal rather than structural: "All things are there in life for those who have the pluck and the stuff" (7). His logic represents the Marxist notion of false consciousness: the internalisation of ideologies supporting capitalism. Franklin was well aware through her work in Chicago not only about the ideological value of such notions as these espoused by Dick, but also about the ways corporations fought back against collective bargaining, pressuring government to call in the national militia, and hiring strikebreakers and legal teams to derail truth claims. She illustrates this when Billy sarcastically explains his own carelessness caused his injury and amputations: "It was all my fault – proved by the company's lawyers ... an' with my education I could have took my choice of – one of the other factories or the diplomatic service" (10). In this comment Franklin illustrates the problems of liberal individualism: that workers have free choice whether to work or not and their individual actions are to blame for their situation.

    Franklin wrote this dialogue with the explicit goal of politicising an audience and encouraging awareness of connections between personal experiences and wider institutions. This amply illustrates the goals of proletarian literature generally and protest plays in particular. Perceived as an instrument in the class struggle, such drama aimed to bring understandings of social life grounded in an anti-capitalist critique to the reader. Its social realism established a "real" narrative world in order to create social awareness and revolutionary optimism.[14] However, although " The Survivors" uses realist drama as a liberatory literary device for uncovering the contradictions of class society and especially the interconnections between wealth and poverty and the personal and systemic violence experienced by ordinary people, it also provides opportunity for characters' introspection as Dick, for example, starts to question his own beliefs and reflect on his experience as a working man. Faced with tuberculosis, he soon comes to his own erroneous thinking about social and economic inequality.

Spoils to the Victor!

The phrase, "the survival of the fittest", and its importance for the central message of the play, reflects the active debates of the time about the science of evolution, questions of progress and degeneration, and its application to human populations. Certain tenets of evolutionary sociology, or what has come to be known as Social Darwinism, were regularly used during this period to explain class inequality, implying that patterns of evolution (who survived and who did not) resulted from the biological processes of natural selection.[15] Although Darwin had initiated this principle, the term "survival of the fittest" and its eventual employment by an emerging eugenics movement originated with sociologist Herbert Spencer, who used these notions to argue that it was natural and proper for the strong to thrive at the expense of the weak because the former were better adapted to social and economic conditions.[16] Several characters in the play struggle with this notion of "the survival of the fittest" and each provides a narrative for its iteration and/or critique. In Act I, for example, after Charlie has a fit of coughing and breaks off his dialogue about union organisation, Dick responds that "it's devilish hard luck but I'm stronger than you. Your dad was consumptive before you . . . I guess a fellow that hasn't got enough stuff in him to rise out of the factory is only getting what's coming to him" (6). Dick thus presents himself at the start of the play in believing Charlie's demise is a natural process of biological selection. He blames the victims for their plight without understanding the structural conditions of economic injustice. Nature rules, and through ambition and hard work individuals might survive or not: "it's the irrevocable law of the survival of the fittest!" he exclaims (7).

By 1908 Charles Darwin's evolutionary theory of descent through modification was the dominant scientific explanation for diversification in nature. As explained

---

14 Candida Ann Lacey, "Striking Fictions: Women Writers and the Making of a Proletarian Realism", *Women's Studies International Forum* 9, no. 4 (1986): 373–384.
15 Robert Bannister, *Social Darwinism: Science and Myth in Anglo-American Thought* (Philadelphia: Temple University Press, 1989).
16 Mark Francis and Michael Taylor, eds., *Herbert Spencer: Legacies* (Abingdon, Oxon: Routledge, 2015).

in *Origin of the Species* (1859), Darwin not only established that all species of life descended over time from common ancestors, but that various patterns of evolution resulted from natural selection, the struggle for existence that all living things share.[17] "Life is all a chance", explains Gerard Grosstin, who employs Dick Dallas. "It's not my fault that I own a factory instead of working in one" (28). "Pshaw!" he cries. "We've had men in our factories all their lives – great husky fellows, and what am I to do anyway? People must die of one thing or another" (29).

In this interpretation of Spencer's application of Darwin's approach, the poor were therefore victims of chance and their own biology. Reformers like Franklin resisted this and borrowed from Darwin's later work in *The Descent of Man, and Selection in Relation to Sex* (1871), which granted that humans have some agency to condition their future through the processes of sex/mate selection. This approach shifted attention away from a random natural selection to sexual selection directed by choice.[18] "[W]e are the people that make conditions" (28) says Avis in response to Gerard's claim about life being a chance. Dedicated to addressing poverty and improving the conditions of working people's lives, reformers, including Franklin, resisted applications of Darwin's biological arguments to discourses on class and poverty, and yet at the same time were seduced by scientific arguments that might bolster their politics.[19] Indeed, science's pre-eminence and authority as the new religion meant that it was forced into service to help explain one of the most important questions of the day: the question of the poor, especially whether there would always be people in poverty or whether this was ameliorable. On this question Franklin was influenced by the scientific theories of evolutionary sociologist Lester Ward, who also helped shape the politics of another of Franklin's favourite writers, Charlotte Perkins Gilman. Both were "crucial" to Franklin's ways of thinking.[20] Ward believed that the real object of science was to benefit society and gravitated to a utilitarian ethic to guide his political thought, which held that enlightenment and the social education of the masses would make possible rational, planned social progress.[21] Like Spencer, Ward took an evolutionary approach, but unlike Spencer followed the Lamarckian notion that evolution occurs as a result of human agency or "telesis" where traits are acquired and passed on to offspring.[22] Ward did not make the case that

---

17 Mike Hawkins, *Social Darwinism in European and American Thought, 1860–1945* (New York: Cambridge University Press, 1997).
18 Angelique Richardson, *Love and Eugenics in the Late-Nineteenth Century* (Oxford: Oxford University Press, 2003), 40.
19 Leslie A. Hall, "Hauling Down the Double Standard: Feminism, Social Purity and Sexual Science in Late Nineteenth-Century Britain", *Gender and History* 16, no. 1 (2004): 36–56.
20 Roe, *Stella Miles Franklin*, 155.
21 Samuel Chugerman, *Lester F. Ward: The American Aristotle* (Durham, NC: Duke University Press, 1939).

knowledge was transmitted directly to descendants through heredity, but rather that the capacity for acquiring such knowledge was hereditary. This environmental approach encouraged progress and human agency and saw Spencer's "survival of the fittest" as "a doctrine of despair".[23]

The Immorality of Philanthropy

When Avis addresses Billy in the first act of the play and inquires how she can "help", she is met with an impassioned response that illustrates one of the most important themes of the play: the shortcomings of philanthropy and the need for structural change. "Help, be damned!" exclaims Billy. "You can't give me back my legs can you?" (9). He suggests she might use her influence to pass protective labour legislation, but is still doubtful if she could "do any good, even there" (10). Many like Franklin, disillusioned by the failure of liberal reform even while they participated in it, began to recognise that only a more systemic transformation could provide a comprehensive solution to society's problems. "I have long recognised the futility – even the immorality of philanthropy" (45), declares Avis, encapsulating Franklin's recognition of the limitations of her own work. According to Socialist Party leader Eugene Debs, whom Franklin heard speak several times, philanthropy was flawed; it might ameliorate social problems in the short term, but was not a sustainable long-term approach.[24]

This critique of philanthropy as a strategy for social justice is demonstrated in three moves during a debate in the second act when various speakers vie for why they should receive the inheritance that Avis feels she does not deserve. First, Franklin satirises members of the Women's Club who moderate the debate, and pokes fun at their philanthropic practices by providing comic relief and political commentary on something close to home: pretentious middle-class "do-gooders". During her Chicago years, Franklin was caught between wealthy reformers like Margaret Dreier Robins, whose independent wealth allowed them opportunities to commit themselves to social reform, and the labouring women with whom she worked directly and in her Stenographers' Union. Although the goals of the NWTUL were to serve working-class women, membership of non-wage earners, middle-class allies, and privileged Clubwomen was encouraged. Not surprisingly, this was its weakness as well as its strength: a fact Franklin recognised by the success of *Life and Labor* in reaching middle-class readers rather than the working women

---

22 Lester F. Ward, *Dynamic Sociology* (New York: Johnson, 1968 [1883]), vii.
23 Clifford H. Scott, *Lester Frank Ward* (Boston: Twayne Publishing, 1976), 88.
24 Marguerite Young, *Harp Song for a Radical: The Life and Times of Eugene Victor Debs* (New York: Alfred Knopf, 1999).

whom it was supposed to serve.[25] Franklin worked alongside Chicago Clubwoman Louise de Kouen and Kouen's colleagues, and although Franklin supported their efforts, as Coleman attests, she often found herself with an "ineradicable bitterness towards the idle rich".[26] With awkward names like Mrs Blueton Dobson, Mrs Braemere Stone, and Mrs Hobson Kalemahir that establish them as their husbands' property, they make up the "Anti-Rust Club" featured in "The Survivors".

These club women rustle around in their seats pretentiously, make comments in loud whispers, and reveal their disdain for real live working-class men. One moves her chair away from Billy and glares at him so that he responds, "Don't be scared ma'am", adding, "I'm helpless" as he taps his knees (43). This critique, however, is mostly affectionate and balanced by Franklin's recognition of their earnest attempt to help the poor. Perhaps it was a coincidence, but Franklin's choice of the debate's convener, Mrs Hubert Kelley, is reminiscent of Florence Kelley, who is considered one of the great contributors to the Chicago Women's School of Sociology.[27]

Franklin's second critique of reformist strategies comes from two characters, each making their bid for Avis' forfeited inheritance, and each demonstrating a particular liberal politics for ameliorating poverty that falls short. Gerard Grosstin declares the necessity of providing "comfortable, attractive and well-equipped libraries, and rest rooms . . . so that the lower classes will gain in contentment and understanding that the employers are their truest friends" (41). Gerard's monologue represents what Franklin's audience would have immediately recognised as *noblesse oblige* or the obligation of the rich to take care of the poor, which functioned as "welfare capitalism", the case for the overlapping interests of capital and workers and its practice of employer-based provisions. Advocates hoped to build a loyal labour force and resist reforms invoked by government through corporate control of labour relations. During Franklin's time in Chicago the McCormick Harvesting Machine Company had links to the Chicago settlement house movement and the Pullman Palace Car Company featured a workers' village in Chicago with a theatre, library, churches, and recreational facilities.[28]

The next speaker is Dr. Splick, a prominent physician and President of the International Tuberculosis Society, who makes the case for the money to be spent on better facilities for tubercular patients. He also insists on educating workers

---

25 Carolyn Daniel McCreesh, *Women in the Campaign to Organize Garment Workers, 1880–1917* (New York: Garland, 1985). See Alice Henry, *Trade Union Woman* (New York: D. Appleton and Co., 1915) for an original account of these divisions.
26 Coleman, *Her Unknown Brilliant Career*, 95.
27 Katherine Kish Sklar, *Florence Kelley and the Nation's Work* (New Haven, CT: Yale University Press, 1995).
28 Stuart D. Brandes, *American Welfare Capitalism, 1880–1940* (Chicago: University of Chicago Press, 1976).

to "avoid dusty occupations and unsanitary conditions" in order to eradicate the disease (42). The use of this monologue is two-fold: to educate about the extent of the public health problem of tuberculosis and its relationship to class inequalities, and to show that focus on this issue is one of amelioration rather than solution, especially when responsibility for the illness is placed on workers and solutions centre on individual behaviours.

The final way Franklin underscores the shortcomings of liberal reform is through the monologues of the last two speakers, who win the debate for Avis' fortune by highlighting the necessity of systemic political and economic transformation. Geraldine Garity, the International Secretary of the Allied Militant Suffragette Association, speaks first after being detained on the street and given "quite a rough handling". Her suffrage monologue provides the mouthpiece for Franklin's New Woman platform: "Get women the vote and if you have any money left teach them – and men how to use it so that . . . they can win a limited workday, a living wage and all that goes with it" (44). She represents what Caroline Howlett has described as a transformative " suffragette femininity" whose representations disrupted traditional gender performances.[29] The last speaker is Dick Dallas himself, who begins by thanking Dr. Splick and explains that it is thanks to the doctor's professional attention that he is well enough to speak today. In this gesture Franklin gives a nod to the medical establishment and its important role in society: one she experienced first-hand through rooming at the home of Dr. Young, a physician who provided her with medical assistance and friendship during these early Chicago years. Dick's suggestions for social and economic justice echo the insights of evolutionary sociology and its resistance to the "paralysing superstition . . . monopolized by the few – the survivors – the fittest" that justifies their "greed and bold cunning" (45-6).

After all have spoken and Avis declares that "Miss Garity and Mr. Dallas have shown me what to do" (47), the strain of the occasion is too much for Dick, who collapses into Avis' arms. The Victorian melodrama of this final act provides what Daniel Duffy declares a "moralised and frequently anguished role" that serves political ends.[30] In "The Survivors", however, this gesture is comedic and somewhat ironic in that it is Avis who catches Dick's swoon, accompanied by "the club ladies offering

---

29   Caroline Howlett, "Femininity Slashed: Suffragette Militancy, Modernism and Gender", in *Modernist Sexualities*, ed. Hugh Stevens and Caroline Howlett (Manchester: Manchester University Press, 2000), 73.
30   Daniel Duffy, "Feminist Discourse in Popular Drama of the Early- and Mid-Victorian Era", in *Feminist Readings of Popular Victorian Texts*, ed. Emma Liggins and Daniel Duffy (Aldershot, UK: Ashgate, 2001), 129. See also Thomas Postlewait, "From Melodrama to Realism: The Suspect History of American Drama", in *Melodrama: The Cultural Emergence of Genre*, ed. Michael Hays and Anastasia Nikolopoulon (London: Macmillan, 1996).

conflicting suggestions" and Billy declaring, "[t]hese old bats aint fit for neither use nor ornament" (48). The swoon also symbolically rebalances and equalises the couple's relationship in mirroring the first act of the play when Dick catches Avis in similar fashion as she slips on the icy pavement. This hybridised protest play, containing all the elements of Franklin's socialist critique, thus echoes Victorian conventions and adapts the specific goals of proletarian literature with a New Woman twist.

A Higher Purpose

A central focus of "The Survivors" is the future of drama that involves a critique of commercial theatre as well as the potential (its "higher purpose" [3]) of protest theatre for progressive social change. Franklin reiterates this notion when she has Avis declare that "drama should carry an ethical message. It should be one of the greatest modern influences for good" (27). This wish comes true when Dick writes the play that fits this bill. "[It] is appealing to the deeper nature of the audience. It is teaching a wonderful lesson. Just listen to the applause!" (50), exclaims Avis when Dick's play is performed in the final act.

In 1908 Chicago had become a popular theatre town, although few plays were local in origin. The city was mostly entertained by touring shows from Broadway and appearances by some of the greatest American and European actors.[31] Both grand auditoriums and smaller stages were built, many in what is known as "the Loop": an area of downtown Chicago that also housed the NWTUL offices. These theatres played host to traditional drama as well as musicals, opera, vaudeville and burlesque, and minstrel shows. Not surprisingly, the sexism and racism of commercial theatre at this time affected staffing, and limited opportunities for writers, directors, and actors. As Avis declares, "there is not much social success for the girl who is interested in the serious issues of life" (11). In this quip Avis critiques commercial theatre that often perpetuated traditional – and often derogatory – representations of individuals and groups. Franklin used "The Survivors" as a way to both critique these practices as well as make the case for drama as an educational strategy of political consciousness-raising.

Not surprisingly, Avis' role in the first act as the beautiful and accomplished actress is not only to provide a love object but also to illustrate the classic New Woman strategy of the *künstlerroman* narrative charting the promise and success of the female artist. Although Dick thought there was "no actress on the American

---

31 Richard Christiansen, "Theater Companies", in *The Encyclopedia of Chicago*, ed. James R. Grossman, Ann Durkin Keating, and Janice L. Reiff (Chicago: The University of Chicago Press, 2004), 817–8. See also Richard Christiansen, *A Theatre of Our Own: A History and Memoir of 1001 Nights in Chicago* (Evanston, IL: Northwestern University Press, 2006).

stage today capable of doing anything but wearing a sensuous Paris gown and disporting herself in some pornographic balderdash for the edification of the moneyed degenerates" (26), we soon find that Avis is no frivolous popular entertainer. She critiques the commercial interests of contemporary theatre, as featured in headlines read aloud by Billy: "IDOL OF THE THEATRE PUBLIC, DISSATISFIED WITH HER ART!" (3). Franklin also uses the sleazy stage manager, Lincoln Freeman, to provide contrast to Avis' principled artistry. When Dick resists Lincoln's financial offer, explaining that creativity relies on "inspiration", Lincoln makes a toast to "cash inspiration" (23), to which Dick "dashes his [glass] to the ground" (24-5). In this move Franklin not only highlights unprincipled commercial theatre, but also underscores Dick's journey from someone whose ideology once supported the likes of Lincoln towards an author whose integrity now refuses such bourgeois claims. Both Franklin's play and the drama Dick writes within the play employ a new social realism that establishes the "real" narrative world in part through such introspection of its characters.

Finally, Franklin's particular approach to protest drama was to hybridise it with the romance tradition and insert a New Woman heroine wisely choosing a suitable egalitarian New Man, whose character and actions are deserving of her love. In contrast Gerard finds his attentions rebuked because of what Avis calls their "incompatibility". On making the case for an egalitarian feminist suitor, she explains that only equality can make love genuine: "Love demands that one's ideals must be in accord or there can be no high attunement of mental companionship" (30). The fierce applause the couple receives on greeting the audience hand in hand as equals and romantic partners illustrates Franklin's hopes for political drama that educates the audience even while it provides entertainment. The final gesture by the heroine of changing the ending of the play and providing a metaphor of sorts for the future of art and society, reflects both Avis' sexual and professional agency. She emerges as a successful professional woman who does not shirk her ethical responsibilities, models art as social progress, and also finds romance. The play teaches the importance of gender equality by reinforcing the knowledge that women can earn their own means through their own talent.

Such a happy-ending, however, is not without its problems. Franklin's own recognition of this is aptly encoded in Avis' comment at the end of the play when she explains to Dick another reason, beyond her love for him, why she felt, in the words of Rachel Blau DuPlessis, to "write beyond the ending", which in this version is actually to retain the template of domestic feminism and stay within its containment.[32] It reflects Franklin's compromise and subsequent apology in

---

32 Rachel Blau DuPlessis, *Writing Beyond the Ending: Narrative Strengths of Twentieth-Century Women Writers* (Bloomington: Indiana University Press, 1985), 4.

terms of the aesthetic form of the drama itself: the "happy ending" expected of commercial art: "Are you unforgivably angry with me for changing the last [act] of the play?" asks Avis. "The audience were so in sympathy with the struggles of the heroine that I had to make it end hopefully. If he had not recovered and won the heroine the public would have repudiated such a cruel and unhappy play" (61).

This dialogue illustrates Franklin's awareness of the constraints of her art. Like other contemporary feminist playwrights, she faced a series of binary oppositions that shaped distinctions between popular and literary drama. The "excesses" of popular realism and the various forms of domestic romantic melodrama that inevitably produced the "happy ending" were set against styles which claimed progress and modernity. The critique of realist drama was in its pretence of naturalness and its masking of the arbitrary aspects of life that lulled the audience into social and political acquiescence.[33] It followed then that feminist protest drama was doubly critiqued because of its feminised content and its realistic style. In *A Stage of Her Own*, however, Sheila Stowell counters these claims against feminist realism and supports their transformational promise by making the case that realism is merely a tool for shaping perception and insisting it can adopt a variety of ideological positions. Such narratives thus worked within – and yet also hoped to transform – traditional dramaturgy, representing "horizons of possibility" associated with various spectatorial readings.[34]

In closing it is also important to note that Franklin leaves us with one final message about the making and consumption of art. Dick's "double toil" of working man and author, made much of in this play, reflects her own double life as an over-worked and underpaid professional activist and a writer. Dick's assumption that he might not survive his toil mirrors Franklin's own fears about surviving in this urban maelstrom. " The Survivors" came after the nervous breakdown associated with difficult adjustments and transitions to life in Chicago, as well as with the stint in the hospital after the tragic news that her sister Linda had died.[35] At this point in writing the play, Franklin may have rejoiced in her own survival and possibly seen her art – if not romance – as her lifeline.

---

33   Roland Barthes, quoted in Terry Eagleton, *Literary Theory* (Oxford: Blackwell, 1983), 136. Jill Dolan also makes this point in *The Feminist Spectator as Critic* (Ann Arbor, MI: UMI Research Press, 1988), 84.
34   Sheila Stowell, *A Stage of Their Own: Feminist Playwrights of the Suffrage Era* (Manchester: Manchester University Press, 1992); Patricia Schroeder, *The Feminist Possibilities of Dramatic Realism* (Madison, WI: Farleigh Dickinson Press, 1996); Judith Mayne, *Cinema and Spectatorship* (New York: Routledge, 1993), 92.
35   Roe, *Stella Miles Franklin*, 127.

2
Like a Thunderstorm

In September 1910, eighteen-year-old garment worker Annie Shapiro walked off the factory floor of the Chicago firm of Hart, Schaffer, and Marx, along with co-workers Esther Feinglass and Bessie Abramowitz. The lives of these Jewish immigrants, who pieced pockets on men's trousers for a few dollars a week, collided with Franklin's, as the walkout escalated into one of the most famous garment workers' strikes in US history, known for its female leadership and organisation that crossed class and ethnic lines, and for its precedent for arbitration that shaped union history. Franklin soon took charge of publicity for the strikers and was swept up into activities that "hit like a thunderstorm" on the Chicago landscape and came to be known as the "Strike of the Forty Thousand".[1] This chapter focuses on Franklin's journalistic and literary responses to this conflict.

Spontaneous strikes were relatively common in Chicago in the first decade of the century and initially newspapers mostly ignored the event. However, strikers paraded with whistles and bells and called workers to join them, and by late October about thirty thousand workers had walked off their jobs despite violent efforts by police and strike-breakers.[2] Tense meetings were held, attended by Franklin, where United Garment Workers' Union President Thomas Rickert did

---

1 National Women's Trade Union League (NWTUL), "Some Facts Regarding Unorganized Working Women in the Sweated Industries," *History of Women*, no. 8623, microfilm (New Haven, CT: Research Publications, 1977 [1914]); Women's Trade Union League (WTUL) of Chicago, "Official Report of the Strike Committee, Chicago Garment Workers' Strike, October 29, 1910 – February 18, 1911", *History of Women*, no. 7161, microfilm (New Haven, CT: Research Publications, 1977 [1911]).
2 Robert Dvorak, "The Chicago Garment Workers", *The International Socialist Review* 11, no. 6 (1910): 358; Amalgamated Clothing Workers of America (ACWA), Research Department, *The Clothing Workers of Chicago, 1910–1922* (Chicago: The Chicago Joint Board and ACWA, 1922).

not take the strike seriously and showed hostility to unionised women, as well as immigrants generally.³ As the days began to get colder, Franklin recorded the temperatures in her diary, worrying how the strikers would fare. The Chicago Women's Trade Union League (WTUL) offered formal assistance that resulted in new responsibilities (including the election of Franklin as Chair of Publicity) and caused Franklin to note the heightened tension in the office where Robins "stormed about".⁴ A Citizens' Committee made up of academics and such formidable reformers as Jane Addams and Grace Abbott investigated grievances that were later submitted as testimony to the Illinois State Senate Investigation Committee.⁵

Eventually in November the "Hart-Rickert Agreement" was made between the garment workers' union and the factory owners, whereby the latter agreed to raising wages and improving conditions, but refused to recognise the union or agree to a closed shop. When Rickert encouraged the strikers to accept this, they decried him as a traitor. As Franklin noted: "Tremendous excitement when it was repudiated".⁶ A Joint Strike Conference Board (JSCB) with representatives from the Chicago WTUL was then formed to handle negotiations. Strikers were suffering and Franklin described the "terrible jam of people … coming for money".⁷ She started the New Year similarly depressed, a condition exacerbated by ill health and the freezing Chicago weather, as well as by the sheer work load: "Crawled into bed feeling cross and ill and disgusted and dispirited with everything", she noted.⁸ Nonetheless Franklin struggled on and by late January 1911 published a cheery call for a fund-raising effort between the Chicago WTUL and the Federation of Women's Clubs. Dubbed "Sweatshop Sunday", it appealed for a "heroic stand for civilized working conditions and the abolition of the Sweatshop from Chicago's Garment Industry!"⁹ The next month Franklin was surprised to hear that Rickert called off the strike without consulting the JSCB or ensuring ratification by the strikers. A "hunger bargain", it occurred "without any consultation".¹⁰ Despite its eventual failure, the strike nonetheless left a legacy of

---

3 Youngsoo Bae, *Labor in Retreat: Class and Community Among Men's Garment Workers of America* (Albany: State University of New York Press, 2001), 88; Miles Franklin, Pocket diary, 12 and 16 October 1910, ML MSS 364/2.
4 Franklin, Pocket diary, 22 October and 1 November 1910.
5 Sophonisba P. Breckinridge, "*Concerning the Garment Workers' Strike (Chicago): Report of the Sub-Committee to the Citizens' Committee*", History of Women, microfilm, no. 8605 (New Haven, CT: Research Publications, 1977 [1910]), 1; Franklin, Pocket diary, 30 October 1910.
6 Franklin, Pocket diary, 5 November 1910.
7 Bae, *Labor in Retreat,* 99; Franklin, Pocket diary, 11 November, 1910.
8 Jill Roe, *Stella Miles Franklin: A Biography* (Sydney: Fourth Estate/Harper Collins, 2008), 141; Franklin, Pocket diary, 11 January 1911.
9 WTUL, "Official Report of the Strike Committee", 30.
10 WTUL, "Official Report of the Strike Committee", 34–5.

solidarity across ethnic and class lines as well as a model of female leadership. It also paved the way for local union control and the formation of the Amalgamated Clothing Workers of America.[11]

Franklin's literary representations of the Chicago garment workers' strike are two-fold. First, her experiences are featured through her role as Publicity Chair and in three articles about the strike published in *Life and Labor*: "Chicago at the Front: A Condensed History of the Garment Workers' Strike"; "Holding the Fort"; and "The End of the Struggle".[12] All articles are unsigned, but are included as Franklin's work in various biographies, mentioned in her diary, and read undeniably as Franklin's prose.[13] These articles redefine creativity as political activism through the lens of New Woman advocacy journalism, which resisted traditional distinctions between news culture and literature, art and political writing. Following Drusilla Modjeska, who describes Franklin's journalism as shaping her fiction, I make the case that Franklin was influenced by Chicago's advocacy "new journalism" that provided accessible print media for radical social commentary.[14] I make a distinction here between the advocacy new journalism more specific to the United States, with its critique of modernity generally, and the power of the corrupt industrialists or "robber barons" in particular, and the broader notion of new journalism associated with British sensation news writing, which "capitalized on social problems" rather than transformed them, and was controlled by corporate influences that ultimately undermined progressive writing.[15] Rejecting the constraints of conventional objective reporting that emerged in the late-nineteenth century in reaction to earlier sensationalist styles, US new journalism defined itself by claiming techniques such as irony, imaginative symbolism, cadence, and prosody more familiar to the novel or short fiction.[16] Although in many ways this was a continuation of partisan nineteenth-century print media, it integrated

---

11 Colette A. Hymann, "Labor Organizing and Female Institution-Building: The Chicago Women's Trade Union League, 1904-1924", in *Women, Work, and Protest: A Century of U.S. Labor History*, ed. Ruth Milkman (Boston: Routledge and Kegan Paul), 22–41; Sue Weiler, "Walkout: The Chicago Men's Garment Workers' Strike, 1910–1911", *Chicago History* 8, no. 4 (1979): 238–49.

12 "Chicago at the Front: A Condensed History of the Garment Workers' Strike", *Life and Labor* (January 1911): 4–12; "Holding the Fort", *Life and Labor* (February 1911): 48–52; "The End of the Struggle", *Life and Labor* (March 1911): 88–89.

13 Margaret Bettison and Jill Roe, "Miles Franklin's Topical Writings: A Listing", *Australian Literary Studies* 20, no. 1 (2001): 97; Franklin, Pocket diary 5, 7 December 1910.

14 Drusilla Modjeski, *Exiles at Home: Australian Women Writers, 1925-1945* (Sydney: Angus & Robertson, 1981).

15 Rita Kranidis, *Subversive Discourse: The Cultural Production of Late Victorian Feminist Novels* (New York: St Martin's Press), xiv.

16 Michael Johnson, *The New Journalism: The Underground Press, the Artists of Nonfiction, and Changes in the Established Media* (Lawrence: University of Kansas Press, 1971).

techniques of fiction and not only expanded the scope of legitimate journalistic reporting, but also fostered a debate about the extent to which journalism might borrow from literature before it violated objective reporting. Through this debate over what counted as "truth", the new journalists thus participated in discussions about literary realism, challenging the journalistic practices of the profession. They insisted that "objective" narrative might be more misleading than stories told from a clearly presented personal point of view, arguing that so-called objectivity did not necessarily guarantee truth.[17] For them "truths" involved inspiring action against social injustice, especially localised corporate greed and corrupt city politics.[18]

Although Franklin had honed her journalism skills before Chicago and continued to write for the Australian press during her time here,[19] she was influenced by the legacy of Henry Demarest Lloyd, father of her beaus, Bill and Demarest. Lloyd senior was an author and *Chicago Tribune* journalist who exposed the corruption of late-nineteenth-century industrial monopolies, especially Chicago-based Standard Oil.[20] Writing in *Life and Labor*, Franklin described him as "one of the first men in America" to recognise journalism's potential "against great social and economic evils". He was, she exclaimed, a "knight" of "modern time".[21] Chicago journalists like Ben Hecht and Henry Justin Smith of the *Daily News,* and Burton Roscoe, the literary editor at the *Chicago Tribune,* followed in this tradition during Franklin's residency, as well as Upton Sinclair, who revealed the brutality of the Chicago stockyards in *The Jungle* (1906). Others like Lincoln Steffens and Ida Tarbell also published in such popular magazines as *Everybody's*, *McClures*, and *Colliers* in order to expose the brutality of Chicago's modern life. In this way, the city provided an exciting and opportunistic milieu from which to hone a socialist feminist-inspired New Woman journalism. Roe describes Franklin working "tirelessly" and learning to write "'on the stone' – that is, dictating copy directly to the typesetter".[22] This is corroborated by Franklin's diary: "No rest or peace in the office"; "Worked like a slave all day on dummy".[23] No sooner would

---

17 Mark Hampton, *Visions of the Press in Britain: 1850–1950* (Champaign: University of Illinois Press, 2004), 35–37.
18 See Phillip H. Ault and Edwin Emery, *Reporting the News* (New York: Dodd, Mead, 1959); J.O. Baylen, "The 'New Journalism' in Late Victorian Britain", *Australian Journal of Politics and History* 18 (December 1972): 367–385; and Hampton, *Visions of the Press in Britain*, 35.
19 S.M. Franklin, "Walter Burley Griffin, Winner of the Federal Capital Prize", *Daily Telegraph* (Sydney), (3 August 1912): 15; S.M. Franklin, "Women to March on the Coliseum", *The World*, (25 August 1912); Alice Henry and S.M. Franklin, "Suffragists Annoyed", *Daily Telegraph* (Sydney) (6 November 1912): 15.
20 Richard Digby-Junger, *The Journalist as Reformer: Henry Demarest Lloyd and Wealth Against Commonwealth* (Westport, CT: Greenwood Press, 1996).
21 S.M. Franklin, "Henry Demarest Lloyd", *Life and Labor* (September 1912): 275.
22 Roe, *Stella Miles Franklin*, 153.

one edition of *Life and Labor* go to press, for example, than Franklin was working furiously on the next one, sometimes writing articles attributed to others. As Lyn Pykett suggests, this link with journalism shaped the market value of New Woman writing at the same time that it allowed women to accessibly represent contemporary concerns for a broad-based audience.[24]

Franklin's second response to the Chicago garment workers' strike is a short, undated, but attributed to 1913, one-act play, "The Waiter Speaks". I have already explored the tradition of protest theatre in Chapter 1, pointing out its role as a liberatory device uncovering contradictions in class society, the interconnections between wealth and poverty, and the personal and systemic violence experienced by ordinary people. However in the years between 1908 when she wrote "The Survivors" and 1913 when it is assumed this play was written, Franklin's approach had matured, sustained by the flourishing protest drama movement in Chicago. Franklin eagerly devoured realist drama, a cornerstone of modern American theatre, at Hull House and the Chicago Fine Arts Building (as evidenced by her attendance, aptly, at Arnold Bennett's play about tabloid journalism, *What the Public Wants*).[25] She was also influenced by suffrage drama and by this time knew the famous English actress and writer Elizabeth Robins, through Robins' sister-in-law, Margaret Dreier Robins. Influence also extended to the thriving Chicago Little Theatre movement, founded by Maurice Browne in 1912, and part of a nationwide movement introducing the artistic principles and experimental techniques of modern drama into nonprofessional theatre at affordable prices. It would provide the foundation for present-day community theatre.[26] "Little" referred to the focus of the plays performed as well as the size of the enterprise.[27] Franklin's diary shows she attended the Little Theatre numerous times in early 1913, perhaps about the time she wrote "The Waiter Speaks".[28] In particular, in February she saw a production of Euripides' *The Trojan Women* there and enthusiastically reviewed it for *Life and Labor*. Franklin closed this review encouraging the Little Theatre to provide more roles for women and suggesting a

---

23 Franklin, Pocket diary, 13 September and 9 October 1911.
24 Lyn Pykett, "Writing Around Modernism: May Sinclair and Rebecca West", in *Outside Modernism: In Pursuit of the English Novel, 1900-1930*, ed. Lynne Hapgood and Nancy L. Paxton (New York: St Martin's Press, 2000), 103–122.
25 Franklin, Pocket diary, 1 April 1910; 1, 19 and 22 January 1910; 31 October 1910; 5, 7 and 25 November 1910; 20 March 1913; "From Near and Far: Drama League of America", *Life and Labor,* (March/April 1911): 93.
26 Bernard F. Dukore, *Maurice Browne and the Chicago Little Theatre* (Urbana: University of Illinois, 1957); Dorothy Chansky, *Composing Ourselves: The Little Theatre Movement and the American Audience* (Carbondale: Southern Illinois University Press, 2004); S.M. Franklin, "Women and War: Chicago's Little Theatre", *Life and Labor* (March 1913): 87.
27 Thomas H. Dickinson, *The Insurgent Theatre* (New York: B.W. Huebsch, 1917), 145.
28 Franklin, Pocket diary, 1 January 1913, 12 February 1913.

"labor play" performed in a "Women's Trade Union League Night".[29] "The Waiter Speaks" may represent Franklin's attempt at such a labour play.

"Short, sharp and political", and illustrating what Shannon Jackson has called "reformance" or the dramatic combination of reform and performance, "The Waiter Speaks" is a "leanly written satire, expressing a great hunger for the feminist cause".[30] It comprises a realist rendition in presenting theatre that mirrors its real-life counterparts in a "slice of life" effect, presenting characters in original settings in the audience's present-day moment. The sketch runs to just short of eight typed manuscript pages and features three unnamed waiters in a "comfortable city restaurant". They serve Mrs Olliver [sic] Dobson, a wealthy philanthropist working as an ally to the striking garment workers (a double for Dreier Robins), and her unnamed secretary (Franklin herself).[31] The three waiters are distinguished by their age, class consciousness, and feelings about unionisation. "Waiter no. 1" is a young man, critical of the restaurant's clientele that disparages the strikers. "Waiter no. 2", the head waiter, identifies with the wealthy business-oriented customers and rejects collective bargaining. "Waiter no. 3", the most experienced, is supportive of the strikers, engaged in the struggle through direct action, and involved with the Waiters' Union. The sketch begins with the Waiter no. 1 taking the women's food order and Waiter no. 2 engaging them in conversation. After the latter leaves to seat a customer, the first returns with the food and talks with the women about the strike. Finally, Waiter no. 3, who is surreptitiously watering plants near Mrs Dobson and her secretary, converses with the women about the strike and his plans for the Waiters' Union. The sketch ends as the first waiter brings the cheque, joins the third waiter in praising the women's work, and accepts a generous gratuity from Mrs Dobson. In the following sections I focus on three central themes represented in Franklin's responses to the garment workers' strike: first, consciousness-raising about the conditions of labour for workers in the garment industries; second, the role of allies in the labour struggle; and third, the need for solidarity across workers and the difficulties of unionisation.

---

29 Franklin, Pocket diary, 5 February 1913; S. M. Franklin, "Women and War: Chicago's Little Theatre", *Life and Labor* (March, 1913): 87.
30 Shannon Jackson, *Lines of Activity: Performance, Historiography, Hull-House Domesticity* (Ann Arbor: University of Michigan Press, 2000), 8; Susan Bradley Smith, "Miles Franklin's Dramatic Ambitions; or, Why Stella Really Came Home", *Antipodes* (June 2007): 18.
31 Miles Franklin, "The Waiter Speaks", ML MSS 445/25, 1. All subsequent references appear in parentheses in the text.

"The Misery"

The dire working conditions of the garment workers and the hardships they endured during the strike were always foremost in Franklin's mind. She was interviewed about this by a reporter from the British Women's Freedom League (WFL) journal, *The Vote,* and declared: "We know what such strikes mean, what has gone before, the misery that makes them necessary, and the misery they cause until a settlement is reached".[32] Franklin's contribution to ameliorating such misery occurred especially in her role as Chair of Publicity where she revealed the strike's human element in order to maintain public sympathy for strikers and to encourage solidarity "against a common oppressor". Franklin's narrative authority to "awaken [the public] to a far deeper understanding of the industrial problem at its door"[33] resided in her immersion in the everyday conditions of the strike, including risking violence and arrest and repeatedly placing herself in the direct line of action. For example, she is described in a *New York Times* article about the strike as a "volunteer picketer" when "[m]ounted police charged mobs of striking garment workers and made numerous arrests". Franklin is noted as "indignant because of the manner in which she had been treated by the police". Her interaction with such police brutality is seconded by Hull-House co-founder Ellen Gates Starr, explaining in the article that they were doing "absolutely nothing against the law". "The only persons violating the law", noted Starr, "were the policemen, who treated us roughly and hurt dreadfully with their clubs some of the poor boys we were leading peacefully by the shops". "Perhaps it would have been a good plan", Franklin is quoted as saying, "to let them take me to jail and just prove to them how little legal foundation they have to stand on".[34] While she did not go to jail, she was called as witness in a test case and prepared her testimony. She was called to court on two occasions, but the case was dismissed.[35] Such experiences helped underscore Franklin's passionate subjectivist journalistic approach.

Narratives of hardship and the abuse of innocent women and children were central in Franklin's advocacy journalism as also was the greed of the manufacturers and their determination to allow violence against those who were bold enough to stand up to intolerable treatment. Franklin starts "Chicago at the Front" with the plural "we" and ends it with a similar refrain, with other collective nouns sprinkled throughout the article. This not only illustrates Franklin's affinity

---

32 Miles Franklin, quoted in A.A. Smith, "Organising Women Workers in America", *Vote*, 16 September 1911: 256.
33 "Chicago at the Front", 4.
34 "Clubwomen Lead Chicago Strike Riot", *New York Times* (2 November 1910): 1.
35 Franklin, Pocket diary, 6 November 1910; 29 and 30 November 1910.

with the subjects of her piece, but also her voice as reporter/narrator inserted into the narrative. This was a participatory project that troubled value-free narrative and reflected new journalism's posture on subjectivity, where reporters were saturated with the issues at hand, and where their values and advocacy shaped the product. And, in Franklin's case, there are sentimental overtones illustrating her feminised approach where strikers endure the bitter cold and babies go hungry:

> With the tramp of thousands of weary feet ... [with] tiny toddlers wailing for milk, with endless difficulties to overcome, we are yet too much in the thick of battle ... The human element, the wonderful patience of the strikers, their heroic endurance under cold, starvation and worst of all, bitter disappointment in their struggle for better conditions touch the heart profoundly.[36]

When the strike was over, Franklin reported, "[w]e are conquered, but we are not defeated ... we may reckon up the losses and gains ... the suffering and destitution ... But far more than this is the sense of solidarity, of mutual understanding".[37]

Similarly, Franklin uses "The Waiter Speaks" for protest and consciousness-raising, immersing herself as a character in the play participating in dialogue about the strike and its miseries. Waiter no. 1 introduces the strikers' grievances in working-class vernacular: "I hope you raise their wages", he tells Mrs Dobson, "and get them conditions of works that are fit for pretty young girls and mens with families [sic]" (5). The average wage for working women in Chicago at this time was about five dollars a week and for men approximately thirteen dollars.[38] With the repeated refrain "it's a waiter that knows", Waiter no. 1 critiques the restaurant's clientele: "They say, these ignorant foreigners, what do they want with higher wages?... they aint half so ignorant as them that comes here to talk of them" (4). This waiter underscores the central grievances of the strike: reduction of wages associated with piece work and increasing complexity of work without remuneration; unjust fines; and the demand for union representation.[39] In his conversation with the women, he explains that his business clientele believes workers should "work in sweat shops all days and all nights too" and admonishes manufacturers who want "young girls ... to starve" (5). This dialogue refers to the increasing mechanisation of factory life that introduced new sewing machines, edge-pressers, and felting machines, and enabled young unskilled immigrant women to obtain jobs previously performed

---

36 "Chicago at the Front", 4.
37 "The End of the Struggle", 88.
38 Bae, *Labor in Retreat*, 3; Carolyn D. McCreesh, *Women in the Campaign to Organize Garment Workers, 1880–1917* (New York: Garland, 1985), 85.
39 WTUL, "Official Report of the Strike Committee", 7–9.

by skilled male labour, although in more tedious conditions and for lower pay.[40] He understands the enormity of the strikers' cause and tells the audience they are "up against a pretty tough proposition" (6).

The uninterrupted – and frequently didactic – monologue familiar to protest drama told a variety of "truths" known to Franklin first-hand through her work with publicity as well as with the picketing committee, which had the two-fold task of both joining the strikers on the picket lines and helping patrol the streets for their protection in order to act as witnesses and testify as needed. The rough handling of strikers and their supporters by police and private detectives inflamed public opinion and helped Franklin's task. She understood the strategic implications of garnering public support at a time when expectations for women – and young immigrant women in particular – constrained both what Franklin could say and the stories about the women she could spin as a journalist. These took shape "over a simple little breakfast [when] the girls talked their hearts out and explained their problems in natural fashion to a few friends".[41] The women's experiences, so simply told, were published the next month in a section called "The Girls Own Stories" as uninterrupted monologue. Franklin reports these "stories" in full, with no summary, editorialising or commentary. For example:

> The foreman said, "If they cannot make it, here is the window and here is the door." I [girl striker] said: "Ain't you ashamed? Ain't you sorry to make those people work an hour and a half for twelve cents?" He said: "Don't you care. In the old country they work for ten cents a day, and in America they make thirty-five cents a day, they can eat beans and they will have plenty to live on" … That made me angry![42]

The article was thus set up from the perspective of the reporter and her "friends". The distanced objectivity of traditional reporting is subverted through intentional participation in the co-creation of truths. In this way Franklin's writing on the strike illustrates central strategies of new journalism that employed techniques borrowed from literature: presentation of full dialogue with conversational speech rather than quotations and summary statements, and the inclusion of nuanced "non-objective" accounts of incremental details of character, relationship, and location. Such narrative inevitably humanised the message and made it immediately interesting and accessible to the reader. It provided education for the public and also allowed the subjects of the

---

40 Alice Kessler-Harris, *Gendering Labor History* (Urbana: University of Illinois Press, 2007). For a broader history see Kessler-Harris's *Out to Work: A History of Wage-Earning Women in the United States* (New York: Oxford University Press, 1982).
41 "Chicago at the Front", 6.
42 "Holding the Fort", 52.

investigation to give voice to their experiences, and develop confidence in their ability to speak in public, build relationships, and go forward in solidarity.

To this end Franklin also had photographs taken of "girl strikers" with "each displaying a badge" announcing she was a "workhouse prisoner" in order to nuance their character and plight. Of course, explained Alice Henry, "that was a good picture to print and printed it was".[43] Franklin provided similar accounts and photographs of the strikers for the *Chicago Daily Tribune* and Henry and Franklin published an article on the strike for the *Englishwoman* magazine.[44] Such publicity encouraged support in part through a sentimental rendering of their voices that invoked a gendered and racialised rhetoric highlighting the women strikers' victimisation as well as their youth and diminutive size. For example, "one of the typical leaders", a "Miss Y", is described in "Holding the Fort" as "a slight, pretty little Russian Jewess, still in her teens". "I was so small", she explained "that the boss could cover me with his coat when the factory inspector came around".[45]

Waiter no. 3 echoes this gesture, describing the striking women as "so many little bits of girls", and adding that "[s]ome of us fellows here have thrown a few dimes together for them" (6). Given the long tradition of anarchism among Jewish garment workers, the critical role of Jewish immigrant women as assertive bread winners of their families, and especially after the extraordinary success of militant Ukrainian Jewish immigrant Clara Lemrich, who sparked the "Uprising of the 20,000" in New York the previous year, it behooved Franklin to de-emphasise any militancy on the part of the "girls". This might explain why Bessie Abramowitz, the outspoken and hardly diminutive union organiser whose walk out helped facilitate the strike and who was also present at this breakfast meeting, was not mentioned by name in the article.[46] "Miss Y" rather than Abramowitz better fit the bill for the image Franklin hoped to portray in order to maximise public sympathies. Not surprisingly, it was the outspoken Abramowitz rather than "little bits of girls" who was hired by the Chicago WTUL to act as liaison with the male-dominated UGW when the strike was over.[47]

---

43 Alice Henry, *Women and the Labor Movement* (New York: George H. Doran, 1923), 118.
44 Harriet Ferrill, "Some Side Lights on the Strike of the Garment Workers". *Chicago Daily Tribune* (13 November 1910): 3; "See Pictures; Forget Strike", *Chicago Daily Tribune* (17 November 1910): 3; S.M. Franklin and Alice Henry, "Why 50,000 Refused to Sew", *The Englishwoman* 10 (June 1911): 297–308.
45 "Holding the Fort", 51.
46 Karen Pastorello, *Bessie Abramowitz Hillman and the Making of the Amalgamated Clothing Workers of America* (Urbana: University of Illinois Press, 2008).
47 McCreesh, *Women in the Campaign to Organize Garment Workers.*

Comrades All

An important message told by Franklin to the reporter of *The Vote* was the reformers' commitment to cross-class alliances as part of the struggle for economic justice:

> [We] recognise that many women who are not compelled to earn their living desire to stand by their wage-earning sisters, and we are the only trade union which allows non-workers to join as allies. It is a splendid idea; it helps women to stand together; it breaks down barriers and class distinctions; it makes us "Comrades All".[48]

Prominent society women took up the garment workers' cause, risking arrest and assault by marching in picket lines, as well as assisting in posting bail, holding benefit functions, and advertising the strikers' plight to the public.[49] In addition, they participated in demonstrations on the streets as recorded, for example, in the *New York Times* article where the reporter explained that police were "dumfounded" when met by "groups of clubwomen and society leaders, who, when arrested, produced calling cards in lieu of bail bonds".[50] Not only were the allies central players in negotiations between manufacturers and strikers, but along with the Chicago Federation of Labor, the Chicago WTUL took over strike relief and plunged into fund-raising that eventually netted over $100,000. They dispensed vouchers for food to be filled at a series of commissary stores, and collections were taken at women's clubs, suffrage organisations, churches, and settlement houses. Dreier Robins even had a plan to provide interest-free loans.[51] After the strike was over and hardships persisted for the strikers and their families, the League continued to provide relief work.[52]

"The Waiter Speaks" is structured around the role of Franklin and Drier Robins as allies who believed in their responsibility to share the human face of struggle.[53] This insertion of real identities easily recognisable to an audience, and the gesture towards their sometimes ambivalent relationship, reflects Franklin's subjectivist stance as playwright and her indeterminate role as a middle-class reformer. The women arrive at the restaurant in mid-afternoon having missed lunch as a result of the work of the strike. "These are terribly busy days", exclaims Mrs Dobson. In

---

48 Franklin, quoted in A.A. Smith, "Organising Women Workers in America", 256.
49 Susan A. Glenn, *Daughters of the Shtetl: Life and Labor in the Immigrant Generation* (Ithaca: Cornell University Press, 1990), 177.
50 "Clubwomen Lead", 1.
51 "The World of Labor", *The Reading Eagle* (20 November, 1910): 17; Franklin, Pocket diary, 17 November 1910.
52 "End of the Struggle", 89.
53 McCreesh, *Women in the Campaign to Organize Garment Workers*, 97.

contrast to the anonymous underling who timidly orders weak coffee, Mrs Dobson is presented as passionate, energised, and with a strong appetite: ostensibly for both food and life. The secretary is ambivalent about ordering dessert, for example, explaining "I don't feel hungry", whereas her boss enthusiastically orders "one of [the] fine large baked apples with plenty of cream". "Laughing gaily", she goes on to reproach her secretary, who suggests she will just have a little bite of Mrs Dobson's apple rather than order her own. "No such thing", Dobson declares. "You just get an apple of your own. I'm hungry" (1).

This dialogue can be read in two ways: it may suggest the ways the secretary – Franklin herself – does not measure up to the vivacious leader who encourages her protégé to seize the moment and "feed" herself: a self-depreciating gesture on Franklin's part; it might also, and I believe more likely, represent a critique of Dreier Robins' entitlement as a privileged woman who takes her food without sharing, as someone who recognises her hunger and feels entitled to satisfy it. Importantly, however, Franklin presents Mrs Dobson as self-actualised rather than selfish; she does not deny her secretary – or the starving strikers – the baked apple, she merely tells Franklin to get her own. That she does not recognise that the secretary may not be able to afford to buy her own dessert in a restaurant is probably closer to Franklin's intentions, although the play seems to indicate that Mrs Dobson eventually paid the bill because she is shown giving the gratuity.

"The Waiter Speaks" represents the commitment of middle-class allies in the face of the struggle as well as working people's appreciation for this work. The two pro-union waiters, for example, speak warmly to them and ask Mrs Dobson to speak at an upcoming Waiters' Union meeting, who eagerly accepts. Indeed, Mrs Dobson with her "vivid coloring" thrives on the work at the same time that the secretary, "a pale and tired-looking young woman" (1), is stressed by the effort. These stage directions, aimed as they are at shaping the interpretation of a real relationship on stage, illustrate again Franklin's subjectivist stance. And certainly Franklin was tired out by the physical and emotional toil of the strike.[54] In comparison, Margaret Dreier Robins was invigorated and saw the struggle between manufacturers and workers as an epic fight "between the forces of good and evil".[55] Mary Dreier, who worked with the New York chapter of the WTUL, described the strike's influence on her sister, writing that it became "part of her very being . . . and burned into her soul".[56] "It is a great fight", exclaims Mrs Dobson in the play: "[i]f we could only get public opinion aroused I am sure it would not stand for

---

54 Franklin, Pocket diary, 6, 7, and 26 November 1910; 9, 11, and 12 January 1911; Verna Coleman, *Her Unknown Brilliant Career: Miles Franklin in America* (Sydney: Angus & Robertson, 1981), 117.
55 McCreesh, *Women in the Campaign to Organize Garment Workers*, 97.

the conditions of work and pay that these young girls are suffering" (3). Like Mrs Dobson, Dreier Robins viewed the League as a "great and glorious cause" inherently tied to the struggle for suffrage.[57] Central here was education for working women about suffrage and its relationship to their economic status. The Chicago WTUL, for example, organised a Wage Earners' Suffrage League to teach women about using the ballot wisely. Suffrage activities alienated some wage-earning women and increased hostility among male union officials opposed to women's citizenship.[58]

Protest and Solidarity

A central focus of attempts dedicated to improve the lives of working people was the need for recognition of the similarities of workers' struggles across the nation, as well as the importance of transnational solidarity. These were central themes of the Industrial Workers of the World (IWW) or "Wobblies", whose international labour union had been founded in Chicago in 1905. Franklin described such focus as the "world-old struggle between human slavery and human freedom" with global class struggle a broad-based war of multiple parties allied in solidarity against injustice.[59] When the strike was over, "the great gift" was "the solidarity . . . that exists today between this huge unorganized group of immigrant workers and the Americanized group of organized labor".[60]

However, it is "The Waiter Speaks" that specifically draws similarities between the poor working conditions of both garment workers and waiters, and demonstrates the similarity of their grievances in making the case for their solidarity. In this regard Franklin establishes dialogue about the poor working conditions of the waiters that puts them on par with the plight of the garment workers and also sets them up as skilled labourers deserving of respect and collective bargaining. The awkward vernacular of the waiters' dialogue is also an attempt at establishing their status as working-class men. For example, Waiter no. 1 uses the inclusive "us" to describe the plight of the working-class people across multiple venues. "I tell you", he exclaims when referring to the restaurant's clientele, "they come here and they speak of us as cattle ... it's a waiter that knows" (5). This repeated motif serves to establish the wisdom of the waiters as witness to the plight of the garment workers and as advocates in solidarity of their struggle.

---

56 Mary Dreier, *Margaret Dreier Robins, Her Life, Letters and Work* (New York: Island Press Cooperative, 1950), 61. See also Elizabeth A. Payne, *Reform, Labor, and Feminism: Margaret Dreier Robins and the NWTUL* (Urbana: University of Illinois Press, 1988).
57 Henry, *Women and the Labor Movement*, 102.
58 Franklin, Pocket diary, 11 October 1910.
59 Franklin, quoted in A.A. Smith, "Organising Women Workers in America", 257.
60 "End of the Struggle", 88.

This issue of similarities across the conditions of working people's lives is raised by Mrs Dobson when she asks Waiter no. 2 how many hours he works daily and is indignant upon hearing his answer of twelve hours. Scholars have suggested that waiters during this period suffered "bondage", being "compelled to work 15 hours and even longer".[61] Their wages were also very low because their labour in many eating establishments was unskilled, and because non-white labour could be exploited if whites were unwilling.[62] Waiter no. 3 alludes to these facts in a remark about fund-raising for the strikers: "We wish it was more but our own conditions are none too rosy" (6). As Mrs Dobson leaves a generous tip, we are reminded that waiters' wages are supported by the generosity of patrons.

"The Waiter Speaks" not only presents a dignified portrayal of hard working waiters but also emphasises the skilled aspect of this labour: an important issue because it provided justification for their union involvement and their strength as a collective bargaining unit alongside other workers. The waiters in Franklin's play are courteous in serving the women and attending to their wants; they hover unobtrusively and arrange cutlery or water plants as they converse with their clientele. Waiter no. 1, for example, remembers that the secretary likes "very weak coffee": a fact which impresses the secretary. He also explains that waiters must "put [their] personalities aside" in emphasising the neutrality of manner needed in this line of work. When discussing the clientele whom he finds abhorrent, the waiter explains the difficulty of "keep[ing] silences" about such bigotry and how "once in a while [he must tell] the truth" (5). In this dialogue Franklin points out that waiters deal with class relationships on a daily basis, using their "truth" as a basis for collective action. The latter is exemplified by Waiter no. 3, who not only supports the strikers but is actively working with the Waiters' Union despite its challenges, explaining that they have to meet secretly "in this land of the free where the bosses can organize, but the workers can't or every one of us would be fired right now" (6).

Although this play dramatises the necessity of unionisation for improving worker autonomy and conditions, it also spells out the challenges associated with class consciousness and the ways workers identify with business and impose status hierarchies among themselves. Franklin uses Waiter no. 2, the headwaiter, to achieve this end, demonstrating how he unwittingly adopts the views of the oppressor class and directs resentment about his situation onto those of equal or

---

61 Matthew Josephson, *Union House, Union Bar: The History of the Hotel and Restaurant Employees' and Bartenders' International Union*, AFL-CIO (New York: Random House, 1956), 13; Mary Lee Spence, "They Also Serve Who Wait", *The Western Historical Quarterly* 14, no. 5 (1983): 16.

62 Philip S. Foner and Ronald Lewis, *The Black Worker: A Documentary History From Colonial Times to the Present, vol. 1: The Black Worker to 1859* (Philadelphia: Temple University Press, 1978).

lesser status by setting himself above the general class of waiters. Franklin shows how he has internalised ideologies that keep him ignorant of the ways power works in his profession and in society generally. From his point of view "anyone" can belong to a union, and "the best ones of the profession don't have to pay no more money than the "bums" who "spill ... over ladies" (3). In response, the secretary makes a humorous suggestion: "Well, couldn't you have a division in your union?" she asks. "The hoboes of the profession who carry things on their arms and spill some of it over ladies could pay fifty cents ... and the experts who know how to wait on a lady could pay double" (3). Such a suggestion would have garnered a laugh from a potential audience at the same time that it illustrates the problems of solidarity among workers.

In this way Franklin's politics and their relationship to writing represent one of the defining characteristics of New Woman fiction: the challenge to and disruption of dichotomies between literature and political writing across multiple locations. While this experience of the garment workers' strike reinforced her politics and understandings of labour issues, it also provided a confidence and narrative authority for literary endeavours presented in both the *Life and Labor* articles about the strike and "The Waiter Speaks". Articulating the plight of garment workers, the role of the allies, and need for worker solidarity in this writing, Franklin modelled the ways the protest tradition responded to the complex social and economic conditions of modernity during this period.

Part II: Marriage

3
That Vexatious Failure

In her critique of marriage and domesticity, Cicely Hamilton, actress and founder of the Women Writers' Suffrage League, declared the " housekeeping trade" the "only one open to us – so we enter the housekeeping trade in order to live". "This", she added, is "not quite the same as entering the housekeeping trade in order to love".[1] Struggles for economic independence and personal fulfilment, and the negotiation of one or the other – the living or the loving – are central themes of this chapter on Miles Franklin's marriage and courtship stories. Franklin eagerly read Hamilton's book, *Marriage as a Trade*, in April 1913, as well as Jane Johnston Christie's *The Advance of Woman* the year before. Their insights about the compulsory nature of matrimony and its relationship to women's inability to survive without male patronage were influential for Franklin, who emphatically believed that the economics of marriage and its domestic practices of domesticity set up marriage as a housekeeping trade constraining women and robbing them of their independence and human dignity.[2]

Franklin's preoccupation with the subjection of women to this particular "vexatious failure" with its reproduction of dominant gender/power relations is represented in a series of short stories, which include the unpublished manuscripts "Teaching Him" (1909); "Mrs. Mulvaney's Moccasins" (1911); "The Illogical Sex" (1911); and "A Business Emergency" (1915).[3] All but "The Illogical Sex" are

---

1   Cicely Hamilton, *Marriage as a Trade* (Detroit: Singing Tree Press, [1909] 1971), 18–19.
2   Miles Franklin, Pocket diary, 20 April 1913, ML MSS 364/2; Jane Johnstone Christie, *The Advance of Woman from the Earliest Times to the Present* (Philadelphia: J.B. Lippincott, 1912). Franklin, Pocket diary, 24 November, 1912. Jill Roe, *Stella Miles Franklin: A Biography* (Sydney: Fourth Estate/Harper Collins, 2008), 151.
3   Mona Caird from the 1888 *Westminster Review*, quoted in Angelique Richardson, *Love and Eugenics in the Late Nineteenth Century: Rational Reproduction and the New Woman* (Oxford: Oxford University Press, 2003), 179; Miles Franklin, "Teaching Him", ML MSS 445/22; "Mrs. Mulvaney's Moccasins", ML MSS 445/22; Mr. and Mrs. Ogniblat L'Artsau

unpublished stories and very little evidence survives concerning their submission or rejection. Through close readings of these stories I examine Franklin's articulation of matrimony as an economic transaction with particular consequences for women's lives, and explore her solution to this problem: the socially and economically independent, spunky heroine. In varying ways each story presents a continuation of Franklin's focus on the economics of marriage as portrayed in *My Brilliant Career,* with its critique of the inequalities of class as well as gender by articulating grievances against the personal and political ramifications of marriage and domesticity. Some of these Chicago marriage problem stories are more radical in critiquing private restrictions and economic tyrannies than others, although all negotiate the matrimonial imperative in their own way. Each also scrutinises cultural and biological destinies rooted in courtship, matrimony, and domesticity from within the romance tradition. As Gillian Beer points out, the romance mode moved beyond realism's engagement with the known world to capture the hidden dreams of that world, making the case for romantic yearning's subversive reach beyond the limitations of everyday reality.[4] And because these stories are "short" and targeted a broad popular market, they contained subversive potential for helping readers rethink and reframe their worlds through the familiar – and pleasurable – tradition of romantic fantasy.

This matrimonial scepticism represents a continuation of Franklin's commitments to the triple grievances of the Australian Women's movement: the condition of marriage and the double standard of sexuality; the exploitation of working women; and women's lack of citizenship and political autonomy, and reflects not only the objectives of *My Brilliant Career,* but also Franklin's suffrage novel, *Some Everyday Folk and Dawn.*[5] In these endeavours she was influenced by late-nineteenth and early-twentieth-century Australian novels about the failure of marriage, such as Rosa Campbell Praed's *The Bond of Wedlock* (1887), Tasma's *A Fiery Ideal* (1897), and Ada Cambridge's *Sisters* (1904). The New Woman stories of Franklin's American years are also influenced by an economic critique of marriage, such as that foreshadowed by Praed, for example, whose protagonist in *The Bond of Wedlock* reveals marriage as a financial transaction. Franklin follows Praed's lead in advocating for women's economic independence and interrogating the sexual double standard that precipitated economic incarceration in marriage and domesticity. Louisa Lawson, the Australian suffragist and writer, and editor of the

---

(aka Miles Franklin), "A Business Emergency", ML MSS 364/58; Grandpa Griddle (aka Miles Franklin), "The Illogical Sex", *Life and Labor* (September, 1911): 287–288. Subsequent references appear in parentheses in the text.
4   Gillian Beer, *The Romance* (London: Routledge and Kegan Paul, 1970).
5   Susan Magarey, *Passions of the First-Wave Feminists* (Sydney: University of New South Wales Press, 2001).

Dawn magazine, similarly provided a strong critique of marriage by making the case for analogies between wives and workers. The headline for a 1890 article led off with the proclamation: "Meeting of the Amalgamated Wives' Association!! Demands of the Women!! Domestic life paralysed!!"[6]

The economic analysis of Franklin's Chicago short stories represents a continuation of these earlier traditions, but also integrates a nuanced version through the specific lens of the New Woman in the American metropolis. In this endeavour Franklin was influenced by the work of Charlotte Perkins Gilman. Although Franklin was familiar with Gilman's *Women and Economics* (1898) before she left for Chicago, and would declare her "incomparably the greatest American woman alive", in the US Franklin heard her speak several times and came to know her personally through Margery Curry Dell, Gilman's agent.[7] In a letter to Rose Scott, for example, Franklin had the following to say about a lecture by Gilman attended in late 1912: "It was a great tonic to hear her tell those women the straight truth. She took out their old parasitic backbones with one clean surgical incision and supplied them with vertebrae based on a biological foundation calling for economic self-respect".[8]

Franklin's interest in the short story form and its usefulness for feminist political ends was also shaped by the increasing popularity of New Women short story collections, especially from the U.K., which provided bold representations of women's freedom. The publication of collections such as Ella Hepworth Dixon's *One Doubtful Hour and Other Sidelights on the Feminine Temperament* (1904) and Sarah Grand's *Emotional Moments* (1908), for example, emerged after the popularity of George Egerton's (Mary Chavelita Dunne) *Keynotes* in 1893.[9] Published in British magazines such as the *Yellow Book* and *Blackwoods Magazine*, and in the U.S. *Cosmopolitan*, these stories were not only instrumental in the growth of the periodical press, helping establish women's voice in popular media, but they also provided potentially subversive content to a mass readership.[10] The usefulness of these examples resided not only in their template for Franklin's feminist political agenda, but also as a result of certain features of their form,

---

6   Louisa Lawson, quoted in Susan Magarey, "*My Brilliant Career* and Feminism", *Australian Literary Studies* 20, no. 4 (2002): 390.
7   Charlotte Perkins Gilman, *Women and Economics: A Study of the Economic Relation Between Men and Women as a Factor in Social Evolution* (Boston: Small, Maynard & Company, 1910 [1898]); Roe, *Stella Miles Franklin*, 155.
8   Miles Franklin, quoted in Roe, *Stella Miles Franklin*, 155.
9   Emma Liggins, "The 'Modern Spinster's Lot' and Female Sexuality in Ella Hepworth Dixon's *One Doubtful Hour*", *Women's Writing* 19, no. 1 (2012): 5–22. Egerton was born in Melbourne.
10 Valerie Shaw, *The Short Story: A Critical Introduction* (London: Longman, 1983); Alice Jenkins and Juliet John, eds., *Rereading Victorian Fiction* (New York: Palgrave, 2000), 6.

which Clare Hanson describes as "hug[ging] the unknown to itself".[11] The short story's brevity, for instance, and the speed with which it might be produced, was well suited to authors whose lives were interrupted by work and domesticity – although in Franklin's case such obstacles did not prevent her from writing novels, and her short stories, what Verna Coleman calls her "pot boilers", were written quickly alongside longer works with hopes of supplementing her meagre income.[12] A relatively common practice at a time when the short story form tended to be viewed as secondary to novels, and authors wrote "unashamedly for money",[13] critiques of marriage and domesticity thus coexisted with the need to satisfy a mass female readership, and represented a two-prong strategy of subversion and commercial gain. As Tony Bennett notes, this writing provided a terrain where "dominant, subordinate and oppositional cultural values meet and intermingle".[14]

In addition, because short stories were more partial and fragmentary with a propensity for ambiguity, they were more easily able to resolve the awkward plot tensions plaguing New Woman writers.[15] When critics refer to the "contradictions" and "emotional confusion" of *My Brilliant Career* with its "to and fro" concerning Sybylla Melvyn's relationship with Harold Beecham, for example, they are responding in part to structural features of the feminist romance imperative that had to deal with the ways romance undercut the heroine's claims for independence, and happy endings (expected by a reading public) might resituate domestic imperatives.[16] The short story form helped, but did not entirely solve, this problem for Franklin. Because writing for the popular market meant she still had to negotiate subversive political ends with the needs of a mass readership, ambiguous, and sometimes contradictory narratives still prevailed, and perhaps help explain why her stories remained unpublished.[17] Indeed, the inability to reconcile these contradictions often resulted in clumsy dialogue and awkward inconsistencies

---

[11] Clare Hanson, "'Things Out of Words': Towards a Poetics of Short Fiction" in *Re-Reading the Short Story*, edited by Clare Hanson (New York: St Martin's Press, 1989), 30.

[12] Virginia Woolf, *A Room of One's Own* (New York: Harcourt Brace Jovanovich, 1963 [1929]), 81; Verna Coleman, *Her Unknown Brilliant Career: Miles Franklin in America* (Sydney: Angus & Robertson, 1981), 118.

[13] Emma Liggins, Andrew Maunder, and Ruth Robbins, *The British Short Story* (New York: Palgrave, 2011), 89–90.

[14] Tony Bennett, "The Politics of 'The Popular' and Popular Culture", in *Popular Culture and Social Relations*, ed. Tony Bennett, Colin Mercer, and Janet Woollacott (Philadelphia: Open University Press, 1986), 19.

[15] Angelique Richardson, "Introduction", in *Women Who Did: Stories by Men and Women*, ed. Angelique Richardson (London: Penguin, 2002), xlix; Eagleton, "Gender and Genre", in *Re-Reading the Short Story*, 62.

[16] Stephen Garton, "Contesting Enslavement: Marriage, Manhood and *My Brilliant Career*", *Australian Literary Studies* 20, no. 4 (2002): 347, 346.

[17] Judy Simons and Kate Fullbrook, eds., *Writing: A Woman's Business: Women, Writing and the Marketplace* (Manchester: Manchester University Press, 1998).

within the story as light-hearted and comedic intent collided with a didactic feminist voice, or the assertive protagonist somehow had to turn her disdain for the flawed suitor into romantic desire. And this is not surprising, for as Chris Willis reminds us, although the New Woman in popular fiction for mass consumption was positively portrayed as healthy, intelligent, and attractive, she always "loses out to the 'womanly' woman", who chooses romance. "[I]f the New Woman is to find a mate she must become as womanly as her less politicised sisters".[18] This was the heart of the problem. These commercial short stories could reach a wider audience, but the New Woman's vocation was inherently depoliticised because her worth was still based upon the ability to become a romantic object, worthy of marriage: the very institution the New Woman writers were hoping to transform. Such a conundrum shaped Franklin's courtship and marriage stories.

"Teaching Him", one of Franklin's earliest Chicago stories, runs to sixteen typed manuscript pages and is undated, but mentioned in her diary in late 1909. Less than a week before working on it, Franklin records reading *Ann Veronica*, a novel published that year by H.G. Wells featuring a bold heroine, who offered a model of feminism's impact on the modern woman: not unlike the self-possessed heroine of this story.[19] "Teaching Him" is set in the home of affectionate newlyweds Mr and Mrs Philip Bohrer. "Mrs Philip" is never referred to by her own name: significant for Franklin's presentation of marriage as a transaction that retains male identity while turning women into the property of men. As she explained in the *Book Lover* several years earlier, "the thought of giving up my own name, even to be Mrs The-Greatest-Gun-Going has ever raised a spirit of protest in me".[20] Mrs Philip, an older self-sufficient woman who established a successful writing career before marriage, teaches her husband about the economic implications of marriage. Subverting the impulse of gratitude for his social and economic protection, she resists *femme couverte* (the notion that upon marriage wives are absorbed into the legal person of the husband) through demands for a salary of her own, which she declares her right rather than her privilege. This move highlights domestic work as productive labour and makes the case for woman's self-sufficiency in marriage.

The second story, "Mrs. Mulvaney's Moccasins", is more traditional in employing an omniscient narrator who explains the characters and presents the

---

18 Chris Willis, "'Heaven Defend Me From Political or Highly-Educated Women!': Packaging the New Woman for Mass Consumption", in *The New Woman in Fiction and in Fact: Fin-de-Siècle Feminisms*, ed. Angelique Richardson and Chris Willis (New York: Palgrave, 2001), 56.
19 Franklin, Pocket diary, 11 and 5 December 1909.
20 Miles Franklin, *Book Lover*, 1 September 1907: 97–98, reprinted as "Letter from Chicago", in *A Gregarious Culture: Topical Writings of Miles Franklin,* ed. Jill Roe and Margaret Bettison (St Lucia: University of Queensland Press, 2001), 32.

classic light-hearted plot of mistaken identity and its romantic almost-happy ending. The story runs to fifteen typed manuscript pages and is undated, attributed to 1911, and reworked at a later date.[21] It concerns a successful author and playwright, Dayton Blanche, who employs a housekeeper named Mrs. Mulvaney. Her special feature is her feet and her bunions in particular. She runs a tight ship and helps Mr Blanche hire a competent stenographer named Joyce Frothingham, who sends Mrs. Mulvaney a pair of moccasins for Christmas hoping they might ease the housekeeper's bunions. Unbeknownst to Joyce, however, the package is addressed incorrectly, and Mr Blanche receives the present and her invitation to dinner. He becomes enamoured even though she regrets the error and avoids his advances. Eventually she sees the author in a new light and professes romantic feelings for him. The story ends on a comic note with Mrs. Mulvaney's bunions at centre stage, thanked for the romance they precipitated. It is ambiguous, however, whether Joyce will trade her dreary work for marriage and/or whether the latter is inevitable.

The third short story was also written in 1911 and published in the September issue of *Life and Labor* under the colloquial pseudonym "Grandpa Griddle". It presents a strong critique of marriage, but also employs the traditional rhetorical device of the "engaging narrator" who performs as the "teller" of the tale, and whose success in mimicking the real-life situation of colloquial conversation is predicated on the fact that the narrator avoids drawing attention to the fictional frame through engagements that work to insist the story is "true".[22] Illustrating Franklin's transnational hybridity as her folksy yarn meets urban New Woman, the story is told from the perspective of the wise elder, "Grandpa Griddle". Running only one full page, or two side by side columns, the story concerns a courtship between two ill-matched people: a traditional, chivalrous young man, Charlie Evvers, and a New Woman, Helen Summers. The story revolves around Helen's response to Charlie's advances.

The last story is "A Business Emergency", written in 1915 under Franklin's penname, Mr and Mrs Ogniblat L'Artsau. It runs to slightly over eleven-and-a-half typed manuscript pages and portrays a frank and more critical portrayal of marriage that reflects Franklin's more mature analysis. The protagonist is Mabel Dodge Reber, an actress who recognised that material comforts procured as a result of her work on the stage might be more easily accessed by marrying the wealthy man with whom she was having an affair. Marriage to Brant Reber was purely akin

---

21 Franklin, Pocket diary, 15 April 1911; Roe, *Stella Miles Franklin*, 145, 146; Franklin, Pocket diary, 8 April 1911.
22 Robin R. Warhol, "Toward a Theory of the Engaging Narrator: Earnest Intervention in Gaskell, Stowe, and Eliot", *PMLA* 101 (1986): 811–18.

to employment and she took it "for all it would yield" (3). Once her "berth" is at risk owing to her husband's new infidelity, Mabel uses all her assets, which include acting skills, to maintain her economic position (9). The story is narrated in the third person from Mabel's dispassionate point of view and ends with a somewhat ambiguous inclination about returning to show business that questions the business of marriage after all.

In the sections below I focus on two interrelated themes as represented in Franklin's short stories: first, the exploration of marriage and domesticity as economic practices that benefit husbands, but result in women's domestic enslavement, financial dependency, and subsequent loss of employment or creative work; and second, the character of the economically independent and self-sufficient heroine with "superior" intellect and integrity that functions as a central trope for the critique and reform of marriage.

Making Their Living Out of Their Loving

Although there is no direct evidence that Franklin read Gilman's *The Home: Its Work and Influence* (1903), it seems very likely. Gilman's central premise that human progress depends on women's liberation from domestic servitude is aptly illustrated in Franklin's Chicago stories. Her views on the dangers of domesticity are reflected in Gilman's insistence that women's economic dependence in marriage meant they must pay off their debt through domestic service: when women are "no longer mak[ing] their living out of their loving, the prostitute, and that more successful specialist, the mercenary wife, will leave the world".[23] It is especially Mabel Reber, the wife in "A Business Emergency", who provides a fine illustration of a self-consciously mercenary wife, although female protagonists in "Teaching Him" and "Mrs. Mulvaney's Moccasins" also trouble matrimony through presentations of its economic basis.

"Teaching Him", for example, begins with a focus on economic self-respect when Mrs. Philip lovingly requests money and responds to her husband's query about how much she needs by saying "[i]t depends on how much I am worth." She declares this "a very poor salary" and begrudges having to show gratitude "like a pauper or poor relation begging alms". She wants "a specified amount" as "a right" and "without any asking" (1–2). These opening lines present Franklin's efforts to portray marriage as an economic contract relying on the unpaid labour

---

23 Charlotte Perkins Gilman quoted in Larry Ceplair, *Charlotte Perkins Gilman: A Nonfiction Reader* (New York: Columbia University Press, 1991), 153. See also Judith A. Allen, *The Feminism of Charlotte Perkins Gilman: Sexualities, Histories, Progressivism* (Chicago: University of Chicago Press, 2009).

of wives and illustrates the precarious economic situation whereby wives must rely on the generosity of husbands. "You don't get anyone to work for you out of love except your mother and wife", exclaims Mrs. Philip (13). Her husband then raises Franklin's central message: "[You] talk ... as if [marriage] were a business arrangement ... Dear one, I shall be afraid that you don't love me if you talk like that" (4, 13). Mrs. Philip replies:

> It's not that I do not love you but love doesn't hold self-respect and a desire for perfect liberty has no intelligence ... supposing ... you give up your business while I supported you and then your only means of getting money was to flatter and coax me for it, how would you feel? (14)

"Teaching Him" was very likely influenced by a debate between Gilman and U.S. suffrage leader Anna Howard Shaw, and moderated by Mary Dreier of the New York WTUL, that preceded the writing of this story in January 1909. Gilman argued the affirmative on the question "Is the Wife Supported by the Husband?" and Shaw the negative. Gilman made the case that women's labour in the home was unproductive, calling such wives parasitical.[24] "An unpaid wife", Gilman declared, was "a domestic servant in the extremely wasteful and expensive class of one servant to one man".[25] Shaw, however, made the distinction between wives and servants. She explained that wives put "something economically valuable" into the husband's income and suggested that wives and mothers should be "compensated with earnings".[26] Opposing Gilman's notion that wives and servants are analogous, Shaw claimed that wives and mothers make a home whereas servants only maintain it. This latter notion, which won the debate for Shaw, is employed in "Teaching Him", representing Franklin's nuanced reading of Gilman's economic treatises. For example, when Mrs. Philip asks her husband how much she is worth as his wife and companion, he is confused and asks: "A salary – you talk as if you were my housekeeper ... but you're my wife." Agreed, explains Mrs. Philip, telling him "you owe me ... something above $900.00" (3).

This story also provides an opportunity for Franklin to show how husbands' economic power over wives maintains class antagonisms between women. She illustrates how female dependence on male generosity encourages horizontal hostility or divisiveness between women and undercuts their dignity as humans: "Kept

---

24 Susan L. Mizruchi, "Becoming Multicultural: Culture, Economy, and the Novel", in *The Cambridge History of American Literature, volume 3: Prose writing, 1860–1920*, ed. Sacvan Bercovitch (New York: Cambridge University Press, 2005), 628.
25 Gilman quoted in Ann Crittenden, *The Price of Motherhood* (New York: Henry Holt, 2001), 62.
26 Shaw quoted in Crittenden, *The Price of Motherhood*, 63.

women" are encouraged to underpay servants and scrimp on household expenses and thus earn "a cruel reputation for meanness in [their] struggles for a little private money" (5), declares Mrs. Philip. Such class analyses were central for Franklin. In this endeavour she deviated from other New Woman writers who did not offer a class analysis, or proletarian writers who did not make these gender distinctions.

Ultimately, however, although "Teaching Him" is a fascinating story in its depiction of the economic foundations of domesticity, its romantic impulse is clumsy. Their affectionate relationship softens Mrs. Philip's demands on her husband, but still the assertive, independent wife who smashes all argument with stunning logic has to end up with a husband whom she describes as "a great Paleozoic blunderbuss": a phrase she utters in uncharacteristically "seductive feminine little tones" (16). And even though this performative femininity might be read as ironic gesture, these affectionate capitulations that soften her stridency at the end of the story are awkward and reflect the difficulties of situating independent women within the romantic imperative.

This difficulty is also prominent in "Mrs. Mulvaney's Moccasins", although its ambiguous ending tends to undercut the romance and potentially underscore feminist scepticism. Here the independent, wage-earning New Woman finds romance with her unappealing employer. His entitlement is necessary for Franklin to make the case about the conditions of women's wage-earning; unfortunately such portrayals then complicate a believable happy ending, although perhaps this is Franklin's point. The story has Joyce, who was initially repelled by her employer, suddenly "astounded by the sudden friendliness . . . upon sight of him" (14). Such ungainly acknowledgement of romantic desire and its resolution might thus be read as Franklin's intentional ironic intent to highlight the extent to which unattractive suitors might promise a better livelihood for the single wage-earning woman than the economic vulnerability of working as a stenographer for the rest of her life. The pathos of such lines as a "loquacity . . . bloomed in her" as "his name slipped from her lips", especially in the context of a comedic story that starts out with a discussion of Mrs. Mulvaney's aching bunions, suggests such an ironic move on Franklin's part. Accepting "marriage as a trade" with better prospects than working as a short-hand typist, and approaching it in such a way that the reader comes to question the turn towards romance, Joyce reveals the romantic predicament for the modern woman at the same time that she highlights for the reader the economic basis of marriage. This is akin to Jane Austen's ironic scripting of Elizabeth Bennet's change of heart over Mr Darcy when she catches sight of his family estate, Pemberley, in *Pride and Prejudice*.

Although both "Mrs. Mulvaney's Moccasins" and "Teaching Him" employ matrimony in varying ways, these stories critique, satirise, and destabilise the marriage plot even as they use it to fuel the narrative. They thus illustrate practices of containment (what Elizabeth McLeod Walls calls a " domestic feminism" revamping nineteenth-century domestic fiction) that were particularly strategic given the romance mandate and the potential mass appeal of New Woman stories.[27] In comparison "A Business Emergency" presents matrimony as distinctly unpalatable, yet still negotiable as a rational economic arrangement. Here a "mercenary wife" uses her husband, for whom she has little affection and no respect, in order to make her living. She understands marriage has "obligations", but insists this is true for "every job, even the stage" (3). Brant was acceptable because he was simple and not "handicapped by any complex mental machinery"; he also possessed "ample means and sound physique" (4). It is therefore no surprise when Mabel responds to Brant's infidelity with the same rational approach:

> She would meet it much as she might the sudden knowledge that one of her high priced rugs had a big grease spot on it or had suffered an attack of moths and was in need of conservation. To her it would be an emergency, to be handled in a business-like way and expeditiously. (1)

Although Mabel feels no jealousy in hearing news of her husband's infidelity, her emotional investment rests in needing to know the details of the affair and its potential implications for her livelihood. Franklin's understanding of marriage as an economic arrangement thus also reflects Cicely Hamilton's insistence on the necessity in marriage, as in any business contract, for articulating participants' rights, especially in the case where one partner is vulnerable as a result of the other partner's proclivity for bad behaviour. Women, for example, needed "the perfect right to know [the] dangers and drawbacks attached to their calling" as wives and sexual partners. Men's "loose living" resulted in "tangible, physical consequences", which invariably affected the women in their lives.[28] Mabel's need to know about her husband's bad behaviour drives the plot of this story and is implicated in its ending when her marriage – and therefore economic livelihood – is once more secured, or potentially given up because to Mabel, "[m]arriage had begun to pall" and the stage once more beckoned. "There were many pebbles on the beach", she exclaimed, "and [on] the stage beach not a few of them [were] gilded" (12).

Armed with this information, Mabel would "never be like Mrs. Reber No.1 and vacate her berth … As soon as the divorce had declared it vacant Mabel stepped into it with the satisfaction one feels in securing a particularly desirable apartment

---

27 Tamara S. Wagner, *Domestic Fiction in Colonial Australia and New Zealand* (New York: Routledge, 2004); Elizabeth McLeod Walls, "'A Little Afraid of the Women of Today': The Victorian New Woman and the Rhetoric of British Modernism", *Rhetorical Review* 21, no. 3 (2002): 230.
28 Hamilton, *Marriage as a Trade*, 73.

over the heads of competitors" (3). Such foreclosure of the romantic imperative makes "A Business Emergency" the most readable of the stories, at least from our contemporary perspective. There is no clumsy attempt to reconcile the couple or to make the case for marriage as a romantic arrangement. The wife's potential return to her acting career might be interpreted as straight-forward rejection of marriage; it might also be read as another ironic gesture underscoring matrimonial bankruptcy as a financially, secure middle-class marriage gets thrown over for the economic uncertainties of life on the stage. Delivered amidst social and literary expectations of marriage as romantic obligation, this "endorsement" of its rational economic aspects serves precisely to reveal its flaws. In other words, in portraying marriage as an economic contract – although importantly a contract between unequal partners – Franklin both undermines it as a romantic endeavour and destabilises it as a rational choice.

A Sane, Sensible Woman

Contrary to New Woman literature of the 1890s that presented outspoken rebellious heroines openly challenging conventional morality and social and sexual norms with astonishing realism and yet who were usually thwarted in their rebellion, New Woman writing after the *fin de siècle* reflected changes in social conventions. It accepted the common presence of the independent woman who in varying degrees both reforms (as in "Mrs. Mulvaney's Moccasins" and "Teaching Him") and transforms (as in "A Business Emergency"), traditional matrimony and courtship practices. As a result, the independent heroine of early-twentieth-century feminist literature was often depicted as a relatively ordinary woman who acted on her desires and was willing to stand up for her beliefs on the matrimonial front. In much Progressive-era New Woman literature, and especially in Franklin's Chicago stories, the spirited protagonist asserts herself and models an independent, urban life, even if she eventually marries. It is through her eyes and voice, and especially her keen logic, as well as through evidence of the flawed manhood of her suitors, that Franklin presents the critique and reform of marriage and courtship practices.

The protagonist of "Teaching Him" is "no maudlin girl in the meshes of an effervescent first passion", but "a sane, sensible woman", who had a successful career before she married (7). Her performance of a housekeeper's work "without having a housekeeper's economic self-respect and independence" precipitates a bold plan with bold words: "Philip, my boy, you've got to be taught!" she exclaims (13, 5). Franklin presents the human capital produced by Mrs. Philip during her spinsterhood as an important asset in marriage and suggests that had Mrs. Philip been less mature, she would have relinquished her plan for economic self-respect upon seeing her husband looking "tired and worn", and thus "sealed the loss of her economic independence forever" (12). Instead she assertively refuses Philip's suggestion for an account in her own name, demands "rights not privileges" (12), and threatens to leave him if he does not accept her terms. Underscoring the economic benefits of wives' domestic labour, Mrs. Philip also refuses all household work, including preparing her husband's dinner, and retires to her study to write. "There!" she exclaims: "That's the last housekeeping I am going to do for nothing" (5-6). The story makes the point that women (at least economically privileged, middle-class women) can be independent without jeopardising their marriageability. It ends with Mrs. Philip articulating her rational argument with spirit and resolve such that "Philip agreed like a very young lamb" (15).

Franklin's depiction of such rebellious behaviour that violates all wifely expectations is a bold gesture and requires a traditional feminine character motivated by love and the backdrop of a happy marriage to make it palatable (and potentially marketable) to a broad audience. A clumsy movement between the strident wife demanding a salary and the affectionate wife whose thoughts about her husband "brought a tug to Mrs. Philip's heart" (7) is Franklin's attempt at reconciling the contradictions. She asserts this by making the case that the lesson is constructed with only Mr Philip's best interests in mind: "He's too good a man" to be allowed to continue in these sexist ways (7-8). And to reassure the more conservative reader, Franklin emphasises that the "intellectual" Mrs. Philip does not violate gender norms. Her husband thinks lovingly of her as "a maze of fripperies", "smelling of the dainty powders and toilet waters dear to the heart of women" (8). And, although she refuses to cook, she does not abdicate responsibility for feeding her husband, but solves the dilemma by ordering food to be delivered for him. Mrs. Philip is thus presented as morally impeccable. From her support of a widowed mother to her concern about those less fortunate, she is shown as compassionate and exceedingly virtuous. Unlike the protagonist in "A Business Emergency", who presents a very different kind of wife, Mrs. Philip's motivation for teaching her husband the lesson about women's economic dependency is self-respect and wifely concern rather than personal material gain.

Accompanying the independent heroine in much New Woman fiction is the flawed traditional male suitor whose lack of integrity, intelligence, and/or ethics provides sharp contrast to the superior intellectual and moral qualities of the protagonist. The "hapless husband" is also a relatively useful device that allows for a critique of both marriage and contemporary manhood without disturbing the narrative conventions of the romance story or disallowing the husband's skills or genius in other (non-domestic) areas. He may be clueless in this sphere, but he is not malicious and thus reformable. Mrs. Philip's intellectual superiority, for example, is enhanced by comparison to her inferior husband, who patronises his cleverly articulate wife and takes time "to formulate thought" (10). This narrative demonstrates the ways men are seduced by traditional femininity into constructing passive and childlike wives who in return are encouraged to hide their cleverness and complicity.

The housekeeper in "Mrs. Mulvaney's Moccasins" is discussed in the third person as an indomitable character, imperious and larger than life, who acts like "the apartment was hers and her employer [the writer, Dayton Blanche] a boarder whom she allowed there on sufferance" (6, 7). Mrs. Mulvaney not only possesses a "masterful personality", but also provides the moral and comedic compass in the story (6). She is hardly a spunky heroine, but most certainly an aged and comedic version of that strong, capable character, and so easily recognisable to the reading public. In comparison, Joyce Frothingham is more reserved: "Tall and quiet and entirely business-like", adept at "obliterating [herself] so far as masculine notice is concerned" (3). It is her aversion to her employer, and then her choice to become romantically involved with him, which reflects her growing independence and self-knowledge. It is a rational choice contextualised in the modern working conditions of urban single women. At first Joyce experiences her suitor, a "stupid employer who did not know [his] place" (11), as quite unpleasant, and "shrank into herself like a rose touched by the frost" (8-9). This analogy mirrors the connotation implied with "Blanche" or loss of colour or bloom. At their next meeting, however, the colour "flamed in her cheeks", when she is overtaken by a sudden flash of temper and flings the moccasins in the waste paper basket. "I have had enough of those foolish things!" she exclaims. "How could you think that I would send you a silly present like that!" (12, 13).

Mr Blanche, like Mr Philip, is presented as a hapless, eccentric, and simple-minded fellow, whose genius is doubtful. With too much time and opportunity to follow that genius, Mr Blanche, "rising author and dramatist who had already risen to an enviable altitude and who was scheduled by himself to rise much higher before he fell to the ranks of the has beens" (1), is shown to take himself too seriously. In this jab at both contemporary masculinity and the cult of literary celebrity, Franklin humorously compares her impeccably industrious female characters to an employer whose "afflatus was so inflated that it had to be loosened to prevent strangulation" (2). Although the heroine ultimately decides to employ her newly found agency by accepting her employer's attentions, if we read between the lines she is saving herself from a life of poverty. Joyce's turn towards romance indicates her own lack of conviction that a poor, overworked office girl would choose the colourless Mr Blanche for any other reason than to leave behind the dreariness and economic vulnerability of her previous life.

Compared to both Mrs. Philip and the potentially soon-to-be Mrs. Blanche, Mabel Dodge Reber is a more complex wife. She is presented as attractive, clever, and accomplished, but she is also made out to be scheming, calculating, and relatively unlikeable. In her case marriage is a better option than her previous life and the class privilege she achieves through marriage allows her to avoid domesticity by employing other women to maintain her home. Unlike the other protagonists, Mabel's independence is thus presented as selfishness. Just as Franklin was particularly adept at portraying the ways traditional marriage encourages men to act badly, the case of Mabel Reber is one that presents the negative moral implications of this economic arrangement on women too. She takes the case of marriage as an economic contract to its extreme and shows how it subverts gender norms so that women act badly too, losing their compassion, kindness, and moral integrity. Mabel, for example, was "no soul-squirmer, or high-brow or feminist", she displays no compassion or emotion beyond self-interest, being neither "fuddled by sentimentality" nor by any "silly high falutin' ideas" (2, 1, 3). Her masculine characteristics include the ways she joked easily with men. "The old maid and the mother-in-law joke" were especially appealing to her, as were "[j]okes about women's lower limbs" (3). However, it is especially Mabel's attitude towards her husband's first wife that reveals to the reader her lack of moral compass. She learned that Brant was married from "the little, tearful, heart-broken wife" (2), for whom she had "no sorrow" and saw as a "fool" (3). Mabel had "many times found amusement" in the ways men deceived their wives "to enjoy her charms" and that experience "gave her cunning" (2–3, 5).

Finally, "The Illogical Sex", the anti-courtship suffrage tale published in *Life and Labor*, features the feminist self-actualised Helen Summers, who rejects marriage in order to become a suffragist. She is "secretary of the Independent Women's Political League" and "addresses street crowds from an automobile", boldly yelling her feminist politics. She rejects the courtship narrative and any mention of marriage. This strong feminist message is tempered by a folksy rendition by the old man, the narrator Grandpa Griddle. He describes Helen akin to the classic bicycling Amazon of New Woman literature: "a great strong athlete ... [with] a form like a well-knit young birch tree as does a man's heart good to see" (287). A vivacious feminist proving that politically astute women also make worthy romantic partners even while they are wary of marriage, Helen is very attractive: "There are always a lot of young fellers showing they have the good sense by wanting to marry Helen", explains Grandpa Griddle, even if she has the "good sense by having nothing to do with them" (288).

Just as Helen is portrayed as morally elevated with "eyes as honest as the day" (287), her suitor is shaped by his flaws, and particularly his views on women. When Grandpa Griddle asks Helen whether she has "made a suffragette of him yet", she describes his inadequacies: "Charlie is a thing of the past", she explains. "No girl of today could endure such foolish views about women" (287). Although Charlie's misogyny is not portrayed as malicious, this moral failing does not win any favours. "I could chew him up for such views" she declares. When he insists, for example, that "no women with any sense would want to vote, and no men of any manliness or brains would want them to", Helen seeks revenge. This entails turning down his marriage proposal because his relative, Jimmy Evvers, had also proposed to her: "I had once nearly married Jimmy and everyone would say, 'Why, she's Mrs. Evvers after all'". The pun on "evver after", which "tickled Helen's fancy", caused Charlie to gasp and sputter: "Would you turn a man down for a little illogical thing like that!" The answer is yes: "[I]f a woman was such an illogical thing that she wasn't fit to vote, she wasn't to be expected to give logical reasons for marrying or not marrying either" (288). Like Mrs. Philip, who used logic to make the case for the productive nature of domestic work, Joyce Frothingham, whose decision to marry was based on the logic of comparing matrimony to women's lowly paid wage labour, and Mabel Reber, whose logic extends to rational reasons why she should reclaim her "berth", Helen Summers also demonstrates logic as a characteristic of the New Woman.

These four New Woman short stories, written at the height of Franklin's engagement with the issues modern American women faced, all present an insistent critique of romance and matrimony and reflect her personal politics during this period. In varying degrees, from endorsing and sustaining marriage to critiquing, transforming, and avoiding it, Franklin interrogates the institution and destabilises romantic imperatives. The subversive content of these stories illustrates New Woman feminism's tremendous shift in consciousness.[29] In varying degrees, from narratives that rethink yet ultimately replicate marriage to those that transform or avoid it entirely, Franklin's stories enacted change within the domestic space of the home while recognising women's right to access the public realm as a source of social and economic sustenance. Although Franklin and her New Woman contemporaries rarely chose formal innovation intentionally, their desires to write about gender relations for modern American women in different and subversive ways disrupted the Victorian traditions from which they sprang and ultimately helped facilitate the development of more modern writing.

---

29 Jane Eldridge Miller, *Rebel Women: Feminism, Modernism and the Edwardian Novel*, (London: Virago, 1994), 6.

4
Her Boldest Throw

Of all Miles Franklin's New Woman writing from the Chicago era, the novel *On Dearborn Street* stands out as her "boldest throw", as well as one of her most compelling narratives about women's sexual agency and the choices they negotiate in its pursuit. Jill Roe explains her summation of the story as Franklin's most courageous New Woman endeavour, stating "[p]ractically all the elements of the New Woman novel are there for the finding … In essence it is a sustained attempt to answer the old question: What do women want?"[1] Such a query is the very one asked by Roswell Cavarley, the novel's male narrator. "God knows what they want!" he declares, considering the modern woman.[2] This question, which rests at the heart of *On Dearborn Street*, sets the stage for the interrogation of the complexities of female sexual desire through the character of the urban New Woman, Sybyl Penelo, who appears as an American remake of the heroine of *My Brilliant Career*. "Where Sybylla Melvyn could not go", says Roe, "Sybyl Penelo could". Both are sexually fastidious heroines, who recoil from sex and yet also claim sexual desire, often in contradictory ways. And if Stephen Garton is correct in exemplifying Sybylla as a link between "the nineteenth-century generation, which condemned sex in all its aspects, and a new generation of activists who emerged between the wars advocating sex reform", Sybyl provides an equally and potentially more striking example of such a function.[3] In its exploration of sexual relationships overshadowed by the spectre of war and its strong case for gender equality, *On*

---

1 Jill Roe, *Stella Miles Franklin: A Biography* (Sydney: Fourth Estate/Harper Collins, 2008), 191.
2 Miles Franklin, *On Dearborn Street* (St Lucia: University of Queensland Press/Australian Large Print, 1987), 167. All subsequent references are to this edition and appear in parentheses in the text.
3 Roe, *Stella Miles Franklin*, 166; Stephen Garton, "Contesting Enslavement: Marriage, Manhood and *My Brilliant Career*", *Australian Literary Studies* 20, no. 4 (2002): fn. 13, 345.

Dearborn Street thus provides what one contemporary reviewer deemed "quotable feminist depth-charges".[4] This chapter addresses those depth charges, and the targets against which they were launched, by focusing on the complex and often contradictory sexual practices of the New Woman. Like *My Brilliant Career* (although I second Roe's assertion that Sybyl is a more sexually mature Sybylla), the story presents frank and subversive representations of the constraints and opportunities associated with the New Woman's pursuit of sexual agency that destabilises courtship and romance traditions.

The New Woman's demand for sexual autonomy was an important aspect of the right to self-determination, as evidenced by the Quaker reformer Alys Pearsall Smith's insistence in 1894 that the New Woman "demands to belong to herself".[5] Although such insistence reflects the lack of political voice associated with women's claim to citizenship, it also represents a plea for personal self-actualisation. New Women demanded the right to be psychologically "free" to make sexual choices irrespective of domestic expectations. This was, of course, a radical notion at the time.[6] Women's rights to sexual autonomy implied the dissolution of the gendered double standard of sexual conduct and ran the gamut from chastity to mutual egalitarian relationships and to "free love". These various sexual practises encouraged female sexual desire in different ways, but each implicitly claimed the right to access and also avoid sexual contact; the right to engage with men who respected women and considered them their equals; and the right to engage in sexual relationships without the constraints of traditional courtship and marriage practices.[7] Still, New Women did not necessarily equate women's liberation with sexual liberation, and although they might endorse "free love" between consenting adults, they tended to eschew promiscuity for its own sake in favour of the ways women might be both "pure" and exhibit sexual agency.[8] They made the case that when women were self-reliant, which in Franklin's case also involved a demand for economic self-sufficiency, they could establish new kinds of sexual relationships with men based upon equality and respect. *On Dearborn Street* reflects these demands. Through snapshots into her psychological journey towards sexual maturity we see the sexually fastidious heroine expressing desire and gaining both

---

4   Review of *On Dearborn Street* available at https://www.kirkusreviews.com/book-reviews/miles-franklin-2/on-dearborn-street/
5   Alys Pearsall Smith, "A Reply from the daughters, II", *Nineteenth Century* 35 (1894): 450.
6   John D'Emilio and Estelle B. Freedman. *Intimate Matters: A History of Sexuality in America* (New York: Harper, 1988).
7   Barbara Welter, "The Cult of True Womanhood, 1820-1960", *American Quarterly* 18, no. 2 (1966): 151–174.
8   Kathleen Blake, *Love and the Woman Question in Victorian Literature: The Art of Self-Postponement* (Sussex: Harvester, 1983); Sheila Jeffreys, *The Spinster and Her Enemies: Feminism and Sexuality, 1880–1930* (London: Pandora, 1985).

independence and sexual self-knowledge. It is precisely through the interrogation of her options that readers learn about the sexual politics of Sybyl's romantic life.

What is innovative about *On Dearborn Street* is that it is told from the point of view of the New Woman's romantic suitor, Roswell, a feminist beau who represents both the positive and negative aspects of the New Man. He functions as a somewhat unreliable narrator who underscores the "fictions" of a masculinist point of view. His "take" on reality, and especially his relationship with the heroine, reveals the flaws in a masculinist acceptance of its own subjective reality as synonymous with objective "truth". As a literary device, the use of the flawed male narrator also helps the novel succeed by presenting Roswell as sufficiently believable, ("more than the author's mask and something less than a god").[9] Such a mouthpiece also works to diffuse the insistent political message and avoid perceptions of the self-serving feminist. My focus in this chapter is on Franklin's feminist social purity negotiation of hetero/sexuality, which was particularly troublesome in advocating both purity and chastity and yet insisting on sexual autonomy and desire. Along with the mature Aunt Pattie character, Sybyl models sexual agency even while the narrative sets her up as a mouthpiece of social purity feminism.

Roswell is an architect with inherited wealth from his adopted Aunt Pattie, whom we learn is actually Roswell's mother. In his early forties, nondescript physically, mildly talented, but very "nice" with a caring disposition and feminist politics, he owns and manages "The Caboodle", a bachelor boarding house/hotel in Chicago's downtown Loop. He falls in love with the beguiling Sybyl Penelo, an independently minded and talented modern woman who works in an office nearby. As Roswell's feelings for Sybyl deepen and they spend more time together, his friend, Bobby Hoyne, appears on the scene. Young and handsome, he presents all that Roswell lacks, including arrogance. Roswell's plan for Sybyl to trounce his friend with superior feminist wit backfires as she is courted by Bobby, who soon announces their engagement. Sybyl refuses to confirm this by declaring it still "might not be fatal" (184). War is declared, but before the couple can execute plans to join the effort, Bobby is tragically killed in an automobile race. Roswell courts Sybyl after loyally taking care of his friend's effects and Sybyl's grief, but marriage proposals are resisted. She decries the constraints of matrimony and is despondent about the war, suffering emotionally on its account. Roswell seeks out Aunt Pattie to help solve this dilemma and together they plan a round-the-world trip where Sybyl can escape from the war and the weariness of her life, including any domestic commitments, and enjoy both a friendship with Aunt Pattie and a maybe marriage with Roswell. He declares matrimony his goal, but the ending is ambiguous with a potential marriage on a potential horizon accompanied by the

---

9   Roy Duncan, "Introduction", in Franklin, *On Dearborn Street*, x.

refrain: "who knows what a day may bring?" (336). In the sections that follow I explore the ways *On Dearborn Street* is a romance, but also a *bildungsroman*: a story about the New Woman's sexual self-discovery and maturation and her broadening outlook on sexual agency that stops just short of marital commitment.

A Saucy Little Sausage

The female protagonists of *On Dearborn Street* illustrate various gendered performances of sexual desire and autonomy. Aunt Pattie is a strong, self-actualised, and relatively one-dimensional feminist character who challenges the constraints of matrimony and shares her frank sexual history. Sybyl, on the other hand, is a more complicated character as befitting the ambiguous and often contradictory debate about women's sexual status, and it is she who illustrates the anxieties that consumed public discourse at the time.

In order to make a compelling case for the independent woman as love object, Sybyl's assertiveness is eroticised in *On Dearborn Street*, even though it is tempered in parts of the novel for the very same reason. We therefore learn at the outset that it is Sybyl's outburst about men's toiletry habits and their inability to clean up after themselves that sends Roswell head over heels in love. From Roswell's perspective, such politics so artfully spoken render Sybyl the woman of his dreams with "the unconscious, God-given impudence of the independent woman richly dowered with sexual attractiveness" (28). He looks on admiringly as she announces that it is "an academic fact" that men "rarely loved anything but themselves" and "neglect no opportunity of drawing attention to the possession of a horn by continuous tooting" (55, 113). She claims her own form of tooting and resists Roswell's censure about use of profanity: "I just love *hell* and *damn*", she exclaims (100). It is this feminist impertinence articulated with passion and confidence that Roswell admires. He soon finds himself falling "gloriously in love" (55).

Throughout *On Dearborn Street* Sybyl asserts feminist agency by consciously disrupting traditional courtship practices. "I hire out my brains by day but not my company by night", she says, and wonders "why shouldn't women be able to command men to entertain them at dinner instead" (35). Still, she allows him to accompany her to the local cafeteria, the Fireside, where she eats because it is all she can afford, and insists on paying her own way (reminiscent of The Hearth, the Chicago cafeteria where Franklin ate many of her evening meals). During these times together, Sybyl treats Roswell as a friend and equal. "I am interested in your *life*. What do you do all day? What did you do last night?" (40), she inquires. Roswell considers these questions and the context of their asking, functioning as a feminist mouthpiece to contrast the egalitarian nature of this encounter to traditional gendered courtship practices.

Another example of Sybyl's resistance to traditional courtship practices is illustrated when she refuses to wait to be kissed. "Oh, as for that silly mistletoe business", she declares, "Why shouldn't I kiss *you*?" The kiss is negotiated, but her distaste for his moustache is made known. "I detest moustaches … they are monstrositios of hideosity", she exclaims. "Why, would you like to kiss me if I had a nasty tooth brush on my upper lip?" (259-260). Roswell admires her critique and responds that he would kiss her "if she had a gopher trap on her face" and will remove his moustache. The New Woman, however, advocates for his right to self-determination just as she demands her own: "If you like it, it is your business". Instead she negotiates a kiss avoiding the worst of his facial hair: "[A]t least … [it's] not one of the weeping willow walrus species, thank heaven" (260).

Such self-determination challenging men's right to call the shots in matters of the heart is especially portrayed in the outtake or abandoned chapter of *On Dearborn Street* titled "Miss Toby's Party: How I Queered a Queer's Party", where Roswell's feminist credentials are tested. Presenting a more calculating and less conciliatory Roswell character, its scornful and absurdly facetious anti-courtship narrative may have been considered too radical for inclusion in the book. The "queerity party" (where queer means odd or out of place), organised by Sybyl and a spinster named Antoinette Toby, involves a secret competition to be won by the woman who brings the most unattractive bachelor, who believes he is worthy of courting his date, to the party.[10] Ironically, the prize is "a set of Mrs Charlotte Perkins Gilman's works" (4). Such audacity in creating a competition showcasing masculine inferiority without concern for the feelings of the men resists gendered expectations for women to put men's feelings ahead of their own in sexual matters as elsewhere. This fierce subversion of gender regimes thus provides women sexual agency to choose and determine their own fate rather than waiting to be chosen and assessed as potential objects of desire. Roswell learns the truth about the party, imagines himself allied with the women, and gets himself invited by the wealthy socialite Sylvia Cheesman, a minor character in both accounts, who serves as a poor contrast to Sybyl.

As Sylvia's "ridiculous admirer", Roswell knows he is not the kind of "specimen" to have been invited unknowingly and firm in this knowledge, sets himself above "the other poor duped members" of his sex, smug at being "so presentable" (4, 3, 5). He plays the part and makes himself look and act ridiculous. In the middle of the party, however, the ridiculousness of the performance is

---

10   Miles Franklin, "Miss Toby's Party: How I Queered a Queer's Party", ML MSS 445/22, 5. All subsequent references appear in parentheses in the text.

revealed even to Roswell. Shocked, he spies "a big dark handsome man" invited to accompany "a golden-haired beauty" and declares: "I felt a little edgy about him being brought as a spectacle". As his role in the ruse is destabilised, Roswell asks another pertinent question: "what on earth did women need? What sort of man did they want?" (5). Franklin thus resists the normalising practices of compulsory heterosexuality, particularly men's entitlement to court attractive women even if they are not attractive themselves. Franklin subverts men's privilege to determine women's worthiness, allowing the women to gauge men's (un)suitability as mates, and in this case even the unsuitability of the New Man who imagines himself beyond such matters.

Still, this portrayal of the independent New Woman and her critique of chivalry and courtship practices tends to be contained within social purity discourses making it clear that Sybyl's sex appeal is not promiscuous. In the novel she is described as "dowered with sexual attractiveness", but also "utterly indifferent" because "her interest centred in other aspects of her life" (28–29). Roswell acknowledges her flirtatiousness, but insists she is "free from carnal appetites" (150). This will all change when she meets the dashing Bobby Hoyne, and it is here where Sybyl's assertive characterisation wains and the social purity argument wears thin. Alongside, and perhaps necessary for, the depiction of her infatuation with Bobby, is a counter-narrative infantilising Sybyl's character, and descriptions rendering her fragile and vulnerable: such a "little wisp of a thing" (265). She is also referred to as "the child" throughout much of the novel and is repeatedly compared to small animals as a way to simultaneously endear and diminish her character. She is, for instance, a "little saucy Tom Tit", "little squirrel", "little puss", "little Tom cat", "little minx", and "scrumptious little quail", as well as – and this perhaps best illustrates her complex femininity – "an imperious and independent little sausage" (245). These allusions to animals suggest a wildness that must be tamed as well as a vulnerability that must be protected; the analogy to food is similarly a traditional linguistic device to objectify and sexualise women, and position them as something to be consumed and controlled. Such diminutions simultaneously endear her as the heroine within romance traditions in terms of domination and protection; they also soften her feminist stridency and present a traditionally feminine sensuality and vulnerability perhaps more palatable to readers. In addition, the similarities here to Franklin are significant. She was petite and known to have shopped for clothes in the children's department. And it was she whom Demarest Lloyd used to call "little rascal".[11] Certainly Franklin was known for her wit and charm as well as for her flirtatious nature, which Paul Brunton suggests she displayed even into old age.

---

11   Roe, *Stella Miles Franklin*, 164.

"Why", asked her grandmother in a letter, "do you encourage them if you do not intend to continue?"[12]

Roswell's patronising behaviours towards Sybyl in the private sphere – and her acceptance of them – can be contrasted with her boldness in the public arena. There is quite a contradiction between the assertive Sybyl who speaks "loudly" and with "a hint of great open spaces", claiming the public landscape of the city, and Sybyl who dances with "the expression of an eager child on her face" (19, 228). Just as Sybyl tentatively learns to dance with Roswell, Franklin notes having her first dancing lessons with Bill Lloyd in October 1913. Both Franklin and Sybyl find themselves dancing in the various ballrooms around Chicago, although one wonders if, like Sybyl, Franklin preferred "solo dancing so that she would not have to be dependent on another" (235).[13] Sybyl's childlike demeanour alongside her recognition of the politics of gender implicit in such dancing illustrate the complex and precarious situations negotiated by the modern New Woman in both literature and life.[14] This juxtaposed dialogue renders itself unbelievable and seems to affirm Sally Ledger's assertion that when it comes to matters of sexuality, the New Woman was "riddled with contradictions".[15] However, like Sybylla of *My Brilliant Career*, who performs gender in ways that disrupt its fixed nature, Sybyl also presents the performative aspects of a multi-faceted femininity that refuses to be fixed.[16] She is a modern woman who resists either/or choices when faced with the New Man treating her as a human and the playboy treating her as a woman. This is the conundrum for the New Woman who hopes for both.

Finally, it is important to remember that this infantilising narrative represents Roswell's voice and his desire. Sybyl does not narrate her own story and most proclamations about Sybyl, and especially those rendering her fragile and child-like, are given by Roswell. The feminist credentials that encourage him to ponder on the institutions of "unbridled masculinism" do indeed allow Franklin a credible feminist narrator to articulate her critique of sexism (11). However, they also allow her to reflect on the sometimes flawed gender practices of New Men who profess to be women's "champion" (he describes the American man, for example, as "a lamentable specimen of arrested development" with the exception of about "five of us" [42]) and yet still demonstrate traditional masculine practices

---

12 Grandmother Lampe, quoted in Paul Brunton, ed., *The Diaries of Miles Franklin* (Crows Nest: The State Library of New South Wales, 2004), xvii-xviii.
13 Miles Franklin, Pocket diary, 16, 20, and 23 October 1913, ML MSS 364/2.
14 Kate Krueger, "Evelyn Sharp's Working Women and the Dilemma of the Urban Romance", *Women Writing* 19, no. 4 (2012): 563.
15 Sally Ledger, *The New Woman: Fiction and Feminism at the* Fin de Siècle (College Station: Penn State University Press, 1999), 2.
16 Ian Henderson, "Gender, Genre, and Sybylla's Performative Identity in Miles Franklin's *My Brilliant Career*", *Australian Literary Studies* 18, no. 2 (1997): 165–173.

that subordinate (10). In this way Roswell's construction of Sybyl's reality is exactly an example of his own insight about the male proclivity to define women's world: "no such institution as WOMAN existed except in [the] frowsy sentimentality with which men regard matters of sex" (11).

Bobby This, and Bobby That

Sybyl and Roswell become friends, but he lacks a "definite plan of conquest" in the love department (55), at least compared to Bobby, who is young, handsome, and rich, and soon kindles Sybyl's desire. However this eligible bachelor has no intellectual curiosity, and cares nothing for reading, science, or philosophy, except for Christian Science, and views women "as a vice to be bracketed with wine" (93). But he does know automobiles and cuts a dashingly handsome figure as a race car driver. If Sybyl is a "fair copy" of Franklin, Bobby is equally so for Demarest Lloyd, who like Bobby was also handsome, very rich, and loved sailing and automobiles, having bought a luxurious new car on a trip to Paris during the period that Franklin was writing about the dashing Bobby, famous race car driver.[17] In addition, Demarest was also a keen follower of Christian Science: a religion Franklin insisted was well adapted to "comfort[ing] the rich".[18] During his sailing travels Franklin and Demarest corresponded regularly and he signed himself "Sinbad the Sailor", addressing her as "Psyche" (the mortal wife who showed undying love to the God, Eros/Cupid). Sybyl's description of the volatile Bobby as "the king of indoor games" (120) is perhaps reminiscent of references in Demarest's letters about "spanking" and other flirtatious gestures.[19] This relationship heated up during 1914 and eventually fizzled out by the end of the year when Franklin referred to him in her diary as a "silly ass". This was about the same time that she had decided the kindly Fred Pischel, perhaps her own Roswell Cavarley and someone whom Franklin had once described as "very dear", was equally problematic.[20]

Sybyl is first struck by Bobby's handsome physique and responds with eyes "softening and darkening with quick responsiveness" (70). Roswell notes the way Sybyl eyed Bobby's "virile spick-and-spanness", tabulating every detail with "swift intuitive glances." Roswell explains that he "catechised her afterwards and she could describe the color of his eyes, the length of his eyelashes, the shape of his teeth,

---

17 Roe, *Stella Miles Franklin*, 166.
18 Miles Franklin, quoted in Roe, *Stella Miles Franklin*, 172.
19 Roe, *Stella Miles Franklin*, 172.
20 Demarest Lloyd to Miles Franklin, 24 and 30 September 1914, ML MSS 364/12; Verna Coleman, *Her Unknown Brilliant Career: Miles Franklin in America* (Sydney: Angus & Robertson, 1981), 164; Franklin, Pocket diary, 21 July 1914; Roe, *Stella Miles Franklin*, 154, 183.

finger nails and feet". Importantly, it seems "she approved of each detail" (70). This frank dialogue portrays her sexual desire. She is neither amused nor offended by Bobby's vacuous prattle about his faith and instead initiates their relationship: "We'll have another séance all to ourselves after business hours. I am one of the heathen aching to see the light" (72-73). Bobby accepts this frank proposal and agrees to a date the next evening.

Like Sybylla of *My Brilliant Career*, who blazes with passion and is enthralled by "something wild and warm and splendidly alive", so Sybyl gains sexual knowledge as her desire for Bobby matures and "lets loose something wild" (81).[21] Such passion is also reminiscent of the protagonist's sexual and social awakening in *V. V.'s Eyes* by Henry Sydnor Harrison, a book Franklin read around the time she was starting *On Dearborn Street*, and about which she wrote a review in *Life and Labor*.[22] When interrogated about her sexual interest in Bobby, Sybyl describes his playfulness as invigorating: "Bobby will let me have some fun. I've never had any fun" (187). Similarly, in response to Roswell's irritation that Sybyl violates her own critique of chivalry when she is with Bobby, she explains that she "love[s] dining in a beautiful place with the orchestra playing … All I have to do is to follow after and look at people" (109). This is presented as a conscious choice in return for a few luxuries after the drudgeries of work. Like the nurse in "Red Cross Nurse", discussed in Chapter 7, these heroines, as well as Franklin herself, dearly want and deserve the luxuries and entertainment that playboys like Demarest Lloyd could provide, despite their dangers. "One gets tired of being alone … I wasn't designed for a nun", Sybyl explains (112).

Soon, however, Sybyl learns of Bobby's "outrageously uncontrolled temper" (81). This is on display after she sends him a package with baby items, including a dummy/pacifier, to make the point that he acts childishly. Bobby finds this amusing, calling her a "sassy little thing", but then threatens to choke her and insists she "use it [the pacifier] while he was looking on". Again her response is amusement that "he only threatened … [and] would be afraid to hurt me" (107). She eventually goes so far as to exclaim, "I can never make up my mind", but "if some man would just take me by assault and battery I'd be so infatuated with his surety of purpose that I'd live happily ever after" (154, 155). These lines and the choice of the bad-tempered playboy/abusive man are distasteful by contemporary feminist standards (even while exploration of the reasons why women stay with men who cause them harm is a source of interest and importance still today), and I am unable to resist echoing Susan Margarey's reaction to the protagonist's

---

21 Miles Franklin, *My Brilliant Career* (1901; Sydney: Angus & Robertson, 1979), 143.
22 S.M. Franklin, "When We Have Time to Read: *V. V.'s Eyes*", *Life and Labor* (October 1913): 364–66.

behaviour with the volatile suitor from *My Brilliant Career*: "How could anyone, even Sybylla Melvyn, hope to combine 'control' with submission to a 'master-hand'?"[23] However, just as Sybylla refused to be cowed and claimed her power from Harold Beecham's loss of control, Sybyl's response to Bobby's willingness to show his feelings – even in negative ways – might reflect her understanding of this emotion as an equalising force. In addition, although this is comparable in many respects to this scene when Sybylla responds positively to the bruises inflicted by her volatile suitor, Franklin weighs in on such problematic violent sexual innuendo in *On Dearborn Street* by having Roswell critique Sybyl's words and announce: "Such assured knowledge of the male of the species left me nothing adequate to say" (107). Franklin is also clear as to Bobby's flaws and intentions in a series of "furious" and mostly illegible handwritten pages titled " When Bobby 'Got' Religion" dated February 1914 where she writes of Bobby's "cocksure conceit" and his deluded acceptance of a religion that sustained his sexism.[24]

Such important feminist commentary, however, is not straightforward in that Sybyl's sexual desire originates in her attraction to Bobby rather than Roswell, and the eventual acceptance of the feminist Roswell is only – and then not always convincingly – expressed at the end of the novel when a romantic sexual relationship with him is promised, but ultimately deferred. In making sense of Sybyl's behaviour, however, it is informative to consider the romance marketplace and the ways the "heart throb" approaches of the sensation novel helped shape New Woman writing.[25] Franklin, like other young women of her generation, most likely read popular romances in which the template for the hero's capture of the heroine – both literally and figuratively – involved his aggression and her submission. These readers understood the romance formula and those expecting a happy ending tended to interpret violent behaviours and the heroine's responses to it in terms of the genre and their familiarity with it.[26]

But what is revealed about Sybyl's motivation for the bad boy is that in the ways of women who become involved with abusive men, she believes she can control him. Such tension "makes it a great game", she says. "We clash – oh, you should hear us clash! It's bang!" (82). Sybyl is resilient by holding her own throughout

---

23 Susan Magarey, "*My Brilliant Career* and Feminism", *Australian Literary Studies* 20, no. 4 (2002), 397.
24 Roe, *Stella Miles Franklin*, 176; Miles Franklin, "When Bobby 'Got' Religion", 1914, ML MSS 445/21.
25 Meg Tasker, "Francis Adams: Realism and Sensation in the 1880s", *Australian Literary Studies* 30, no. 3 (2015): 79–95.
26 Katherine Cooper and Emma Short, eds., *The Female Figure in Contemporary Historical Fiction* (London: Palgrave, 2012); Laurie Langbauer, *Women and Romance: The Consolidation of the English Novel* (Ithaca: Cornell University Press, 1990).

this conflict and by refusing to be cowed. Nonetheless, despite this show of spirit, the reader, along with Roswell, wonders where the assertive young feminist has gone. We are perturbed by Sybyl's "Bobby this, and Bobby that" (80), a development Roswell finds increasingly confusing and something that prompts him to ask: "Why is Bobby so absorbing?" To this Sybyl's responds: "If I put a ribbon around my neck or a new twist in my hair I feel that Bobby sees and enjoys it, but if I were dressed in a mother hubbard, it would be all the same to you" (80). Given that Sybyl is initially described as dressed unconventionally with no embarrassment about her looks, this illustration of feminine body conformity comes as somewhat of a surprise. Yet such expressions of conventional femininity also represent Sybyl's agency as she subverts notions denigrating such feminine practices by claiming them as her own, again without embarrassment. She wants the New Man to indulge her in these feminine performances, even if they are traditional ones and potentially oppressive. This point is underscored when Franklin allows Roswell to recognise the behaviour for what it is: a gender performance, a "burlesque" if you will: "When she indulged in such nonsense – a dainty, ironical burlesque of the charming-for-her-dinner business incumbent upon women, I was infatuatedly entertained" (89). Similarly, the constructed nature of femininity is also revealed as Roswell watches the ways Sybyl performs this new version of femininity and declares, "You are a little snare and a fake ... You are only a wraith which isn't there when it is struck at" (86). Like Sybylla's paradoxical performance in *My Brilliant Career*, where there is a "'playing up' of conventional roles", Sybyl's heteronormative gestures seem overdone in their rendering of traditional femininity, thus underscoring their performative aspect and potentially destabilising the literal message.[27]

The complexities of this novel are underscored by Franklin's conscious articulation of Sybyl's contradictions, implying her understanding of the complexities of sexuality and its relationship to women's freedom. Roswell, for example, calls her a "curious mixture" of femininities (125). Here Franklin resists gender binaries by pointing out the ways women might be both critical of patriarchy and systems that support a chivalrous heteronormativity *and* willingly participate in it as a form of sexual agency. Could feminist politics coincide with the heteronormative practices of traditional courtship? Does practicing coquetry invariably mean women condone their subordinate status? Ahead of her time, Franklin's exploration of femininity through the gendered sexual performances of her feminist heroine resists traditional duplicities: Sybyl was "a curious mixture of cave woman and the over-feminised girl so prevalent in American society" (125). Such apparent contradictions produce a

---

27 Henderson, "Gender, Genre, and Sybylla's Performative Identity in Miles Franklin's *My Brilliant Career*", 172.

complex sexuality refusing to be pinned down that illustrates Franklin's attempts to craft a more nuanced rendering of the New Woman.

The Banquet of Love

Sexual politics in *On Dearborn Street* were shaped by the onset of World War I, a "far-reaching calamity" (183) revealing "the worst elements of a materialistic civilization resting on brute force" (324). War meant that "millions of the mental and physical flower of half a dozen nations were using every device of modern science, every piece of strategy, and straining every nerve to slaughter and mutilate each other in the most terrible way" (208). For Sybyl, the situation is a madness "killing [her] by inches". Such "grim torture" dampened her ardour, so that she could no longer contemplate love or romance and was "dying of a broken heart" (210). Franklin's heart was also breaking: "So sick about the war that I am really paralyzed", she wrote.[28] This anguish precipitated a nervous collapse that led to the amiable New Man's rescue. "Fred found me sick", Franklin explained, and "took me home to his mother who nursed me out of a bout".[29] It seemed she spent this respite reading Karin Michaelis' novel, *The Dangerous Age* (1910), which featured a heroine fast approaching the "dangerous age" when she has to decide whether to return to a marriage, take a lover, or maintain her self-imposed solitude. This was close to home for Franklin, who at almost 35 years old was fast approaching such an age.

Militarism thus represented for both Sybyl and Franklin the global rendering of masculine vice as men were turned into beasts: a caricature inflamed by reports of German atrocities against Belgian women and the high rate of sexually transmitted infections reported among the troops. In essence it was men's capacity for vice and brutality that dampens Sybyl's sexual desire. Also, because heterosexual relationships were inherently connected to reproductive matters, Sybyl's response to war's "ghastly nightmare" (314) was shaped by the new social and economic conditions it brought, as well as by the grim future it promised for children in "a world denuded of all sanity". Because Europe was "strewn for hundreds of miles with other women's sons, husbands, [and] sweet-hearts", Sybyl, like Franklin, found the "spiritual devastation staggering" (208), and refuses to be another "sacred producer of cannon fodder" (299). War exacerbates Sybyl's ongoing resistance to marriage: "[It] has finally decided it for me", she explains. "I am never going to marry" (263). *On Dearborn Street* thus provides a number of practical reasons why women should not marry in

---

28 Franklin, Pocket diary, 22 August 1914.
29 Franklin, Pocket diary, 31 August and 1 September 1914.

this context, not the least of which is that it affects female desire. Sybyl is "turned off" sexually by the thought of male vice magnified by war.

Toward the end of *On Dearborn Street* when two men have routinely proposed to Sybyl (one of them on a weekly basis) and she is still uncertain about matrimony, having accepted and resisted and accepted again, we learn the real reason for her hesitancy through conversation with Aunt Pattie: "Men" and the physical and emotional aspects of a sexual relationship with them, which Sybyl claims as her own "sex fastidiousness" (272). For Sybyl, and indeed for Franklin, who learned from Rose Scott that marriage was desirable "only if it could be 'a comradeship full of sacred responsibilities'", this "fastidiousness" is grounded in responses to men's proclivity for promiscuity and extramarital relationships that caused women emotional turmoil, shame, and physical harm, and infected them with sexually transmitted diseases.[30] This is a frank representation of the problems of heterosexual relationships with men who visit or have visited prostitutes and who engage in adulterous affairs that indicate dishonesty and untrustworthiness. Even among supposedly enlightened men who advocate free love, their critique of matrimony tended to provide another opportunity to exercise male sexual privilege. As Roe notes, Franklin was "scathing about the fevered sexual experiments of bohemian associates in Chicago".[31]

Sybyl responds to her deflated ardour in dialogue with Aunt Pattie: "[I]f [men] weren't such ravening creatures . . . In the feast of love women can sit down to a banquet of soiled and broken meats or go hungry. I prefer to go hungry" (271). This decision represents a trade-off between freedom and domesticity, as well as recognition of a taboo topic: the consequences of sexual activity for women under either of its guises because in domesticity women not only endured compulsory motherhood and the risk of sexually-transmitted infections but also what today we would call marital rape. Such behaviours promoted what Emma Liggins refers to as the "husband-fiend". He was a frequent character in New Woman romances (for example, in Sarah Grand's *The Heavenly Twins* [1893] and Emma Brooke's *A Superfluous Woman* [1894]), and makes his appearance in *On Dearborn Street* as Aunt Pattie's "diseased husband", whom we learn precipitated her own sexual maturation. Liggins emphasises that New Woman literature responded to problems of male sexual excess by pointing out the restrictions on sexual knowledge for women and the necessity of "choice" for mitigating this danger.[32] "Choice" is illustrated in Sybyl's bold claim: "Well, I am free to choose', she exclaims. "I prefer

---

30 Magarey, "*My Brilliant Career* and Feminism", 392.
31 Roe, *Stella Miles Franklin*, 157.
32 Emma Liggins, "Writing Against the 'Husband-Fiend': Syphilis and Male Sexual Vice in the New Woman Novel", *Women's Writing* 7, no. 2 (2000): 175.

loneliness to what the economic dependence of women has made of love – the cruelty to my sister women … their brutal commerce which has defiled even love" and brought "degradation and danger" to women's lives (273). Sybyl makes this clear when she asserts that "passion, the flame of love's fire is always extinguished … [by] disease in the palace of love" (274).

These strong words about the causes and consequences of prostitution that defile love and render its banquet a series of "soiled and broken meats" (271) explain why Sybyl would prefer a platonic relationship with Roswell over a sexual one. Like the cross-dressing Max in Katherine Cecil Thurston's *Max* (1910) or Sue Bridehead in Thomas Hardy's *Jude the Obscure* (1895), Sybyl's fastidiousness is expressed through her comfort with more platonic friendships with men. The question remains, however, why Sybyl would profess such squeamishness with Roswell and not with Bobby, although it is unclear whether her articulated desire with Bobby would have led to a sexual relationship given that he is conveniently removed before this is tested. Knowing Bobby's playboy character, it would seem his banquet might be more soiled than Roswell's, at least on the face of it. Although these incongruities threaten to destabilise the novel, some sort of equilibrium is maintained by the fact it is the onset of war, and Sybyl's extreme reaction to it after Bobby's death, that shapes her reaction to male vice.

This chapter revealing Sybyl's "sex fastidiousness" is the only one where Roswell abdicates his role as narrator. Instead it is presented entirely through dialogue between Aunt Pattie and Sybyl where the latter's knowledge about men is confronted by the older woman in ways that encourage Sybyl's maturing sexual agency. Aunt Pattie's response to Sybyl's angst about male sexuality is two-fold. First, she provides an optimistic response to Sybyl's sexual meticulousness in her announcement that not all men are "ravening creatures". "When you've lived as long as me", she explains, "you'll be astonished by the virtue that individual men display" (271–272). She makes the case that men suffer from their own socialisation, "plunged into it with the terrific force of a marching regiment" (272). Sybyl agrees, but is not entirely convinced. Aunt Pattie then focuses directly on Roswell's sexual history, encouraging Sybyl to agree that if Roswell is innocent in this regard, Sybyl will accept him.

The second part of Aunt Pattie's response to Sybyl's rigid social purity defence occurs when she reminds Sybyl that because he is known as her adopted son and there is "some doubt as to his origin", Roswell assumes that his uncertain parentage is the reason why Sybyl rejects him. This is the set-up for Aunt Pattie's next comment, which subverts the social purity argument: "He is afraid to grasp his happiness owing to one set of superstitions and you repulse yours on account of another. You really are a well-matched pair" (276). This claim for the "superstitions" associated with social purity feminism is crucial in not only articulating Sybyl's short-sighted assumptions about male sexuality, but Franklin's too, which promotes a nuanced reading of Franklin's association with this position. Aunt Pattie continues to dismantle inflexible notions of feminine sexual behaviour by providing context, through her own personal experience, for the reasons why women might "stray" from purity practices of chastity and monogamy. She explains that Roswell thinks he is the product of an illicit affair between his father and his father's mistress when in actual fact she (Aunt Pattie) is his mother and it is she who had the affair. She wanted to be a mother, but her husband's sexual indiscretions rendered him infertile. She left him, and with no care for what people might think, had a sexual liaison with a man who "was nothing but an incident". "Lots of married women are irregular", she explains. "More men than ever dream of it are deceived, and deserve to be – it helps even the score" (280). Eventually Aunt Pattie reconciled with her husband, he adopted Roswell, and they were able to "eliminate the past and buil[d] always on the present" (280): a situation that bolsters her optimism about American manhood, including hopes for the sexual behaviours of her own son. It could be claimed that Aunt Pattie models the social purity advocacy for rational mate selection, although perhaps not in the way social purity feminism usually intended.

For her part Sybyl declares this sexually frank story "splendid". She is unfazed and thrilled by such assertive sexual practices: "Oh, tell me more", she exclaims. "[I]t is like a book!" Sybyl agrees that it is "the desire of dozens of women ... to go forth boldly and have a child when they think fit". Most, she asserts, "have not the pluck that you had". And, in an afterthought and to insist on the economic issues shaping such "pluck", Sybyl adds that not all were as financially independent as Aunt Pattie and therefore able to make such choices (280).

To Be Let Alone

On Dearborn Street's response to the New Woman demand for sexual autonomy is unique in its forthright discussion of heterosexual relationships and its demands for women's sexual agency. We read, for example, Sybyl's declaration that it would be "paradise" to be able to "let one's self go in love" (275), and her intimate request to "hold me tighter and tighter and closer and closer and kiss me and kiss me till I cannot breathe, and never let me go" (287). Alongside such passionate dialogue, however, are demands for a desire to be left alone. "OH [sic], the thought of marriage spoils it all", says Sybyl to Roswell. "You'll be for ever buzzing in my ear about how you love me and kissing me and persecuting me all the time. I don't want to be loved or married. I want to be let alone" (331). Like Sybylla of *My Brilliant Career*, who refuses to endorse any stable and unified model of identity, Sybyl is a curious mixture; she articulates sexual desire, but requests to be left alone to claim freedom from domesticity. This desire for a relationship and yet to be free of sexual contact, which implied health and independence, was a paradox and central defining feature facing New Women like Sybyl – and Franklin. Demarest Lloyd, who also claimed the name "the Bull" for himself, called Franklin "Hornbreaker", which presumably referred to such sexual reticence.[33]

In her relationship with Bill Lloyd during 1913, for example, Franklin appears to have maintained her chastity, the loss of which would have created a vulnerability she abhorred. Celibacy represented freedom. As Cicely Hamilton explained, the "modern distaste of the celibate has its root in ... an over-sexed and mentally lax generation". She declared "a good deal of respect for the celibate, who should have nothing to be ashamed of".[34]

Franklin handles this perennial choice between love/domesticity and vocation/loneliness in *On Dearborn Street* by invoking Aunt Pattie's wisdom and the respect the New Man offers for his (maybe) bride. Aunt Pattie instructs Roswell not to "irritate" her, explaining that "[s]ex is always a disturbing element, divinely stimulating to the fit but it can be wearying and repulsive to the frazzled". She tells Roswell not to "pursue her too closely, but to 'let her alone'". This refrain is repeated over and again, as in: "Leave her alone when you are bewildered ... begin reading at the next page that is opened, even if it slightly disconnects the thread of the story" (333). Such instructions set the stage for Sybyl to be loved without giving much in return; Roswell wins Sybyl and she wins an independence of sorts that allows her to avoid the interpersonal intricacies of maintaining an emotional and sexual relationship.

It is no surprise that the closing of the novel is one that negotiates between passion and responsibility. Franklin achieves this through a fantasy ending where Sybyl and Roswell escape with Aunt Pattie on a voyage away from war and from matrimony, even if there is the hint that the couple might marry in some faraway place. The threesome escaping the war with a glimpse of marriage illustrates Franklin's contradictory hopes of love and companionship, minus the actual commitment, and her advocacy for spinsterhood and the community of women. In other words, Sybyl's sometimes competing and contradictory demands result in a quest only satiated by this ending that both gestures towards, and resists, matrimony, and claims a sisterhood of sorts through the inclusion of Aunt Pattie, who by the end of the novel has developed a strong friendship with Sybyl. When Aunt Pattie tells Sybyl that it is she who would make a good partner for Sybyl, the latter offers her wish for that too. This homosocial gesture is heightened by Aunt Pattie's description of their potential relationship: comfortable friendship and mutual companionship:

---

33 Demarest Lloyd to Miles Franklin, 24 and 30 September 1914.
34 Cicely Hamilton, *Marriage as a Trade* (1909; Detroit: Singing Tree Press, 1971), 247–8.

> "I'm the person you should marry," said Aunt Pattie promptly. "I shan't be buzzing in your ear that I love you. In fact I don't care whether I love you or not. I find you agreeable and entertaining."
> "I wish I could marry you" [said Sybyl]
> "We'll go on a long honeymoon together which will be as good." (331)

This dialogue is spoken in front of Roswell, who, like the enlightened New Man he has become, adds: "And I'll be little Tommy Taggy-Tail and come along in the rear." He even accepts Sybyl's disparaging quip that he "wouldn't come far enough in the rear" and Aunt Pattie's retort that he would if she were "in control". She tells them at least he might be "useful to buy tickets and make out routes and find out when to catch boats and trains" (332). Therein lies the usefulness of men.

Representing the ambiguous and often contradictory practices of femininity in the new century, *On Dearborn Street* responds to the New Woman demand for sexual autonomy and produces a narrative unique in its forthright discussion of heterosexual relationships and its bold demands for women's sexual agency. The fact that the playboy arouses Sybyl's passion, and the kind New Man is instructed to leave her alone, is part of the puzzle of the novel. Representing the ambiguous and often contradictory practices of femininity of the period, the novel articulates the claim for a nuanced womanhood that is both independently human and "feminine", and which pursues public vocation as well as romantic love. She mercilessly critiques men yet indulges in heterosexual coquetry and flirtation; she strides out into the public world and yet timidly tries to learn to dance. In this way Sybyl not only reflects the Edwardian heroine who is "ordinary" and "fallible" and "certainly never ideal", she also models the contradictory and often ambiguous gender performances that characterised this uncertain and transitional moment.[35] Roswell puts it this way: "She was most unconventional in some ways and unbelievably Victorian in others" (234).

---

35 Jane Eldridge Miller, *Rebel Women: Feminism, Modernism and the Edwardian Novel* (London: Virago, 1994), 110.

5
The Chicago Spinsters

> I'm free! Thank God! They say any fool can get married but it takes a devilish clever woman to remain an old maid, so that is the distinction I covet. When a man becomes too vigorously engaged to me, I change my geographical location and then he jilts me. I just love to be jilted. It relieves me of the responsibility and leaves the other fellow a friend for life.[1]

So declares Sybyl Penelo, the modern urban New Woman from Miles Franklin's *On Dearborn Street*, whom we met in Chapter 4. Eager to avoid "the evil effects" of marriage, this New Woman actively rebuffs proposals from suitors on a weekly basis.[2] In these lines, as in much of her New Woman writing during this period, Franklin's spinsters take centre stage as compelling characters critiquing gender injustice and modelling purposeful lives. This chapter focuses on these literary spinsters as intentional political acts, resuscitating the "old maid" as a positive rather than a negative, unenviable character. These mature, unmarried women find love and some eventually marry; others eschew matrimony by living full, independent lives. As illustrative of the former, more reformist take on the spinster, I discuss Miss Hilton in Franklin's short story, "Uncle Robert's Wedding Present" (1908) and Miss Eleanora Haskett from the unpublished novel "When Cupid Tarried" and its dramatic rendition, "The Love Machine" (1909). Representing spinsters who revolt by resisting marriage and leading a satisfying, productive, and independent life is Sophie Mortimer from Franklin's 1913 play "Aunt Sophie Smashes a Triangle".[3] In these narratives Franklin presents empowered spinsters

---

1 Miles Franklin, *On Dearborn Street* (St Lucia: University of Queensland Press/Australian Large Print, 1981), 184.
2 Franklin, *On Dearborn Street*, 302.
3 Miles Franklin, "Uncle Robert's Wedding Present", ML/MSS 445/21; Miles Franklin, "When Cupid Tarried", ML/MSS 445/18; Miles Franklin, "The Love Machine", ML/MSS

who debunk cultural stereotypes, model independent behaviour, and provide opportunities for unmarried women to emerge with dignity and respect.

In the nineteenth century women who did not marry were at best treated as sacrificial angels: pathetic virgins entombed by the demands of aging parents or siblings' children; at worst they were ridiculed and pitied as human failures bringing shame and scorn on their families.[4] Despite this denigrated social status, working-class spinsters had always worked alongside their married sisters in agricultural and industrial labour, while genteel women who were destined to be poor because of their marital status might seek employment as ladies' companions, teachers and governesses, or seamstresses.[5] The Sydney *Bulletin* was known for portraying such "redundant" women as "dangerous" because a desperate desire for a husband would result in men "find[ing] themselves trapped into marriage and burdened by domesticity". In addition, when sexual instincts were thwarted, repressed spinsters might become bitter, fanatical, and "kill joys" in future relationships.[6] At the other end of the spectrum, sexual activity of the "promiscuous" urban working-class spinster needed regulation in order for her eventually to "take her place" among the mothers of the race.[7] In Australia, as in the US, such regulation required "Citizen Mothers", who might populate the Empire and consolidate nations. Such efforts were precipitated by increased numbers of spinsters after World War I and fears of racial degeneration as birth rates among white, middle-class women fell.[8] Spinsters were therefore not static or monolithic cultural icons, but shaped by class, race, nation, and social location.

445/2; Miles Franklin, "Aunt Sophie Smashes a Triangle", ML/MSS 445/25. All subsequent references appear in parentheses in text.

[4] Ruth Freeman and Patricia Klaus, "Blessed or Not? The New Spinster in England and the United States in the Late-Nineteenth and Early-Twentieth Centuries", *Journal of Family History* 9, no. 4 (1984): 394–414; Martha Vicinus, *Independent Women: Work and Community for Single Women, 1850–1920* (Chicago: University of Chicago Press, 1985); Nina Auerbach, *Woman and the Demon: The Life of a Victorian Myth* (Cambridge, MA: Harvard University Press, 1982).

[5] Carroll Smith-Rosenberg, *Disorderly Conduct: Visions of Gender in Victorian America* (New York: Oxford University Press, 1985).

[6] Katie Holmes, "Spinster Indispensable: Feminists, Single Women and the Critique of Marriage, 1890–1920", *Australian Historical Studies* 29, no. 110 (1998): 78; Sheila Jeffreys, *The Spinster and Her Enemies: Feminism and Sexuality, 1880–1930* (London: Pandora, 1985), 173.

[7] Julie Tisdale, "Venereal Disease and the Policing of the Amateur in Melbourne During World War I", *Lilith* 9 (1996): 35–50.

[8] Marilyn Lake, "Between Old Worlds and New: Feminist Citizenship, Nation and Race, the Destabilisation of Identity" in *Suffrage and Beyond: International Feminist Perspectives*, ed. Caroline Daley and Melanie Nolan (Auckland: University of Auckland Press, 1994), 277–94.

In response to such cultural surveillance and derision, many spinsters led marginal lives, ending their days in poor-house and charity institutions. Still, even while such women suffered economically and socially, defined by what they could not have, their experiences as women who disrupted notions of female sexual subordination by resisting heterosexual relationships, or choosing celibacy, or each other, positioned them as subversive subjects.[9] Kay Whitehead makes this case in her discussion of spinster teachers, who in choosing celibacy accessed personal power that "fuelled ambitions, which could have been constrained by marriage".[10] This is not to say, of course, that spinsters during this period were outside the control of fathers and brothers in terms of their lived experience, only that by avoiding the oppositional logic associated with marriage, they emerged as potentially radical, transgressive figures, often resented by men whose control they had escaped. Rather than only representing rejected women, the spinster started to emerge as "the figure for whom no man was good enough, a woman of integrity who would not compromise her intelligence or her bodily autonomy".[11] As Susan Cotts Watkins notes: "Where there are many spinsters we must question the centrality of marriage".[12] The "independence" of the unmarried woman thus coalesced with the "freedom" of the New Woman.[13]

By the late-nineteenth century, with access to higher education and employment and with a growing openness about the fragility of happiness in marriage, independent middle-class women in the US were no longer regarding marriage as necessary for financial support or self-respect, and were increasingly free to live outside the parameters of family control.[14] Sheila Jeffreys also makes the case that in the UK between 1906 and 1914 many spinsters were "choosing to remain single and were articulating their decision in political terms" in response to the double standard of sexual conduct subordinating women, and because they enjoyed more legal rights (despite their cultural marginality) than married women. Katie Holmes also makes this point in reference to Australian spinsters,

---

9 Rita S. Kranidis, *The Victorian Spinster and Colonial Emigration* (New York: St Martin's Press, 1999), 19.
10 Kay Whitehead, "The Spinster Teacher in Australia from the 1870s to the 1960s", *History of Education Review* 36, no. 1 (2007): 6.
11 Holmes, "Spinster Indispensable", 88.
12 Susan Cotts Watkins, "Spinsters", *Journal of Family History* 9, no. 4 (1984): 311.
13 Susan Magarey, "History, Cultural Studies and Another Look at First-Wave Feminism in Australia", *Australian Historical Studies* 27, no. 106 (1996): 104.
14 Lillian Faderman, *Surpassing the Love of Men: Romantic Friendships and Love Between Women from the Renaissance to the Present* (London: Junction Books, 1981); Naomi Braun Rosenthal, *Spinster Tales and Womanly Possibilities* (Albany: State University of New York Press, 2002).

emphasising that what was at stake for them was their freedom and sexual autonomy.[15] The English New Woman writer Ella Hepworth Dixon illustrates these assertions in an 1899 Humanitarian essay, "Why Women Are Ceasing to Marry". She boldly defended the spinster and critiqued the notion that women acted out of "selfish reasons" in order to "shirk the high privilege of maternity and domestic life . . . [and] compete with men".[16] A key aspect of Dixon's response to this concerned the tricky system of chaperone, which was on the decline, but still constrained women and encouraged them to make rash marital decisions in pursuit of minimal autonomy. Access to freedom, from getting an education to going to the theatre and taking up space in public arenas, Dixon explained, was a privilege for which "the girl of twenty or thirty years ago was ready to barter herself to the first suitor who offered himself and the shelter of his name".[17]

Despite the inevitable backlash resulting from such disruptions of women's domestic "nature", New Woman literary spinsters emerged as vibrant and attractive characters, elevated in the name of public visibility and service. They were portrayed as distinctly "modern", no longer hopelessly unfashionable, but also representing "disorder and rebellion".[18] By declaring that women could choose to lead fulfilling lives outside of wedded domesticity, spinsters of all types were increasingly depicted as resisting patriarchal social norms, and encouraging debate about definitions of femininity and what it meant to be a woman, including whether marriage was her absolute destiny and what kinds of sexual practices might be possible outside matrimony. In addition, self-fulfilled characters worthy of love and respect were portrayed as sympathetic protagonists and more psychologically complex characters whose lives did not neatly fall into patterns of romance and domesticity circumscribed by the traditional nineteenth-century novel.[19] As Jane Eldridge Miller explains, because marriage was no longer the only ending in these stories, authors with spinster protagonists "were forced to work in opposition to dominant narratives of romance and marriage which had traditionally been used to tell stories about women".[20] For example, novels such

---

15 Jeffreys, *The Spinster and Her Enemies*, 89.
16 Ella Hepworth Dixon, "Why Women Are Ceasing to Marry", *Humanitarian* 14 (1899): 391.
17 Dixon, "Why Women Are Ceasing to Marry", 394.
18 Emma Liggins, ed., *Odd Women? Spinsters, Lesbians and Widows in British Women's Fiction, 1850s–1930s* (Manchester: Manchester University Press, 2014); Smith-Rosenberg, *Disorderly Conduct*, 247.
19 Ann Heilmann, *New Woman Fiction: Women Writing First-Wave Feminism* (New York: St. Martin's Press, 2004); Charlotte J. Rich, *Transcending the New Woman: Multiethnic Narratives in the Progressive Era* (Columbia: University of Missouri Press, 2009).
20 Jane Eldridge Miller, *Rebel Women: Feminism, Modernism and the Edwardian Novel* (London: Virago, 1994), 76.

as E.M. Forster's *Where Angels Fear to Tread* (1905), Mary and Jane Findlater's *Crossriggs* (1908), and F.M. Mayor's *The Third Miss Symons* (1913) boldly resist traditional narrative conventions concerning these previously pitied and/or despised spinsters.

In this way New Woman literature normalised the spinster protagonist and positioned her as "one element" in a variety of feminine archetypes for cultural consumption that was able to reach a wide audience in the popular periodical press.[21] The Anglo-Caribbean author Annie E. Holdsworth's collection of short stories, *A Garden of Spinsters*, is case in point, as illustrated by one of her sassy protagonists, who declares: "In my grandmother's time women were old maids at 25; but these days in the days of bicycles there are no old maids".[22] Popular plays like Cicely Hamilton's *Just to Get Married* (with the audacious line spoken by the New Woman heroine, Georgina: "Surely you're not romantic enough to imagine that all married women of your acquaintance have selected their more or less unsuitable husbands out of pure affection!"[23]) as well as those by George Bernard Shaw also reached a broad audience. In 1913 Franklin attended a Chicago performance of Shaw's play *Candida*, which made the case for spinsterhood by questioning Victorian notions of love and marriage.[24]

Franklin followed the lead of other New Woman authors in resisting tropes associating bachelors with eligibility and sexual agency, and spinsters with frigidity and sexual naivety, and joined them in creating attractive "old maids" choosing romance for themselves and helping negotiate romance for others. Eleonora Haskett and Miss Hilton, for example, mature into compelling characters eventually choosing – and especially in the case of the former, never giving up on – romance and marriage. Such practices, of course, were hardly revolutionary in still presenting women within normative standards of matrimony, and even in "Aunt Sophie Smashes a Triangle", which presents the empowered – although conventionally beautiful, intelligent, and accomplished – spinster Sophie Mortimer resisting marriage, her talents are employed to save a marriage. These spinster manuscripts are typical of Franklin's domestic feminism that both endorses traditional matrimonial heteronormativity and seeks to critique it, reflecting as they do her own contradictory and sometimes ambiguous narrative about the trade-offs between love and vocation.

---

21 Rosenthal, *Spinster Tales and Womanly Possibilities*, 6.
22 Annie E. Holdsworth, *A Garden of Spinsters* (Leipzig: Tauchnitz, 1904), 251.
23 Cicely Hamilton, quoted in *New Women Plays*, ed. Linda Fitzsimmons and Vivien Gardner (London: Methuen, 1991), 31. See also G. L. Harding, "Feminism and the Propagandist Drama", *The Freewoman*, 14 December 1911, 76–78.
24 Miles Franklin, Pocket diary, 10 April 1913, ML/MSS 364/2.

The Spinster Narratives

The earliest of Franklin's spinster narratives discussed here is "Uncle Robert's Wedding Present", a short story of fifteen-and-a-half typed manuscript pages. Dated September 1908, it concerns the negotiations of a spinster, Miss Hilton, for Brenda, a young friend who is engaged to be married. Brenda was raised by a single mother, Mrs Pinchton, who taught her daughters to use their feminine wiles to secure a husband. The choice of "Pinchton" echoes the scrimping and scraping state of the family's economic situation that relies on a cantankerous benefactor, Uncle Robert. Disappointed by his unwillingness to finance her marriage, Brenda summons Miss Hilton, who writes Brenda's thank-you note to Uncle Robert with an assertive tone that catches his attention and respect. The note then prompts Uncle Robert to visit the young couple and results in him underwriting the wedding and hiring her new husband as a partner in the firm. " Uncle Robert's Wedding Present" ends happily with the spinster revealing herself as the narrator and romantically involved with Uncle Robert, who is transformed into a potential mate. This story is innovative in its switch at the end from an omniscient narrator hovering above the story to the use of the first person, which encourages the reader to rethink the original narrator's point of view through knowledge that it was Miss Hilton all along. Such a device precipitates the dismantling of truth claims of the original omniscient narrator and the revelation of its unreliable nature, drawing attention to the fictional frame of the story.

The second manuscript, "When Cupid Tarried", written in 1909 and reworked as the play "The Love Machine" later that year, was referred to by Franklin as the "Cupid Story". It is typical of Franklin's New Woman writing in its new realist focus on romance and marriage, but is set in "Cosmopolita" (Illiwah Point, Sydney[25]) rather than Chicago or New York and mirrors the fantasy ending of *On Dearborn Street*. The play is also reminiscent of H.G. Wells' 1895 novel, *The Time Machine*, and reflects modernity's preoccupation with science and technology, and the emerging genre of science fiction. The story features a young tomboy scientist, Harrie, who resists traditional femininity and creates technology for social purity ends in the form of a machine to help lovers choose their mates. The story also features her spinster aunt, Eleonora Haskett, who is negotiating Harrie's cousins' marriages and finds her long lost love in the form of a professor, who is helping Harrie build the love machine. As the invention progresses, the nieces find their suitors, and ask Harrie to help with various trysts. Harrie forgetfully – or perhaps purposefully, the motive is not clear – mixes up the couples, who profess love for

---

25 Jill Roe, *Stella Miles Franklin: A Biography* (Sydney: Fourth Estate/Harper Collins, 2008), 135.

5 The Chicago Spinsters

the wrong suitor after sitting in the love machine. Along with this convention of mistaken identity is that of gender confusion. Harrie dresses as a boy to try and rectify – and enjoy – the increasingly comedic mess that occurs as a result of the love machine, but wins the heart of one of the potential suitors in the process. Although acting as a boy while falling in love with the man who befriends the boy is a classic dramatic trope, as is the homoerotic gesture of the man falling in love with the boy-woman whom he has befriended, these performances allow Franklin a strong feminist character who eroticises cleverness as well as resists traditional femininity. As Eleonora eventually reunites with her former love, the point is brought home that the two most authentic and egalitarian love matches (the spinster and the scientist) are those done without the aid of the machine.

The machinations of Victorian realist romance are present here in plotting, character, and form, but this story and its dramatisation uses fantasy and whimsy to achieve its ends, which question – if not transform – the traditional romantic ending. Still, the novel is especially tedious for the contemporary reader because of its length, its extended list of characters who are difficult to tell apart, and its contrived plot. Compared to the subtle irony and light touch of *On Dearborn Street*, its polemics feel heavy-handed and it suffers from an exceptionally didactic tone. The farce and slapstick rendering of comedic action is better suited to the play, which reads more easily. Despite these flaws, the various versions of the Cupid Story emphasise that non-traditional women (both spinsters and scientists) still find love, and all women have rights to rational mate selection. In addition, Franklin inserts the sphere of the feminine into the technology of modernity by declaring women creators and recipients of a fantasy love machine, and also questions modernity's optimism for harnessing technologies to solve social problems.

The third spinster narrative discussed here is "Aunt Sophie Smashes a Triangle: A Domestic Comedy in Four Acts", which runs to sixty-two double-spaced manuscript pages. It features the ebullient spinster, Sophie Mortimer, who reins in her brother, David, the philandering husband, saves his marriage, and also saves the mistress, Elaine Powell, from a life of disrepute through joining the fight for woman suffrage. This play provides a good example of the ways theatre might potentially be employed not only to provide models of empowering spinsters, but also as a site for feminist campaigning itself.[26] The first act features Alice, the cuckolded wife, deep in domestic drudgery, and her husband eager to leave for the office so he can meet his paramour. The spinster, Sophie, arrives, confronts Alice about the infidelity, and encourages her to "disappear", spend some time at a sanatorium under an assumed

---

26 Kate Newey, "Women's Playwriting and the Popular Theatre", in *Feminist Readings of Victorian Popular Texts*, ed. Emma Liggins and Daniel Duffy (Aldershot, UK: Ashgate, 2001), 153. See also Sue-Ellen Case, *Feminism and Theatre* (New York: Methuen, 1988).

name, and let David fend for himself. The second act features the lovers together and includes Elaine's lament about not wanting to be a home breaker. She suggests they separate knowing that each might summon the other. The third act takes place at "Rest Haven Sanatarium" [sic], where, according to Sophie's plan, both Elaine and Alice have sought refuge and become friends, although their identities are not revealed to each other. In the final act David arrives, having been summoned by Elaine, and Alice is overjoyed, thinking he has come for her. Elaine, newly awakened to the politics of marriage, privately confronts David on his cowardice, and scornfully ends the affair, declaring he must not humiliate his wife by revealing the truth to her. She asks Sophie about joining the suffrage campaign, hears that "the world is open to young woman now", and is rewarded with exciting and socially responsible work (61).

In the sections below I first discuss Franklin's debunking of negative stereotypes about unmarried women by crafting attractive spinsters who are worldly and intelligent. Second, I illustrate how having established her spinsters' assets, Franklin subverts convention by portraying them negotiating romance for themselves and others. Third, I discuss Franklin's response to tropes about spinsters' responsibilities for "municipal housekeeping" or work in the public sphere that assumedly replaced wifely, domestic obligations.[27] Embedded in all these themes are both critiques and endorsements of the traditional romance narrative, producing what Jill Davis has described as complex sexual politics representing both "progressive ideas and patriarchal reactions" where portions of an audience or readership would accept and others reject different aspects from different sets of meanings.[28] Like the interpretation of any text, such nuance requires understandings of the "delicacies of interpretation" that provide both effective vehicles for feminist enlightenment and pleasure as well as a route for more conservative reading and spectacle.[29]

Beauty, Intelligence, and Generosity

A central aspect of the devaluation of the spinster was her supposed lack of conventional feminine beauty.[30] As Miller, explains, representing "unnaturalness and uselessness . . . a kind of death-in-life", the spinster was usually a physically

---

27 Eileen Janes Yeo, ed., *Radical Femininity: Women's Self-Representations in the Public Sphere* (Manchester: Manchester University Press, 1998).
28 Jill Davis, "The New Woman and the New Life" in *The New Woman and Her Sisters: Feminism and Theatre, 1850-1914*, ed. Vivien Gardner and Susan Rutherford (Hemel Hempstead: Harvester Wheatsheaf, 1992), 22.
29 Newey, "Women's Playwriting and the Popular Theatre", 154.
30 Laura L. Doan, ed., *Old Maids to Radical Spinsters: Unmarried Women in the Twentieth-Century Novel* (Urbana: University of Chicago Press, 1991).

unattractive character, who prompted pity.[31] These tropes would be resisted in the new century, but progress was unsteady and Virginia Woolf, for example, gave us the physically unattractive Miss Kilman in Mrs Dalloway: "a hideously ugly, bitter, hard-done-by humbug of a religious zealot in a smelly raincoat".[32] Most New Women writers, however, attempted to reshape these stereotypes by either branding their spinsters with physical attractiveness or offering a more deliberate challenge in subverting notions that a woman's worth is determined by her appearance. Although in *My Brilliant Career* Franklin follows the latter route by pointing out Sybylla's unconventional looks, her tendency in these Chicago manuscripts is to follow the former and create attractive spinsters conforming to traditional standards of feminine beauty. Their disruption of conventional femininity resides in being mature women, although beautiful ones nonetheless. Overall, Franklin's spinsters are no Miss Kilmans. One explanation for this can be found in the marketing of the New Woman in the US by the first decade of the new century, when popular commercial presses realised she was a marketable commodity only if she was presented in ways that appealed to a mass audience. As a result, "high-minded heroines" were "scaled down and prettied up" for popular consumption.[33] Because the potential opportunity for education was enormous, authors like Franklin hoping to reach a broad audience were keen to showcase these positive portrayals of the modern woman.

Miss Eleonora Haskett, for example, is "a beautiful dame of anything over forty", described as "the embodiment of all that is refined and beautiful in her sex" ("Love Machine", 2, 53). Similarly, in the novel she is described as equally beautiful with hair more becoming than the "bright locks of teens". Wearing a gown that "revealed her beauty of line", she demonstrates "indescribable pathos and attraction". Compared to such a dazzling spinster, the illusion of "undeveloped youth" is described as merely "insipid" ("When Cupid Tarried", 271–2). The spinster from "Aunt Sophie Smashes a Triangle" is another attractive woman whose mature looks attract a host of admirers. With "an elegant diaphanous waist", she is "less drab of manner and gesture" and takes "more pride in her personal appearance" than Alice, her married sister-in-law (8). In this play Franklin turns the unattractive spinster stereotype on its head by implying that compulsory domesticity renders women unattractive. Alice, described in the stage notes as "a plump, unspectacular, little woman", displays

---

31 Miller, *Rebel Women*, 87.
32 Sybil Oldfield, "From Rachel's Aunts to Miss La Trobe: Spinsters in the Fiction of Virginia Woolf", in *Old Maids to Radical Spinsters*, 92.
33 Chris Willis, "'Heaven Defend Me From Political or Highly-Educated Women!' Packaging the New Woman for Mass Consumption", in *The New Woman in Fiction and in Fact: Fin-de-Siècle Feminisms*, ed. Angelique Richardson and Chris Willis (New York: Palgrave, 2001), 54.

"the colorlessness, the lack of individuality of women too closely immured in 'Woman's Sphere'" (1). In this way Franklin's spinsters resist the cultural derision of the homely character who is too ugly to catch a man. Franklin also renders maturity itself attractive and confronts the aging process, an issue that most New Woman writers tended to avoid.[34] An exception among Franklin's mature spinster protagonists is the adolescent tomboy, Harrie, but she is also an attractive young woman despite her scientific priorities.

Franklin's spinsters also possess brains as well as beauty, and each one is portrayed as exceptionally articulate and worldly. In this regard Franklin again sexualises intelligence and creates spinsters whose cleverness is a source of their sexual allure and power. For example, when Sophie Mortimer puts ambition and social purpose ahead of romance and resists male attention in order to prepare a speech for a "great [suffrage] meeting", her suitor is undeterred, and describes her as "one of the most interesting women I have ever met". He finds the fact that she has "such a splendid grip on herself and consequently gets so much out of life" as particularly attractive (36, 50). Similarly the spinster in "Uncle Robert's Wedding Present" is "self-poised" and possesses the positive outlook and congenial spirit as a result of "having suffered none of the coarsening disillusionment of the average marriage" (13, 7). This sage spinster strides into the public downtown area to give Uncle Robert a "talking to" and demonstrates an assertiveness he finds most appealing. And finally Harrie's cleverness, as illustrated in her scientific pursuits and her lack of concern for gender proprieties, is also exceptionally appealing to her suitor.

Rather than being represented as mean and embittered, Franklin's spinsters demonstrate another asset: kindness and generosity. Miss Hilton takes it upon herself to support Brenda and responds to her with compassion and care. Eleonora Haskett also guides her nieces with a generous spirit despite their thorny matrimonial problems; she also supports Harrie's ambitions and her experiments that explode and terrorise the family. She even manages to forgive the house servant who sits in the love machine and insults her under its spell by declaring: "At your time of life, you ought to be thankful to have someone love you" ("Love Machine", 16). But it is especially Sophie Mortimer who demonstrates kindness and feminist solidarity in her support of the mistress, and the latter who in turn befriends the wife. At the end of the play the newly empowered mistress berates David for his cowardice, pulls off the necklace he has given her, and kindly arranges it so that Alice will think it is a present to her from David. This ending mirrors Charlotte Perkins Gilman's story, "Turned", in which the wife and virtuous mistress unite and together confront the villainous husband.

---

34 Emma Liggins, "The 'Modern Spinster's Lot' and Female Sexuality in Ella Hepworth Dixon's *One Doubtful Hour*", *Women's Writing* 19, no. 1 (2012): 12.

Cupid's Interest

Despite cultural constructions of the unlovable spinster, romance is in the cards for Miss Hilton: one of those women who "have loved, then do love, then will love" (8). This late-life relationship is presented as joyful and fulfilling, resisting stereotypes about romance as the province of the young. "Each generation thinks it has the only patent on love, believing that it could not exist without it. Youth," she declares, "never pauses to wonder what grey-haired folk use as a substitute" (9). It is at the very end of the story that Miss Hilton reveals herself as Brenda's "'old maid' friend", and professes that "love when the bride is almost twice twenty and the bride-groom considerably more . . . lead[s] to a very gratifying radiance" (16). This ending, including Franklin's destabilisation of the term "old maid" by the use of quotation marks, establishes the eligibility of mature spinsters and their agency in matters of the heart.

Miss Eleonora Haskett also finds love and "entered upon her hour" ("When Cupid Tarried", 273), but of all Franklin's spinsters, her story is closest to the conventional spinster narrative and is used to illustrate negative social conventions about them. In surveying her life as an unmarried woman, for example, Miss Haskett had "fad[ed] from a young and beautiful girl surrounded by adulation, to an elderly woman on whom no man cast eyes of desire" (11). In this dialogue Franklin reminds readers of the reality of the spinster's plight and emphasises culture's role in its construction: "Eleonora", writes Franklin, is caught by "androcentric spinsterhood, with youth subtracted like an asset" (12). Similarly, in "The Love Machine" Eleonora laments "the bitterness and waste of a lonely life" (11) and laments "the humbug of mock womanliness" that prevented her from articulating her love for the professor in her youth (26–27). Although these descriptions sit awkwardly amidst dazzling descriptions of her, they are useful in first presenting the traditional cultural constructions of the spinster that Franklin seeks to subvert. A more self-actualised spinster would have left little space for critique.

Like the Misses Hilton and Haskett, Sophie Mortimer is also eligible and worthy of romantic interest, having "done some fellow out of the nicest thing in the world" (42). She debunks the myth that spinsters are unworthy of heterosexual romance, resists the lure of romance as women's ultimate achievement, and notes how a "spinster has to endure that venerable [pro-marriage] wheeze" on a daily basis, declaring it "enough to drive one to suicide". "Imagine the horror of being yoked to one individual day in and day out for the term of your natural life!" she exclaims (12–13). Sophie does not, however, reject romance outright. On inviting Elaine to join her in the "the healthy absorbing action" of the suffrage campaign (53), she gives another convincing reason for independence: the promise of real romance: "Love comes more readily to the busy people than those who sit down and wait for it" (61).

Finally, Franklin also debunks the myth that spinsters have little knowledge of love, romance, and marriage by creating characters that help negotiate romance in the lives of others. In this endeavour she just barely avoids re-inscribing the gossipy, busy-body spinster stereotype. Miss Haskett, for instance, is "a fairy godmother" when it comes to helping her nieces secure a marriage ("When Cupid Tarried", 9). She takes on this role with bravery and courage, working to enhance their status on the marriage market. In similar fashion Miss Hilton engineers Brenda's marriage as well as her own, demonstrating an "exquisite sympathy" for the needs of the young couple (7). And finally it is Sophie's cleverness that saves her sister-in-law's marriage as well as the reputation of the mistress, thus safeguarding her for future matrimonial options.

It will come as no surprise to readers who know Franklin's work that she does not engage with cultural references of the spinster as lesbian, given her relatively dismissive attitude towards that notion even while she celebrated women's friendships and community.[35] What she does engage is the eugenicist aspect of social purity feminism that made the case for women to be economically empowered to be able to choose their sexual partners and therefore maintain their role in the struggle for progressive evolution.[36] The choice of unmarried women to accept marriage and leave spinsterhood behind, or reject marriage and remain a committed spinster, was thus central in this regard. In this way the ability to choose the right man (in the cases of Misses Hilton and Haskett), avoid the wrong one (in the case of Elaine Powell and several of the cousins in the Cupid Story), and decide to remain single (in the case of Sophie Mortimer), were all aspects of women's freedom, autonomy, and rational mate selection.

A Wider Outlook

Alongside presentation of spinsters' assets, Franklin argues for their involvement in public life. A central component here is the denigration of its alternative: domesticity. Uncle Robert insinuates this by sending Brenda a wedding gift of a "wash tub" containing a variety of kitchen utensils (8). Franklin also uses Uncle Robert to illustrate a classic double bind inherent in traditional matrimony. Women may act in weak and frivolous ways to attract men and secure economic livelihoods, but they precipitate disgust in those ensnared: "All young and healthy and not one

---

35   Roe, *Stella Miles Franklin*, 537.
36   Mike Hawkins, *Social Darwinism in European and American Thought, 1860–1945* (New York: Cambridge University Press, 1997), 258.

got spirit enough to tell me to go to the devil!" he declares (3). Similarly, she also uses Mrs Pinchton, Brenda's harried mother, to demonstrate the negative economic consequences of a dependent wife who "rear[ed] her daughters wrongly" (2). As in all her critiques of domesticity, Franklin seeks to explain the misogyny expressed by men rooted in a system requiring women's social and economic dependence.

As already mentioned, "Aunt Sophie Smashes a Triangle" also contains a strong critique of marital domesticity through comparisons of Alice Mortimer's domestic burdens to the unencumbered and vivacious options of her spinster sister-in-law. These representations of everyday intimacies, instances of what Kirsten Shepherd-Barr calls the "intimate realism" of everyday life, portray Alice, for example, as unhappy and frazzled.[37] As David reads the newspaper, she is sewing a dress, trying to handle two rambunctious teenagers, and organising the house-servant. Witnessing this, Sophie delivers many comedic lines such as suggesting marriage might be seen as "a case of measles". When the sobbing Alice calls it a "[p]retty long case of measles", Sophie revises her analogy to "something more lasting – paralysis for example" (14). This sets up the spinster's interest in public life as a rational and attractive choice compared to the drudgery of domesticity.

By the early-twentieth century women were forging new paths in education, business, and public life generally, often utilising traditional notions of femininity associated with care and domesticity and extending them to the public sector in professional employment and various forms of public philanthropy.[38] Understanding the difficulties of combining family and careers and the inevitability of marriage ending an intellectual life, educated middle-class women often chose this vocation of social responsibility where meaningful work was the centre of their life. Martha Vicinus, for example, writes of the ways unmarried women "believed passionately in the morally redeeming power of work; paid public work would give them dignity and independence".[39] Already accustomed to putting other people's needs above their own as maiden aunts or parental caretakers, they slid easily into this civic duty: a credible undertaking, but one still diminished by cultural norms endorsing the sanctity of marriage and representing such service as sublimated domesticity.[40]

The normalcy of spinsters leading full lives in the public sphere was a central cultural preoccupation during this period when the marriage problem was being debated. *The Ladies Home Journal,* one of the most widely read American women's

---

37 Kirsten E. Shepherd-Barr, "'It Was Ugly': The Maternal Instinct on State at the *Fin de Siècle*", *Women: A Cultural Review* 23, no. 2 (2012): 216.
38 Alison Mackinnon, *Love and Freedom: Professional Women and the Reshaping of Personal Life* (Cambridge: Cambridge University Press, 1997).
39 Vicinus, *Independent Women*, 6.
40 Susan L. Katz, "Singleness of Heart: Spinsterhood in Victorian Culture" Ph.D. dissertation, Columbia University, 1988.

magazines in the new century, for example, took up the issue of the public-minded spinster with a vengeance, often describing them "with respect and admiration" as well as reinforcing traditional notions.[41] It emphasised the implicit choices women must make; they gave up careers and intellectual lives to marry because the responsibilities of the home were "clearly deemed inimical to professional accomplishments" and spinsters embodied freedom precisely because they were not obligated to a husband and children.[42] It goes without saying that Franklin was a prime example of this in representing the civic-minded spinster who combined a need to support herself with desires for socially meaningful work and resisted the loss of independence associated with matrimony. "The personal cost of singledom", explains Jill Roe in her analysis of Franklin's romantic endeavours, "remained high, but where was the resting point if not in marriage?"[43]

Franklin provides illustrations of spinsters engaged in public life in each of the manuscripts discussed here, but also encourages potential readers and audiences to consider cultural expectations associated with such civic duty. In other words, she asks them to think twice before assuming that all spinsters, when denied the supposedly ultimate satisfaction of love and marriage, would "naturally" turn to altruistic public service. For example, Eleonora Haskett of "When Cupid Tarried", the least subversive of all the manuscripts in terms of its representation of empowered unmarried women, embraces the privileges of her class and resists expectations of public service. And, although Eleanora of "The Love Machine" supports spinsters doing public work when she declares that they "may turn to being a blessing to their fellows and to the uplifting of mankind", she still "rejected the serious works of life … [and] recognised that being a boon to one's fellows is against natural law … at best a vain and empty substitute for having really lived" (12). In this example Eleonora is presented as a somewhat pretentious character, but her portrayal resists the expectation of the publicly engaged spinster who is denied marriage and a family and therefore has nothing better to do.

Although the Cupid Stories resist assumptions that all spinsters turn to public service, "Uncle Robert's Wedding Present" encourages readers to question the motives of those who do. Uncle Robert, exclaims Brenda, is a "selfish" bachelor in comparison to sweet "old maids" like her friend, Miss Hilton, with their hearts of gold, whose existence is to serve others. Spinsters, gushes Brenda, "keep their souls pure and sweet and sympathetic and unselfish to help others over the unhappy parts

---

41 Rosenthal, *Spinster Tales and Womanly Possibilities*, 40; Patricia Searles and Janet Mickish, "'A Thoroughbred Girl': Images of Female Gender Roles in Turn-of-the-Century Mass Media", *Women's Studies* 3 (1984): 261–81.
42 Rosenthal, *Spinster Tales and Womanly Possibilities*, 74.
43 Roe, *Stella Miles Franklin*, 193.

of life" (12). It is easy to imagine Franklin writing this tongue-in-cheek narrative irritated by – or perhaps even fuming over – those people who thought unmarried women were involved in public life for altruistic ends rather than recognising spinsters' needs to support themselves economically.

A central aspect of the cultural preoccupation with the marriage problem and spinster's choice to serve a public rather than a husband were anxieties already mentioned about anticipated dangers of spinsterhood thwarting "normal" sexual and domestic "instincts". It was feared this "lust of exercising power" might turn them into feminists as compensation for the denial of their "natural" biological destinies.[44] Franklin recognised this trope and dealt with it by exaggerating her spinsters' feminist public achievements simultaneously with their marriageability. The attractive and sexually alluring Sophie, for instance, was not only a suffragist, but a leader described as working on a speech for an important suffrage meeting where she is "going to be one of the stars" (36). She also has "a couple of magazine articles crying for her" (49).

Such stellar public achievements are derided by her brother, whose declarations are simultaneously made to appear disingenuous and discredited coming as they do from the adulterous husband. David tells Sophie she is "crazy", insinuating her problem is "too much suffrage and emancipation" and suggesting she "marry and get back to normality" (38, 41). He labels her suffrage work "[s]kyhooting rot" (42), even though such rot eventually entices his mistress to choose socially responsible work and leave him. This dialogue illustrates the ways anxiety about empowered spinsters who turn to feminism was used to discredit them and to imply they hated – or wanted to control – men: "You old maids and suffragettes think you're going to turn out a man like a tailor's dummy – a creature that won't move or act unless you press the button" (40), says David. Finally, a key aspect of negative cultural constructions of spinsters as rabid feminists was that such civic-mindedness was caused by past rejections from men. "I took to suffrage", Sophie explains, "not to replace love by it as some nincompoops imagine … I want the women of the future to have a wider outlook" (17). During this dialogue Franklin manipulates gendered space as the masculinised geography of David's office is invaded "by one righteous female after another". These invasions result in David's literal retreat from the stage at the same time that his intentions are revealed as disingenuous. Men who oppose suffrage and the rights of spinsters "lose both the argument in hand, and, gradually, physical space on the stage".[45]

---

44 Jeffreys, *The Spinster and Her Enemies*, 173.
45 Susan Pfisterer and Carolyn Pickett, *Playing with Ideas: Australian Women Playwrights From the Suffragettes to the Sixties* (Sydney: Currency Press, 1999), 199; Penny Farfan, *Women, Modernism, and Performance* (Cambridge: Cambridge University Press, 2004).

Such a range of spinster narratives from containment of traditional romance and courtship to their subversion provided new scripts for the audience and reader. Indeed, the varied accounts of the spinster in these manuscripts allowed for a range of potential extra-textual identifications that encourage sympathy with her plight. This staging of relations of identification, what Laura Green describes as "cementing an ontological alliance between the protagonist and the reader", is enacted in part through feminist realist strategies that depict varying degrees of self-awareness on the part of protagonists.[46] Miss Hilton, for example, reflects on her opportunities for love and her options with Uncle Robert, Elaine Powell comes to recognise her freedom, and Sophie Mortimer considers domesticity and rejects it. Like most New Woman heroines, including Franklin herself, they give spinsterhood a good run and provide marriage with a healthy dose of scepticism.

---

46 Laura Green, "'I Recognize Myself in Her': Identification with the Reader in George Eliot's *The Mill on the Floss* and Simone de Beauvoir's *Memoirs of a Dutiful Daughter*", *Tulsa Studies in Women's Literature* 24, no. 1 (2005): 57.

Part III: Men

6
Moral Squalor

Franklin was keen to join her New Woman sisters in identifying the ways men's errant sexual behaviours subordinated women emotionally and economically, threatened the stability of the family and society, and created a public health threat.[1] "Innocent" wives were robbed of their dignity and forced to endure health and reproductive dangers as an explicit consequence of husbands' adultery and liaisons with prostitutes and its risk for sexually transmitted infections. This "moral squalor", which illustrated sex in the context of danger and disease, was a serious and often very perilous issue; it was also something Franklin faced in her personal life as well as in her relationships with working women through the NWTUL.[2] Such narrative authority, focused through the lens of social purity feminism, was expressed in Franklin's writing in two ways: she made frequent use of the sexual behaviours of flawed male characters to illustrate misogyny as part of her critique of American manhood, but she also used the psychological journeys of these suitors to highlight the ways men might reform their ways, participate in more egalitarian interpersonal relationships, and might therefore model gender transformation.

This chapter discusses these strategies through a focus on adultery and prostitution as two examples of moral squalor. First, I revisit two manuscripts already discussed to illustrate Franklin's adultery narratives: the short story, "A Business Emergency", from Chapter 3, and the play, "Aunt Sophie Smashes a Triangle", discussed in Chapter 5. Second, I focus on the play, "Virtue", in order to explore

---

1 Lucy Bland, *Banishing the Beast: Sexuality and the Early Feminists* (New York: New Press, 1995); Beryl Satter, *Each Mind a Kingdom: American Women, Sexual Purity and the New Thought Movement, 1875–1920* (Berkeley, CA: University of California Press, 2001).
2 Sally Ledger, *The New Woman: Fiction and Feminism at the* Fin de Siècle (College Station: Penn State University Press, 1999), 21.

Franklin's response to prostitution.³ Also written under the pseudonym Mr and Mrs Ogniblat L'Artsau, it is usually attributed to post-1915 when Franklin was residing in London, but "Virtue" is included here as an example of Franklin's Chicago manuscripts because she most likely started the play while still in Chicago, and because Franklin biographers describe the play as "representative" of her New Woman American years.⁴ The play is set in Chicago and New York in its present time.

A focus on Franklin's feminist social purity approach to understandings of male vice begins with a reminder of the conflation of the moral and the medical. This is aptly illustrated in the politics of the social purity movement generally and its language of "health" as a euphemism for morality. Male vice was associated with impurity, uncleanliness, and disease, as the terms "squalor" and "social hygiene" attest.⁵ In addition, this approach relied on the popularity of biological explanations for social relations, which assumed men's "natural" tendency to promiscuity, and transformed purity, long accepted as women's lot and destiny, as a moral virtue. In this Franklin employed evolutionary sociologist Lester Ward's notion that women's acquired trait of genetic superiority functioned as a counter to men's exaggerated sexual desire. The case was made that women were innately more "racially" aware compared to men's predisposition to mate indiscriminately, whose lust made them less mindful of the consequences of procreation. As a result, women were better custodians for the future because they possessed a "moral biology" and were poised as "managers of male passion". British social purity feminist Frances Swiney put it this way: "women are always the pioneers to the humaner and nobler civilisation".⁶ For Franklin, however, this moral imperative also necessitated women's political and economic independence, as illustrated in the strong moral crusades in Chicago invigorating the city's suffrage campaigns and helping win state-level woman suffrage in 1913. Franklin was surrounded by such demands as "Votes for Women and Chastity for Men" that illustrate this preoccupation with problems of male sexual behaviours in the context of women's rights.⁷

---

3   Miles Franklin, "Aunt Sophie Smashes a Triangle", ML MSS 445/25/2; Mr and Mrs Ogniblat L'Artsau [aka. Miles Franklin], "A Business Emergency", ML MSS 364/58; Mr and Mrs Ogniblat L'Artsau [aka. Miles Franklin], "Virtue", ML MSS 445/28/6. All subsequent references appear in parentheses in the text.
4   Jill Roe, *Stella Miles Franklin: A Biography* (Sydney: Fourth Estate/Harper Collins, 2008), 156.
5   Angelique Richardson, *Love and Eugenics in the Late Nineteenth Century* (Oxford: Oxford University Press, 2003), 49.
6   Richardson, *Love and Eugenics in the Late Nineteenth Century*, 50; Frances Swiney, *The Mystery of the Circle and the Cross, or The Interpretation of Sex* (London: Open Road, 1908), 29.
7   Bland, *Banishing the Beast*, 48.

The Affinity Business

Male adultery, or what Franklin in "Aunt Sophie Smashes a Triangle" (46) called "the affinity business", was a central concern for feminists of all stripes, serving as it did as prime example of male entitlement and a reflection of men's exaggerated sexual desire. And, although adultery was a central component of social purity feminism's critique, the public was simultaneously apprehensive, fascinated, and shocked by it.[8] Traditional literary attentions to male adultery were silenced due to moral concerns and censorship worries, or it was normalised, in part by turning the attention to female adultery instead: a drastically less frequent, although more noted and sensationalised, issue with its focus on ostracism and social stigma, loss of children and livelihood, suicide and madness.[9] As the "Marriage Question" gained steam, however, authors of various stripes started to borrow from print journalism and the language of the divorce courts and wrote about adultery, usually from the moral perspective of the betrayed party that allowed relatively "chaste" accounts of these transgressive practices. Henry James' *The Golden Bowl* (1904) is case in point, as also are Ford Madox Ford's *A Call: A Tale of Two Passions* (1910) and *The Good Soldier* (1915).[10] Still, despite the increasing sexual frankness of the period, literary narratives about adultery were relatively bold for the time and most authors tended to treat it cautiously, with the exception of the sexually sophisticated sensation novels of the late-nineteenth century that did not intentionally politicise gender so much as capitalise on the "Edwardian vogue ... [for] naughtiness".[11] Caution about the moral implications of writing about adultery was especially pertinent for women authors hampered by the sexual double standard. Franklin's adultery narratives thus represent a relatively courageous act, especially "A Business Emergency", which includes descriptions of a woman's illicit sexual relationship, told through the detached and ironic narrative voice of the wife/ex-mistress.

Between 1913 and 1915 Franklin spent an inordinate amount of time with Bill Lloyd, recording numerous outings with him, including seeing *The Creditors*, a Swedish play about, aptly, a love triangle.[12] In particular, the union with Bill helps

---

8 Barbara Leckie, *Culture and Adultery: The Novel, the Newspaper, the Law, 1857–1914* (Philadelphia: University of Pennsylvania Press, 2015).
9 Tony Tanner, *Adultery in the Novel: Contract and Transgression* (Baltimore, MD: Johns Hopkins University Press, 1979).
10 Donald J. Greiner, *Adultery in the American Novel: Updike, James, Henry, 1843–1916* (Columbia: University of South Carolina Press, 1987); Bill Overton, *Fictions of Female Adultery, 1684–1890: Theories and Circumtexts* (New York: Palgrave Macmillan, 2002).
11 Jane Eldridge Miller, *Rebel Women: Feminism, Modernism and the Edwardian Novel* (London: Virago, 1994), 71.
12 Miles Franklin, Pocket diary, 20 February 1913; 9 May 1913; and 11 February 1913, ML MSS 364/2.

put a certain spin on the analysis of "A Business Emergency", as evidenced by several mentions in her diary in 1915, including Franklin's cynical note: "Bill made a long call in the afternoon and told me what a joy life was and talked around his latest mistress and plans to see her more conveniently. I listened attentively." It was the next month when Bill called on her again wanting "advice on whether he should confess his sins of marital omission and commission" that she "got an idea for a story".[13]

Little Brown Bird and the Fallen Woman

Although Franklin was keen to blame men for sexual transgressions and improprieties, she was especially critical of domestic slavery and took every opportunity to make the case against domesticity broadly defined. For Franklin firmly believed that as well as stunting self-control, domesticity turned women into drudges whom men learn to despise and therefore cheat. This is a central point of Charlotte Perkins Gilman's 1903 text *The Home: Its Work and Influence*, which was an important influence on Franklin's understandings of domesticity. "It is not easy", explains Gilman, "to maintain the height of romantic devotion for one's house-servant". The pain of male adultery, what Gilman described as "the sad record of sorrow and sin", is directly related to these dangers of domesticity. Adultery occurs because "love strays from that domestic area to follow a freer bird in a wider field". The "best-loved women of all time" she writes, "have not been the little brown birds at home". Both Gilman and Franklin are insistent that it is "not marriage which brings this danger, it is domestic service". They do not blame women for their husband's infidelity; rather compulsory domesticity as an aspect of contemporary marriage is at fault for turning wives into unattractive, uninteresting people. Such inequity is not lost on Gilman: "Of course, when a man marries the queen of song he expects her to settle at once to the nest and remain there".[14] In other words, the irony is that men expect all women, even those "free birds" they chase to avoid domesticity, to eventually turn into the little brown birds at home.

Following Gilman's theory, Sophie, the spinster in "Aunt Sophie Smashes a Triangle", responds to her married sister-in-law's frumpy appearance and domestic orientation as "enough to alienate any male creature without a moral sense", adding, "[n]o wonder David neglects you". And when Alice insists it is "terrible to be a woman and be cast aside", she responds it is equally bad "to let yourself be cast aside" (10, 11). It is important to note that while Franklin follows Gilman's treatise on domesticity as the cause of "false sex relations" when she allows Sophie to berate

---

13 Franklin, Pocket diary, 13 January 1915; 14, 20, and 22 January 1915; 10 and 18 February 1915.
14 Charlotte Perkins Gilman, *The Home, Its Work and Influence* (New York: McClure, Phillips, 1903), 281.

Alice and blame her "curse of virtue" (10), she paints David in a negative enough light as to encourage a potential audience to recognise not only his foolishness, but the injustice of Alice's plight as the cheated-upon wife.[15] Similarly, although the domestication and meek demeanour of the first wife in "A Business Emergency" are blamed for the demise of her marriage, it is spoken by the dispassionate and morally corrupt second wife, Mabel, whose self-serving ethics work to highlight the injustice of the first wife's domestic situation.

While Franklin is critical of the "brown bird at home", she has more sympathy for the "fallen woman", perhaps a reflection of the fact that in Chicago she derided domesticity and indulged a married suitor of sorts. A key character in New Woman literature about male infidelity and prostitution, the fallen woman carried a strong political charge and emerged in the nineteenth century as a transnational trope violating broad codes of feminine behaviour and sexual purity, employed in various contexts to represent the anxiety, degradation, and pollution of the nation.[16] However New Women writers like Franklin sought to represent, rehabilitate, and support her through demands for economic freedom as well as checks on male vice and sexual excess, especially through her alliance with other women and wives in particular.[17] In "Aunt Sophie Smashes a Triangle", for example, Sophie "saves" the mistress, Elaine, but also asks Alice to help rescue her as a potential fallen woman. "I want you to have the true mother spirit towards that deluded youngster", implores Sophie. "You owe this girl a motherly duty. Try and rise to a little of the new ideal of motherliness which considers the happiness of the world at large" (17, 18). She employs an evolutionary argument: "Don't be like an animal that considers only its own offspring. That kind of motherliness is being replaced by something more worthy of a decent human being" (17). In May 1913 Franklin recorded seeing a sentimental social purity play, *The Necessary Evil,* which used a similar sanctified notion of worldly maternalism to protect the fallen woman. Franklin was friends with its playwright, Charles Rann Kennedy, and his wife, and noted in her diary "worked on Aunt Sophie play" after the performance.[18]

A plea for the importance of feminist solidarity in combatting male infidelity is notably absent in "A Business Emergency", but its opposite, portrayed by the unlikeable non-feminist character undeserving of sympathy, produces a somewhat

---

15   Charlotte Perkins Gilman, quoted in Larry Ceplair, *Charlotte Perkins Gilman: A Nonfiction Reader* (New York: Columbia University Press, 1991), 156.
16   Sos Eltis, "The Fallen Woman in Edwardian Feminist Drama: Suffrage, Sex and the Single Girl", *English Literature in Transition, 1880–1920* 50, no. 1 (2007): 27–49.
17   Lynda Nead, *Myths of Sexuality: Representations of Women in Victorian Britain* (Oxford: Basil Blackwell, 1988); Katie Hansord, "Symbolism and the Antipodes: The Fallen Woman in Caroline Leakey's *Lyra Australis*, or *Attempts to Sing in a Strange World*", *Australian Literary Studies* 30, no. 3 (2015): 121–133.
18   Franklin, Pocket diary, 15, 4, and 22 May 1913.

similar effect. Potential readers are encouraged to dislike the calculating wife and recognise her cruel response as morally corrupt, knowing also that Mabel is incapable of the generosity necessary for feminist solidarity. For example, she humiliates her husband's paramour by insinuating she is a prostitute, the actress/prostitute being a common trope of this period. "Of course you are a *professional*" she declares. "You must ply your trade where and how you can and I don't suppose you are in business for your health" (10–11). In this she reminds the reader of the public health implications of adultery and its relationship to sexually transmitted infections at the same time that she models feminine divisiveness. Franklin's moral here is that Mabel is unable to act in feminist ways and show support for other women because the rational arrangement of her marriage as an economic transaction, which results in bad behaviour for both men and women, has shaped her selfishness and lack of compassion. Still, despite her unattractive character, Mabel is not a fragile fallen woman, ruined for life. She has agency, ambition, and skill. She may lack a soul, but she violates all notions of the traditional fallen woman.

No More Originality than a Turnip

In her analysis of male philandering, Franklin makes the point that men are inherently morally lax, and are simple, easily seduced creatures. As social purity feminism biologised morality, arguing for women's ethical superiority and their role in choosing marriage partners, it argued that men's sexual promiscuity was shaped by their proclivity to be influenced by flattery and seduction both inside and outside marriage. Also, importantly, this was something all men faced.[19] For example, both "Aunt Sophie Smashes a Triangle" and "A Business Emergency" portray the vice of relatively ordinary men, illustrating the ways contemporary manhood was susceptible to lust and vice without necessarily involving malicious intent. This underscores the biological argument for moral vice showing up in places least expected and not merely representing the idiosyncratic traits of a few bad apples. Franklin's relatively benign male characters possessed by male vice are, however, distinct from the more calculating lust of Phipps Toby from the play, "Virtue", discussed later in the chapter. They are also different in kind from the violent persona of Colin Maynard in "Red Cross Nurse" explored in Chapter 7, and the volatile playboy Bobby Hoyne from *On Dearborn Street*, already discussed in Chapter 4. This does not make them innocent of male vice, however, as we shall see.

The particular danger of David Mortimer, described in the stage notes as "an average American paterfamilias" (1), lurks in the fact that he is such an ordinary

---

19   Martha H. Patterson, *The American New Woman Revisited* (New Brunswick, NJ: Rutgers University Press, 2008).

chap rather than someone who goes out of his way to subordinate women. And it is his "ordinariness" that bears the brunt of much of the comedy. Sophie describes her quotidian brother in the following way:

> He's not bad, as men go. I know him thru and thru. He's a rather good-looking, averagely successful man who would never have risen above a floor walker if his family hadn't made a groove for him to fall into. He's all right in his place – a useful, humdrum husband and father – a family provider, but he's not adapted to breaking into the Don Juan business. (18–19)

His son, the minor character David Jr., is more cutting in describing his father as "an old back number" and declaring that a "girl must be pretty hard up for something in pants when she takes to Popper" (24, 25).

Sophie's plan to save the marriage capitalises on the fact that David, who "never abounded in originality", is "indolent, comfort-loving and selfish" (19, 15). Despite this mediocrity, David's masculine entitlement is still on display: "I'm not doing anything more than sitting still and taking what's coming to me" he explains when confronted with his adultery. "You couldn't expect the lilies of the field to do less than that. You know what women are" (28). In this way, even ordinary men with no malicious intent make fools of themselves with their mistresses and yet can still exclaim that women are "getting too darned independent" in assuming "Nature's law isn't good enough for them" (6).

Sophie's knowledge of adultery is explained through dialogue concerning her own experience with a married man in her youth, which serves as education and warning about adultery. Her paramour is also characterised as having been relatively ordinary: the "man next door", who was easily seduced by comfort and attention. Sophie explains that he had a "nice soothing way" and "went around saying pretty things to youngish women". She also describes his "pose" to encourage sympathy "about marrying when he was too young" and confesses she was "romantic and inexperienced enough" to believe she was "the one woman ordained by God to really appreciate him". Compared to her guilt about not letting their affair break up his marriage and pain his family, Sophie's ex-paramour had "no similar scruples about wasting a woman's life" and instead "rested secure" on her honour (15–16).

The adulterer in "A Business Emergency" is similarly ordinary, overly entitled, and not very smart or particularly attractive. Even though the straightforward tone of the story makes it clear that Brant's vice is a serious matter, he is still depicted as a relatively lightweight character, albeit wealthy enough for Mabel's taste. Like David, his ordinariness, and the entitled way he undertakes his infidelity, makes him all the more dangerous in this regard. When Mabel confronts him in the restaurant she tells his new mistress exactly what she thinks:

> There's nothing to him. I guess if it weren't for his money there would not be many [who would] sit up all night for the joy of his conversation. No woman with any pep would sacrifice herself to his genius if he hadn't the price of a good time. (11)

Declaring him such an "easy mark", she finds his overly entitled masculine predictability amusing. "He has no more originality than a turnip", she declares, chuckling to herself. "Paying the bill was always his strongest point" (7, 8).

Virtue

Living between the centuries placed Franklin in a location to both revere and trouble the notion of "virtue", or what Franklin understood as sexual agency associated with a particular moral standing. It ideally positioned her to provide an economic critique of new sexual expressions she believed masqueraded as "freedom" but constrained women in the same old dilemmas. "Virtue", a long-forgotten protest play about economic servitude and the perils of prostitution, employs such a critique.

This play problematises the "moral squalor" associated with sexual predation and prostitution through the character of its male protagonist, Phipps Toby, who also makes a very brief appearance in *On Dearborn Street*, and is featured in the London manuscript, "Sam Price from Chicago" (1921).[20] The potential fallen woman is a salesgirl named Maisie Pierce whose sexual agency and reputation is jeopardised when impoverished and desperate, she solicits Phipps, and is persuaded to become his mistress. She subsequently falls in love with his feminist friend, Royce Burbeck, who treats her with kindness and respect. Maisie also befriends Royce's sister, Hattie, a society girl and Phipps' fiancée, who dreams of joining the war effort. Again Phipps' older sister, the spinster Antoinette Toby, helps save Maisie's "virtue" and her relationship with Royce, and liberates Hattie so that she can avoid marriage and follow her dreams. Phipps is finally reformed at the end of the play and provides a relatively hopeful message about the future of American manhood.

My objective in exploring "Virtue" is two-fold. First I emphasise the ways the character of Phipps Toby is employed to illustrate a facet of male vice: the tendency for indulging in prostitution, particularly the predation upon economically vulnerable women. Second, I address what Franklin understood to be the pitfalls of "sexual liberalism" through Phipps' embrace of modern sexual practices that encourage women's economic, physical, and emotional vulnerability. Here I

---

20   Miles Franklin, "Sam Price from Chicago", ML MSS 445/17.

emphasise the ways Franklin believed these sexual practices – often characterised as liberatory – were modern takes on traditional misogynous behaviours.

Maisie's Peril

"Virtue" opens after Maisie has accompanied Phipps back to his uptown New York apartment. She hungrily eyes the food Phipps is preparing and tells him she has eaten nothing "but for a few crackers for days". She works long hours in a shoe store, earns only $6 a week, and is described as "pale, tired and dispirited" with cheap clothes "the worse for wear". Her impoverishment is the reason for soliciting Phipps that evening, a fact recognised by Phipps, who tells her: "I saw you were new to the business. That's what interested me" (1). Maisie's economic vulnerability casts her as a target for sexual predation and the potential "white slave" market.

It is important to remember that along with Jane Addams and other social purity reformers, Franklin worked in anti-"white slavery" advocacy addressing prostitution and its causes in the metropolis.[21] Despite the slippery nature of the definition and extent of white slavery, the phenomenon was essentially a gendered and racialised construct in response to women's increased presence in department stores, offices, dance halls, and other public places, and (especially non-white) men's participation in "vice" that included gambling and alcohol consumption as well as the commercial networking of vice through organised big business.[22] The white slave panic associated with urban sexual immorality proved "an elastic cultural resource for a range of political agendas" and prompted "strange alliances" across multiple political positions that in 1910 helped pass the Mann Act criminalising the transfer of women across state lines for "immoral" purposes.[23]

Although the issue of prostitution is central to "Virtue", it is essential to recognise how vaguely and imprecisely prostitution was defined at this time, not only in terms of the construction of white slavery, but also concerning its relationship to an accelerated pace of economic and social change and the cultural shift towards consumption, gratification, and pleasure that facilitated a commercialisation of sex and fuelled anxieties about the "moral vacuum" in urban centres.[24] These developments from Victorianism to modernity transformed

---

21 Mark T. Connelly, *The Response to Prostitution in the Progressive Era* (Chapel Hill: University of North Carolina Press, 1980); Brian Donovan, *White Slave Crusades* (Urbana: University of Illinois Press, 2006); and Margit Stange, *Personal Property: Wives, White Slaves, and the Market in Women* (Baltimore, MD: Johns Hopkins University Press, 1998).
22 Ruth Rosen, *The Lost Sisterhood: Prostitution in America, 1900–1918* (Baltimore: Johns Hopkins Press, 1982), 133. See also Emma Liggins, "Prostitution and Social Purity in the 1880s and 1890s", *Critical Survey* 15, No. 3 (2003): 39–55.
23 Donovan, *White Slave Crusades*, 20, 2.
24 Jane Addams *A New Conscience and an Ancient Evil* (New York: Macmillan, 1912), 215.

relationships between the sexes and encouraged a movement from homosociality to a thriving and commercially profitable heterosocial culture.[25] In *Cheap Amusements*, for example, Kathy Peiss emphasises that the extent of sexual intimacy involved in these encounters was difficult to establish, although it is known that "charity girls", those who traded sexual favours for male attention and gifts but refused money exchange, were commonplace.[26] Also widespread were occasional prostitutes who moved in and out of prostitution when unemployed or in need of extra income, referred to as "amateur prostitutes" by the Association of Moral and Social Hygiene.[27] With this in mind it is not clear whether Maisie is willing to trade sexual intimacies or merely an evening's companionship in return for a meal: "I just had a fit of desperation. It would have passed. It always does", she says (5). Phipps, however, recognises the bargain:

> It was a mighty dangerous fit tonight ... [you could] die of this game – for that's what it comes to, you know. A good-looking girl like you shouldn't have to go hungry if you played your cards right. (1–2)

Like the "slum angels", the vulnerable rural and immigrant working-class girls who moved to Chicago and fell prey to sexual predation as depicted in Addams' *A New Conscience and an Ancient Evil*, Maisie is constructed as naïve, trading her "virtue" for economic survival.[28] Franklin understood this trade of sexual and economic assets and sought to highlight the disparity between the freedom of men and the vulnerability of women moving into public spaces in the city. For example, when Phipps realises Maisie is in love with his friend, Royce, he tells her: "I shall have to feel it my duty to explain our arrangement and inform Royce that you are a woman of no virtue" (57).

Franklin thus uses Phipps to demonstrate the ways men's sexual predation hurts women on many levels. "It really means selling myself, selling my *virtue*?" she cries on realising the consequences of the bargain (5). "Let it be a straight business proposition" he responds, suggesting he support her so that she can finish a stenography course. He promises that after six months she will be free to leave: "I'd give you food and clothes and a good time. It ought to be comfortable for you and a

---

25 John D'Emilio and Estelle B. Freedman, *Intimate Matters: A History of Sexuality in America* (New York: Harper, 1988), 171–201. See also Gail Reekie, *Temptations: Sex, Selling and the Department Store* (Sydney: Allen & Unwin, 1993).
26 Kathy Peiss, *Cheap Amusements: Working Women and Leisure in Turn-of-the-Century New York* (Philadelphia: Temple University Press, 1986), 110.
27 Julia A. Laite, "The Association for Moral and Social Hygiene: Abolitionism and Prostitution Law in Britain (1915–1959)", *Women's History Review* 17, no. 2 (2008): 211.
28 Addams, "Introduction: Slum Angels", *A New Conscience and an Ancient Evil*, ix.

good chance for me" (4). Again Maisie resists but realises her reputation is already sullied. "Well, I found you tonight", she is reminded (4). He claims his sexual object with such lines as "you're mine already", and by his announcement that "[b]y every right of decency, I'm the only man who could ever have any claim on [you] now" (57, 60). As final example of Phipps' predatory malice, he goes back on his word and tries to prevent Maisie from leaving him after the six months is up.

Franklin also highlights Phipps' propensity for vice by using Maisie as the mouthpiece during her growing independence from him, which again exemplifies Franklin's disruption of the trope of the fallen woman. Maisie acts opportunistically to survive and support her material needs, but she survives and emerges with a renewed and assertive sense of herself, telling Phipps what a potential audience already knows: "I wouldn't marry you if you were a Rockefeller … If you were the only man in the world I'd turn my back on you" (27, 58). Instead of being a timid fallen woman, Maisie shows up the predatory Phipps as a cad and a coward whose vice implies he has no respect for women, including his fiancée. "You treat a protected girl one way and a helpless one another" (27), she notes. Alongside pointing out the class-based perils of male vice, this dialogue also serves as a bold reminder of the double standard of sexual conduct allowing men to have multiple sexual partners. Supposedly engaged to Hattie, yet keen to keep Maisie as his mistress, Phipps admits: "Most men's hearts *are* divided … several times. Nature meant them to be polygamists. It is a false promise to attempt anything else" (39).

Franklin's analysis of male vice on the topic of prostitution was shaped not only by the Chicago cultural milieu and the social and scientific discourses of the time but also by her personal relationships. As "Virtue" suggests, even (and, perhaps, especially) progressive, relatively well-meaning men, and sometimes men who espouse feminist politics, are capable and culpable when it comes to sexual promiscuities that harm women. Biologising this situation and seeing men's susceptibility to vice as unavoidable and inherent, and not necessarily involving a malicious intent, may have helped Franklin make sense of her fondness for Bill Lloyd, despite his failings. The bottom line, however, was that Bill had a history with prostitutes. "When he wanted me to marry him", explained Franklin, "I said scornfully I cd [sic] not undertake the heavy burden competing with all the 'sporting' women in town".[29] Just as Phipps Toby may represent the merging of both Lloyd brothers with whom Franklin was involved, it is no less surprising to find the heroine protagonist of this play illustrating the dangers and opportunities of trading chastity for economic security: a scenario Franklin also faced with both brothers.

---

29 Roe, *Stella Miles Franklin*, 170, 206.

The Point on Which You Are So Old-Fashioned

When Phipps' sister, Antoinette, critiques his "modern" views on sex, he responds by calling this "the point on which you are so old-fashioned" (39). This quote sets the stage for Franklin's critique of the ethical traps of sexual liberalism itself: a stance responding to the sexual orthodoxy of Victorianism through a resistance to traditional institutional contexts like marriage and monogamy and by broadening the range of legitimate sexual behaviours. Endorsed by radical thinkers and sexologists, such ideals were reflected in sexologist Havelock Ellis' endorsement of "trial marriage" before legal matrimony. Such thinkers considered that the state's infringement on women's bodily integrity through regulation of sexual matters was problematic; they also believed in women's right to sexual desire.[30] In a sense Maisie's relationship with Phipps is set up as a "trial marriage", albeit a coerced one.

Sexologists, and the cultural radicals like Edward Carpenter, Floyd Dell, and Ellen Keys who were influenced by them and who self-consciously adopted a new ethic and style of personal life, did not advocate prostitution, and they had much in common with social purity feminists in their responses to modernisation and their involvement in radical causes such as feminism and socialism.[31] Indeed, they were not "pro" sex in a way that is easily recognisable today, given the profoundly different sexual economy that shapes our perceptions of them. Tending to deny sexual promiscuity or license *per se*, sexual liberals or "free lovers" often claimed they were working for a relaxation of external controls in order to produce a greater sense of sexual responsibility and personal control, which included notions of harmonious, monogamous true love. However, even though as Leslie Hall suggests, "they were fighting, on somewhat different fronts, a common enemy that privileged the (white, upper-/middle-class, heterosexual) male in both actual law and in social practice", there still arose a gender distinction epitomised by sexologists' encouragement of male sexual desire and social purity feminists' call for its opposite: restraint.[32] Franklin's critique of sexology was its simultaneous support for men's sexual excesses alongside what she considered its disingenuous call for sexual reform, a stance Peter Kirkpatrick describes as the "predatory

---

30 D'Emilio and Freedman, *Intimate Matters*, 224; Joanne Passet, *Sex Radicals and the Quest for Women's Equality* (Chicago: University of Illinois Press, 2003), 1–6. See also Paul Robinson, *The Modernization of Sex: Havelock Ellis, Alfred Kinsey, William Masters, and Virginia Johnson* (New York: Harper and Row, 1976); and Kevin White, *Sexual Liberation or Sexual License? The American Revolt Against Victorianism* (Chicago: Ivan R. Dee, 2000).
31 Lucy Bland and Laura Doan, *Sexology Uncensored: The Documents of Sexual Science* (Chicago: University of Chicago Press, 1998), 1–7.
32 Leslie Hall, "Hauling Down the Double Standard: Feminism, Social Purity and Sexual Science in Late Nineteenth-Century Britain", *Gender and History* 16, no.1 (2004): 37.

masculinist milieu" of Bohemian men who used women sexually in the name of sexual liberalism or "free love".[33] As Jill Roe explains, Franklin was critical, for example, of free-love advocate Edith Havelock-Ellis whom she met and heard speak.[34] Like many other women of her generation, Franklin understood the often potentially dire consequences of sexual activity, and found the morality associated with sexual experimentations of some of her contemporaries "revolting". Free love was "just another term for promiscuity and thoughtless exploitation of women by men".[35] In this regard she was especially critical of Floyd Dell whose misogynous sexual liberalism revealed his feminist politics to be disingenuous.[36] As Franklin explained in her later years, "death was preferable to 'living in sin' to one of my codes and sensitiveness".[37]

Franklin's critique of sexual liberalism in "Virtue" first disrupts the notion that it is a positive practice for women. Phipps is used both to illustrate and discredit the ideologies of sexual liberalism, which are constructed as modern and progressive, but actually reinforce the same old gender hierarchies. In the stage directions, Phipps' apartment is "bright, shining, and up to date [with] no frowsiness [sic] or clutter". Similarly he is described as a modern businessman: an "average young man of the day ... [who is] making good in [commerce]" (1). Phipps also justifies his behaviour in "modern", so-called liberating ideas, and dismisses Maisie's concern about losing her "virtue" as prudish and out-of-date, calling her "old-fashioned" when she resists a more permanent sexual relationship with him. "What is *virtue*?" he asks. "The thing you mean is kept on file by a few old maids who have no call for it since our grandmother's day". He declares her "a little hayseed back number" whom he needs to "educate" in the ways of the modern world (6).

Phipps tries to seduce Maisie into becoming his mistress and tells her he is a "modern businessman ... not a monk. I don't pretend to be St Anthony, but I'm all right for all that" (5): a reference to the saint known for recovering lost people and things, and perhaps suggesting a nod to middle-class social purity reformers who "rescued" young women from a life of vice. That Phipps does not pretend to be St Anthony suggests this playboy's distance from them at the same time that the addition of the phrase, "but I'm all right for all that", is his way of stressing a benevolent intent. He presents himself, for example, in the role

---

33 Peter Kirkpatrick, "Dulcie Deamer and the Bohemian Body", in *Wallflowers and Witches: Women and Culture in Australia, 1910–1945*, ed. Maryanne Dever (St Lucia: University of Queensland Press, 1994), 18. See also Emma Liggins, "Introduction", 'New' Female Sexualities, 1870–1930", *Critical Survey* 15, no. 3 (2003): 3.
34 Franklin, Pocket diary, 14 May 1914; 13 December 1914.
35 Roe, *Stella Miles Franklin*, 157, 145.
36 John Hart, *Floyd Dell* (New York: Twayne, 1971), 3.
37 Roe, *Stella Miles Franklin*, 184.

of "rescuer", reminding Maisie of the potential consequences had someone less benevolent responded to her plight. "What if you had met another fellow?" he asks (5). The dialogue reveals, of course, that the arrogant Phipps who imagines himself a free love advocate is no better than men who accept prostitutes. The fact that he lies to Hattie, and goes back on his word in trying to keep Maisie with him after the six months is up, ultimately reveals him to be worse than the ordinary "john" who keeps his side of the bargain by paying to have his sexual needs met.

In addition, "Virtue" provides an opportunity for Franklin to tackle the argument articulated by sexologists at the turn of the century that non-marital sexual experiences provide women with positive assets in a changing world. Such thought, endorsed by Havelock Ellis, held that sexual experience was neither a threat to moral character nor a drain on vital energies, but a crucial aspect of individual and social well-being. Ellis makes this clear when he declares sexual activity "the chief and central function of life ... ever wonderful, ever lovely".[38] As Jeffreys explains, "sexual activity with men was [considered] vital to the health of women ... without it she became either bitter and twisted or gushingly sentimental": the spinster's lot.[39] Franklin references this notion that sexual experiences outside of marriage provide women with positive assets when Phipps insists Maisie is "only half a woman" without the relationship he can offer. "Holding on to virtue", he says, is no way to go through life "unless you're a crank reformer or a suffragette". He refuses to take no for an answer and tells her to "get into the game!", insisting that the "enlarged experience" of being his mistress will be a future asset. He insists she will be "fit to go anywhere when we get thru [sic] here" because she "can't help picking up something that will be useful". Ultimately, he declares, "you'll have bought more than you sold ... a rattling good bargain, I call it" (5, 6).

Although Phipps tries to insist that she has more to gain from the arrangement, the play makes clear that his sexual pleasure takes priority. This is aptly demonstrated when toward the end of the play Maisie reminds Phipps of his insistence that the arrangement would increase her assets ("You said when I went to your flat that ... it would improve me, that people would think more of me") and Phipps admits this was a ruse to manipulate her ("If you were fool enough to believe *that*, it was your own look out" [56]). Such declarations from someone whom the audience is encouraged to see as dangerous and predatory highlight the injustice of Maisie's situation and disrupt the argument that a sexual relationship with Phipps is positive for her.

---

38 Havelock Ellis, quoted in Paul Robinson, *The Modernization of Sex: Havelock Ellis, Alfred Kinsey, William Masters, and Virginia Johnson* (New York: Harper and Row, 1976), 31, 28.
39 Sheila Jeffreys, *The Spinster and Her Enemies, Feminism and Sexuality, 1880–1930* (London: Pandora, 1985), 95.

A Hopeful Narrative

Although Franklin uses these stories and scenes to shed insight on the sexual perils of male vice and to hold men accountable for their actions, she presents a range of narratives from the pessimistic vision of contemporary manhood in "Business Emergency" to a somewhat more hopeful view in "Aunt Sophie Smashes a Triangle" and eventually to a more optimistic narrative in "Virtue". The former story starts and ends with the assumption of adultery and the critique of marriage; there is little hope in Brant Reber for American manhood except perhaps his predictability and relatively simple nature. Similarly, David Mortimer is hardly reformed and returns to his marriage perhaps only with slightly more sense about the negative consequences of his infidelity, although his son illustrates a more optimistic model for manhood. David Jr delivers lines that support his spinster aunt, articulate his mother's domestic burden, and chastise his father's adultery. The title of the play, "Aunt" Sophie, also reflects the ways the play is shaped by, or potentially imagined through, his youthful and hopeful feminist perspective.

The hopefulness of "Virtue" is demonstrated in the pro-feminist character of Royce Burbeck, who disrupts misogynous notions of manhood and resists male vice. Set against Phipps, who takes advantage of Maisie's vulnerability, Royce notices her fatigue and worries about her wellbeing. He acknowledges his egalitarian aim as the single moral standard of sexual conduct and professes hope that he might be "as decent as I'd expect the girl I marry to be". When Phipps exclaims that such a girl "won't appreciate that", Royce's response is guided by a strong feminist ethic. "It's a matter of conscience, not her appreciation", he declares (11). Phipps' disdain for Royce's values and his insistence that such virtue is "out of date" further accentuate the differences between Phipps, who represents male vice, and Royce, who illustrates the feminist hope for the future of manhood (11). Antoinette's summation of Royce also highlights his role as a feminist ally: "Any woman who couldn't fall in love with [Royce] deserves an anti-suffragist husband", she exclaims, adding: "Men are growing up since the days when I indulged in serious love affairs … I look forward to an epoch when men will have to quit making such a fuss about women's virtue while they concentrate on their own" (43, 45, 49).

In the end, despite Phipps' construction as a misogynist, Franklin offers a last-minute plot twist and redeems him too. Phipps appears in a comedic drunken stupor, but soon an audience would realise he is actually pretending to be drunk to provide Hattie with a way to repudiate him so that she does not have to suffer being humiliated when she learns that Phipps does not want to marry her. He explains he decided to "pull this stunt" once he understood that "poor little Hattie was the one getting the worse deal" (72). Such a final gesture on the part of Phipps restores Antoinette's affection for her brother, ending the play on a light note, and leaving the audience with the suggestion that there is hope for the future of masculinity. Phipps' transformation is thus revealed in the final act as he demonstrates self-knowledge and insight about Hattie and her needs.

Similarly, Royce also demonstrates his own psychological journey and his character evolves towards a more nuanced feminism. Although he is "a prince among men" (61) and shows compassion for Maisie, he admits Maisie's "mistake" would still be a problem for him. "Intellectually I know that it ought not to be, but instinctively, yes, it would be a great blow to me", he declares (45). Through the next act he attempts to deal with this reality and is eventually able to accept Maisie on her own terms by thinking of her "as a young divorcee who had a brief marriage in which she had not been happy" (62). This introspective process is further revealed: "I thought at first it would [be a blow] but I've walked a good ten miles on it … [and] it's not made any difference" (6). This self-reflection serves two purposes. It stands in contrast to Phipps, who although reformed, has not yet reached these understandings, and it works to humanise Royce himself by revealing the ways even egalitarian New Men have to cope with the baggage of gender that shapes their relationships with women. Modelling modified conventions of realism, "Virtue" presents nuanced and introspective male characters who are transformed throughout the play.[40] Royce and Phipps reflect on the demands of conventional gender and are transformed in the process. In contrast, "A Business Emergency" and "Aunt Sophie Smashes a Triangle", employ male characters that are relatively fixed in order to illustrate sexism and/or offer contrast to more evolved female characters.

Maisie is also transformed and embarks on a psychological journey towards self-knowledge and empowerment, reflecting a lively protagonist articulate about her rebellion and self-conscious about her feminism. Maisie is no fallen woman. Her decision to solicit a potential sexual relationship in return for economic sustenance, and to embrace a certain kind of "marriage", occur as socially subversive acts rather than mere acceptance of the status quo. Franklin's creation of the Maisie character illustrates the ways New Woman writing "consistently problematized, deconstructed, demystified, or rethought 'womanliness' … in order to find ways of figuring female interiority and of exploring and dramatizing the effects of prevailing social institutions on individual female lives".[41] Maisie rethinks her situation and emerges empowered, illustrating a fractured female subject who struggles with social institutions and practices, navigating the contradictions between conventional femininities and the pressures of modernity. Feminist realist

---

40   Sheila Stowell, "Rehabilitating Realism", *Journal of Dramatic Theory and Criticism* VI, no. 2 (1992): 81–88.
41   Lyn Pykett, *Engendering Fictions: The English Novel in the Early Twentieth Century*. (London: Edward Arnold, 1995), 57–8.

reappraisals are thus evident in Maisie's ambiguous and multiple social locations and desires as potential prostitute, mistress, friend, and shop-girl: all identities constructed in and through her shifting socio-economic status and sexual agency and vulnerability. In other words, Franklin not only observed and detailed relationships and the intricacies of the domestic, but created situations and characters that contextualised and reframed these material realities as demonstrated in the exercise of gendered power between Maisie and Phipps or class relations between Maisie and Hattie. Lyn Pykett declares such strategies "proto-modernist gestures [of] impressionistic realism" that move beyond mere detailing of material reality to nuance and challenge social structures.[42]

This challenge to gender practices is the mainstay of these scenes and stories about male vice and presents the basis of social purity feminism's insight on the dangers and inequitable gendered consequences of sexual desire. Franklin thus presents re-enactments of social limitations and expectations shaping women's sexual agency, demonstrating how societal values and institutions might be dramatically expressed and resisted through the reform of American manhood. In contrast to conventional literary romance traditions, love is sustained only between equals and those who have actively chosen this route. The only marriage on the horizon for the three female characters, for example, is Maisie's companionate, egalitarian relationship with Royce, the hopeful feminist candidate, while Hattie and Antoinette as well as Elaine, escape matrimony – like Franklin herself – to lead fulfilled lives as feminist activists.

---

42 Pykett, *Engendering Fictions*, 75–76.

7
Courage and Confession

In late 1914, as war raged in Europe and Miles Franklin was distressed by work, love, and a world gone mad, she wrote a "curious story" titled "Red Cross Nurse and Armored Chauffeur", amended in her handwriting with the subtitle: "Confessions of a Frustrated Grandmother", and known simply in discussions of Franklin's work as "Red Cross Nurse".[1] This *bildungsroman*, which presents a moral journey towards sexual maturity and loss of innocence, tangles with the staples of Franklin's ongoing feminist project: gender politics, marriage, sexuality and desire, and encapsulates, like much of her New Woman writing, the anxieties of the period, including the white slave panic and the outbreak of World War I. It breaks new ground for Franklin, however, in its frank portrayal of physical and sexual abuse. My objective in this chapter is a continued focus on male vice, but with particular attention to violence against women and its consequences for female sexual agency. I interrogate two representations of American manhood implicated in this violence: the volatile abuser and the passive New Man, who betrays the victim's trust. I also explore ways this story both illustrates and resists traditional "white slave" discourse through characterisations of victims and perpetrators.

This fragmented novel of approximately 160 typed and hand-corrected manuscript pages, which includes several pages of handwritten addenda numbered as ½ and ¾, is set in an unnamed American city in its present day. The story is told from the first-person perspective of an anonymous protagonist, "the nurse": a young woman, trained in medicine and needing to support herself. This narration allows an expression of the psychological pain and confusion caused by violent masculinity through a focus on internal perspectives and self-awareness on the part

---

1   Verna Coleman, *Her Unknown Brilliant Career: Miles Franklin in America* (Sydney: Angus & Robertson, 1981), 165; Miles Franklin, "Red Cross Nurse and Armored Chauffeur", ML MSS445/3. All subsequent references appear in parentheses in the text.

of the victim/survivor. Ultimately this awareness is unsatisfying from the point of view of the contemporary reader, but nonetheless represents the survivor's social and sexual agency.

Reminiscent of Franklin's fond relationship with her own grandmother, "Red Cross Nurse" begins with the protagonist declaring her grandmother "the supreme love" of her life (1) and explaining this record is left for a potential granddaughter (hence the subtitle) in case of the nurse's death. This mysterious acknowledgment is explained at the end of the story when she joins the war effort and is subsequently injured. The record is also left "as an explanation for James Denvir" (4), a kindly bachelor who employs her to provide convalescent care after an automobile accident. He soon falls in love with the nurse and proposes. She finds "interest in him deepening", but requests "some experience to make me sure of myself" (9, 10). When James agrees, she uses this freedom to pursue a relationship with Colin Maynard, a wealthy and dashing, yet selfish and egotistical playboy. The nurse is initially flattered by Colin's attentions, and both attracted and repelled by all he represents. She assumes she will not only enjoy and win this game, but will ultimately reject and diminish Colin through authentic desire for James. This reasoning is reminiscent of Sybyl Penelo's desire to tame the dashing Bobby Hoyne in *On Dearborn Street*, discussed in Chapter 4. Instead, however, the nurse embarks on a roller-coaster relationship that involves kidnap, physical assault, and much emotional turmoil. Because of the cultural prohibitions around discussions of rape and the assumption and suspicions of women's fault in gender violence, there is no explicit mention of sexual abuse or rape, only indirect inference. The nurse bravely resists these attacks and survives by promising silence and agreeing to marry Colin within the week. She writes to James hoping for rescue, but her letter crosses with one from him withdrawing his proposal. Shaken, the nurse registers the depths of James' betrayal and comes to believe that Colin is the worthier suitor.

The next pages making up chapters fifteen through eighteen are missing until the final chapter of the story about the nurse's service with the Red Cross, working as a volunteer behind the front lines. Anticipating Colin's arrival as the armoured chauffeur, she is injured by shrapnel. The narrative seems to assume that the nurse has accepted Colin's romantic advancements, but it is not clear whether a critique of, or focus on, marriage is an aspect of the missing chapters, although the mention of a granddaughter might imply a child resulted from the violent relationship with Colin. It is also not clear whether the term "confession" implies remorse about the sexual improprieties of this trial relationship, or regret associated with her decision to stay with him. It might also signify her guilt associated with physical and sexual abuse at a time when women were readily perceived as responsible for the abuse directed at them and were encouraged to internalise such notions. The story ends with a plea for Colin's safety: hardly a satisfactory ending from a feminist point of view, but one that also establishes the moral failings of contemporary manhood in both their "nice" and brutal aspects. Like "Virtue" discussed in the previous chapter, "Red Cross Nurse" thus serves as a cautionary tale about experimental relationships through exploration of the vulnerable protagonist's psychological and moral journey where she acknowledges sexual desire and comes to understand its implications. As in both the romance and *bildungsroman* traditions, the goal is maturity, and for the protagonist of "Red Cross Nurse" that means a loss of innocence and recognition of men's "true nature" and its relationship to vice (109 ¾).

"Red Cross Nurse" subscribes to all the conventions of the romantic novel: the search for self, the central place of the heroine's emotional experience, and the quest for love and marriage, including the trope of the competing suitors. However, although it contains the conventions of Victorian literature, its hybridity also incorporates a modern focus on the singularity of the individual female subject and is written in the first person voice that reinforces the heroine's individuality and a psychological journey that squarely encompasses a romance of experience inscribing the modern woman's life.[2] The fact that the protagonist of "Red Cross Nurse" is nameless and lives in an unnamed city, underscores the generalisability of this female subject to "any woman" of the New Woman trade, encouraging reader identification. Its bold illustration of men's interpersonal violence and its frank illustration of a young woman's sexual desire, her "fall", and her survival, all ultimately resist the traditional romance template.

A Tale of Two Suitors

Changing notions of American manhood, as well as their relationship to war, are problematised in "Red Cross Nurse" through two key characters hoping to win the nurse's affections. They represent opposing illustrations of masculinity in flux during this period: the loyal, honourable gentleman, who presents self-restraint and control as epitomised by James Denvir; and the pleasure-seeking, body-centred playboy represented by Colin Maynard, who is infused by the erratic volatility of modern militarism. The former models "powerful self-control and a delicate refinement", offering the sincerity and self-restraint that characterised essential qualities of nineteenth-century middle-class American manhood (14). These qualities rested in mastery and self-denial and privileged honour and integrity through the control of impulses

---

2   Susan Sheridan, *Along the Fault Lines: Sex, Race and Nation in Australian Women's Writing* (St Leonards, NSW: Allen & Unwin, 1995), 52.

and emotion.[3] Such control reflected a "spermatic economy" and represented a disciplined and renunciatory image of the body and social and economic life that also underpinned imperialism and military prowess.[4]

By the new century and as economic forces decreased the usefulness of self-restraint, a rougher, more bodily centred notion of manhood appeared that prioritised rugged individualism, sexual prowess, and bodily strength. These changes worked in tandem with, and were exacerbated by, modern, technological warfare that would test and break more traditional codes of masculinity.[5] As the slaughter of mechanised warfare tested belief in heroism, producing modern combat as a social, embodied and psychological experience, it shaped notions of manhood among combatant nations.[6] These new bodily centred masculinities took shape, were infused into the mainstream, and were sustained by increased opportunities for commercial leisure that encouraged middle-class men to experience the pleasures of consumer culture in saloons, music halls, and sporting spectacles rather than identify with disciplinary practices of work.[7] Colin epitomises this depiction of middle-class American manhood that reflects the opportunities for pleasure and consumerism arising as a result of US modernity. Compared to James' civility and self-restraint, Colin's hedonism follows its fancy at will: "When any other amusement called or any other action or adventure was more to his pampered taste, he went off ... and forgot all about me", explains the nurse when discussing Colin's temperament (14). The class privilege inherent in these behaviours is important for Franklin and she references them in depictions of Colin as "the Duke of Fifth Ave" (23), who enjoys "lordly freedom from all limitations and sordid struggle to make ends meet!" (16–7).

---

3   Michael Kimmel, *Manhood in America: A Cultural History* (New York: Free Press, 1996); Gail Bederman, *Manliness and Civilization: A Cultural History of Gender and Race in the US, 1880–1914* (Chicago: University of Chicago Press, 1995).

4   Donald J. Mrozek, "The Habit of Victory: The American Military and the Cult of Manliness", in *Manliness and Morality: Middle-class Masculinity in Britain and America, 1800–1940*, ed. J. A. Mangan and James Walvin (New York: St Martin's Press, 1987), 147–8; Michael Paris, *Warrior Nation* (London: Reaktion Books, 2000); Michael Carnes, *Meanings for Manhood: Constructions of Masculinity in Victorian America* (Chicago: University of Chicago, 1990).

5   Alison Fell, "Gendering the War Story", *Journal of War and Culture Studies* 1, no. 1 (2007): 53–58; Graham Dawson, *Soldier Heroes: British Adventure, Empire and the Imagining of Masculinities* (Routledge, 1994).

6   Joanna Bourke, *Dismembering the Male: Britain, Male Bodies and the Great War* (Chicago: University of Chicago Press, 1996); Jessica Meyer, *Men of War: Masculinity and the First World War in Britain* (New York: Palgrave Macmillan, 2009).

7   Kevin White, *The First Sexual Revolution: The Emergence of Male Heterosexuality in Modern America* (New York: New York University Press, 1993).

Franklin's focus on these particular examples of contemporary masculinity again represents a continuity of concern. As Stephen Garton explains regarding *My Brilliant Career*, Franklin is:

> wrestling with a real social issue as well as a revulsion to the nature of manhood born of reading and personal experience. Here we glimpse … [her] sense of a deeper malaise in the gender order, one grounded not just in a feminist critique of the politics of masculinism but an uneasiness about the very nature of manhood itself.[8]

Garton makes the point that representations of masculinity in *My Brilliant Career* emerge as toxic factors poisoning heterosexual relationships, suffocating women, and imprisoning both women and men. By 1914 Franklin's take on this toxic masculinity is more nuanced as a result of insight and experiences with vulnerable working women in Chicago, the onset of war, as well as personal experiences with men. Her perspective on this, however, is no less severe.

Certainly there is strong evidence for the origins of this tale of two suitors in her romantic relationships in Chicago. After Demarest Lloyd's return to the city in early 1914, Franklin spent more time with him, finding his manner and lifestyle both attractive and repulsive. He had courted her throughout the preceding year with dinners, theatre, and visits to the cinema, simultaneously it seems while she was also seeing a lot of his brother, Bill. Demarest at one point advised Franklin to keep "our little secrets" from him.[9] In 1914, however, the relationship with Demarest was definitely heating up. After a dinner date on Valentine's Day, 1914, Franklin wrote in her diary that "Demi [was] a conceited and inexplicable boor in every way but interesting study", adding "shall pursue him for copy".[10] Franklin's relationship with Demarest would eventually peter out in 1915, although he subsequently married and that wife would divorce him for cruelty many years later.[11] However, just as Fred – and perhaps Bill Lloyd to some extent – resembles James Denvir, Demarest most definitely precipitated Colin Maynard. And it is during a vacation in Boston on her birthday, 14 October 1914, when a date with "Demi" provided the basis for the plot of " Red Cross Nurse":

---

8   Stephen Garton, "Contesting Enslavement: Marriage, Manhood, and *My Brilliant Career*", *Australian Literary Studies* 20, no. 4 (2002): 339.
9   Demarest Lloyd to Miles Franklin, 8 October 1913, ML MSS. 364/12.
10 Miles Franklin, Pocket diary, 14 February 1914, ML MSS 364/2.
11 Jill Roe, *Stella Miles Franklin: A Biography* (Sydney: Fourth Estate/Harper Collins, 2008), 184.

> Demi came at 2.45 … Afterwards we went driving … and went to the Crown at Providence, R.I. for dinner … [then] dancing. Then back to Newman's for supper and started home. D. had too many cocktails (5) and champagne (2 bottles) and was highly dangerous. We didn't get home till nearly four. He was desperate and brutal in an unprecedented degree when drunk. Escaped death and tragedy by N. small margin![12]

Within a week Franklin reflected on writing "a movie-play-novel" about the episode and by November started to type up the story. That she considered the story a potential movie script is revealing, and reflects the increasingly frank and popular narratives of the period that had commercial potential. These had something in common with nineteenth-century Victorian "sensation" stories: a term "applied disparagingly" to a broad range of crime, mystery, horror, and romance fiction. Reflecting a popular taste for the gothic, sensation novels are best remembered for their "violent yoking of romance and realism" and many were serialised in the popular press of the day. Although at their height before Franklin's time, sensation romance still littered the popular press in the first decade of the new century and had potential for an emerging movie industry.[13] Franklin's decidedly feminist take on a narrative resembling sensation fiction reflects her unique hybridised strategies as well as hopes for commercial success. She would continue work on the manuscript over the next month and on Boxing Day was "typing Red Cross Story for agent".[14] No other communication survives about its publication.

Darling Sissy Boy

Initially claimed the nurse's "rock of refuge" and "the most refined and gentle of men", James Denvir is described by the heroine in glowing terms that underscore her respect for him as the feminist New Man (9, 7). The reader is encouraged to appreciate the promise of a marriage proposal from an educated man of such integrity and progressive politics, and to see James as a panacea for women's lot in life. He holds much promise for social purity feminism in modelling a platonic, spiritual bond between like-minded companions. His offer of love, is a "spiritual kinship" that "reflect[s] a high purity of mind" (9). The couple soon found themselves in territory "reserved for lovers", where he showed "a robustness of

---

12 Franklin, Pocket diary, 14 October 1914.
13 P.D. Edwards, "Sensation Novels", in *Victorian Britain: An Encyclopedia*, ed. Sally Mitchell (London: Garland, 1988), 703–4; Winifred Hughes, *The Maniac in the Cellar: Sensation Novels of the 1860s* (Princeton, NJ: Princeton University Press, 1980), 16. See also Ana-Isabel Aliaga-Buchenau, *The "Dangerous" Potential of Reading: Readers and the Negotiation of Power in Nineteenth-Century Narratives* (New York: Routledge, 2004).
14 Franklin, Pocket diary, 18 November 1914; 26 December 1914.

virility" proving there was "no lack of fire", but still he was "repelled by the thought of unions built only on a physical attraction" and "always exercised a self-control which bespoke unlimited tenderness and an unselfishness" (9, 10). This is a "progressive model" of romance whose gentle manner might avoid the dangers of sexual passion.[15] If these personal assets were not enough, James is also very open-minded when it comes to courtship. He agrees with "unselfish generosity" to the nurse's request for freedom to "have some fun" before she settles down. James tells her to feel herself "quite free" in this regard (10).

This characterisation of the New Man's positive assets for the New Woman is soon disrupted by James' aunt, who reveals that her nephew is a "darling, sissy boy", who has been "bossed by his sister since ever he was born". She warns the nurse that he "hasn't an idea in his head that she hasn't directed … It's she you have to marry not Jim" (11 ½). Given this narrative about the influential sister, it is tempting to conjecture that Franklin was using Fred Pischel's relationship with Emma, his sister and Franklin's friend, as a model. Certainly Jill Roe makes the point that he apparently he did not have "the same stuffing" as Emma.[16] Also, just as Colin goes off to war, the nurse claims that James avoids having to fight by claiming academic pursuits (and also, presumably, his age). In this regard it is interesting to note that Demarest Lloyd was "an uncomplicated patriot" whereas Fred Pischel was a German American whose allegiance to the Allies might have been more complicated.[17]

The aunt's warnings about the sissy boy, however, are ignored, and the nurse's estimation of James only increases, especially after the abusive incidents when she continues to compare James, "innocent as a dove and as wise as a serpent" (48), to the brutal Colin. As the violence exacerbates, the "thought of James Denvir rose before [her] like a paradise regained" and she identified with him a "sense of deliverance and safety" (93). The nurse copes with the shame of physical and potentially sexual assault by maintaining her faith in the New Man as well as by the knowledge of his willingness to intervene and protect her. However, when she receives the letter breaking off their relationship, she finds he is indeed "a milksop" tied to his sister's apron strings. It seems this sister warned him about the nurse and he believed her. In trying to make sense of such a turn of events, the nurse asks herself why James did not trust her. Anguish of this betrayal runs deep:

> Had he cared for me as he had seemed to do, surely he would have thought it worthwhile to come on and see for himself what was transpiring and try to rescue

---

15 Tara MacDonald, *The New Man, Masculinity and Marriage in the Victorian Novel* (New York: Routledge, 1996), 1.
16 Roe, *Stella Miles Franklin*, 183–4.
17 Coleman, *Her Unknown Brilliant Career*, 161

me, if necessary from evil influences. But no, and oh, how humbly I had believed in him! (109)

After his betrayal, the nurse's critique of the New Man is strong and relentless. His measured masculinity of restraint is ultimately revealed as weak and "fake". She describes this particular brand of masculinity as "shoddy" and with no substance (107). James no longer represents paradise for her. "I was not shut out from paradise" she exclaims, "so much as paradise had become a fake affair – a far harder blow to bear to the soul than the other way about" (107). At this she throws in her lot with the better evil: a "lunatic" rather than "that sniveling, hypocritical spineless James" (109 ¾). He is disrobed as the ultimate wolf in sheep's clothing. The story disrupts the domestic bliss associated with the tale-of-two-suitors tradition and teaches how good men, even feminist New Men, can still betray women and impose a different kind of violence.

Cold-Blooded Monster

In direct contrast to James is Colin, the eminent rich playboy, who is both selfish and insincere: "I failed to unearth one instance of his ever having done an unselfish or generous act to any one", explains the nurse (20). And, while James is tender and loving, Colin is lustful and aggressive, becoming increasingly belligerent as he drinks. He thus represents the new, potentially degenerate, American man who is self-directed, impulsive, and pleasure-seeking, and who can easily become violent and turn into "a cold-blooded monster" (89). The nurse is attracted by his physique and energy for life, even while she finds his deceit and selfishness repelling. Again mirroring Sybyl's experience with Bobby Hoyne in *On Dearborn Street*, the nurse describes (and enjoys) Colin's physique and represents his more bodily centred masculinity compared to James: "He shone like a wax model and the movements of his muscles were a delight" (17). During these early "irresponsible days" (22) of their courtship, the nurse does not realise the potential dangers that Colin poses and infantilises him as simple and non-threatening: "I wanted to take him on my knee and dandle him and call him Cute, cunning, little Collykins" (20–21).

After the agreement with James to pursue her fancy before settling down, the nurse eagerly and with great anticipation agrees to meet Colin for an evening out. He collects her in his new car and offers her a fur that signifies wealth and chivalry. The automobile, its speed and power representative of modernity and an extension of his potent masculinity, is a "magnificent machine, dark blue and shining". The nurse delights in the way he "handled it like a master", excited about getting to the open road where it swept along "like a roaring torrent". They "took to the hills at fifty miles an hour, the descent at 20 and 40 and the levels at 60 and 70". "Ah!"

7 Courage and Confession

she exclaims, thrilled by the speed, excitement, and adventure (33–34). Once they arrive at the restaurant, Colin dominates the conversation and orders her food. This foreshadowing of his abusive nature that parallels contemporary profiles of dominating men is set against the gullible nurse who is "well pleased", still beguiled by his chivalry and attention (34). Again like Sybyl, the nurse enjoys "a little dancing after dinner", content with some "perfectly innocent fun and pleasure, free from all guile" that she had "so fiercely craved" (35). These are her frank, yet innocent, desires, stated to establish her lack of responsibility for what would take place during their next outing. In these pages Franklin responds to cultural notions (still present today) that women are culpable for men's violence.

As the relationship progresses, he invites her out again and hints they will be gone for several days. The nurse goes along with his threat of elopement as mere flirtation. He becomes intoxicated and announces he has arranged for their marriage: "I have a license in my pocket", he declares and a justice ready to perform the deed" (45). She cannot believe this is happening: "In spite of what we hear of men … we are blessed with a blind delusion that the man we know cannot be as bad as all the others" (46). Her response is "to pitch the drink clean in his face … and then walk out with cool disgust", but she feels "bound by the conventional horror of making a scene and a newspaper scandal which would have surely followed" (46–7). She is also constrained by a lack of money for alternative transportation and fears about what people might think should she go begging for help. Embarrassed about this situation, "convention again held [her] … tight" (52). Colin continues to drink, imbibing his fifth cocktail and more champagne, and becomes increasingly belligerent and dangerous. The role of alcohol in this declaration that he is "free to do" whatever he pleases (49) is an important feature and one highlighted by the Temperance movement's influence on social purity feminism. Even though there is no evidence of Franklin's association with this movement, she appears to have understood the role alcohol played in interpersonal violence. Unfortunately Colin is "one of the very worst types of drunks". Like the "desperate and brutal" Demarest, Colin turns into a "terrible demon" (68).

The physical violence begins in his car where he "laid violent hands" on her, "threatening to break [her] … neck" (55). She tries to escape by jumping out of the car, but he follows and soon catches up with her, acting contritely, and proclaiming he "wouldn't really hurt a hair of her head" (57). When the nurse scorns him, he roughly hurls her back into the car, drives them to a wooded area, and tells her: "[you can] scream your little head off and no one would hear you" (59). Soon they are "struggling amid the pricking underbrush" and he attacks her again with a "grip like a vice" (60). When she tries to defend herself and bites him on the cheek, his rage increases "with the ferocity of a famished tiger finding its prey". She fights for her life, but he gags and chokes her, pins her down, and attempts to strangle her. The threat of rape accompanies these physical assaults as the heroine declares, "I was defending that which was dearer than life itself" (62). The nurse's horrified description of Colin's rage allows Franklin to comment on misogyny, the victimisation of women, and the relationship between men and militarism: "He was like unto several big nations attacking a smaller one" (62). This line is one among many as "Red Cross Nurse" teems with comparisons between male vice in interpersonal relationships and depictions of war as natural extensions of a globalised masculine moral destitution. This was the "staggering calamity" that so shocked and depressed Franklin.[18] Militarism's casualties, and especially the production of men's violence against women in war, as well as male military hysteria or shell shock as a crisis of manhood, were deemed examples of this "medical and moral abyss of sexual excess" or what the nurse describes as the "frantic orgy" of "male hysteria" (152, 155).

Colin's physical assault of the nurse continues alongside the insinuation of rape as the nurse declares her "inherent right to remain inviolate" (66). Colin insists she precipitated the assault, telling her that she encouraged it. "[You] led me on to the very last lap and then when I was getting down to business fluttered off like a butterfly", he exclaims, insisting that it is her "insolence" that "brought this upon [her]" (76, 81). As a form of survival she agrees to marry him within the week providing the marriage is kept a secret and unannounced. Delivered to the foyer of her apartment building, she assumes she is safe and wanting to show her disdain in parting, gives him a "little smack" to show she is not conquered (89). This provokes the final and most serious attack when he beat her until "things went black", falling upon her "like a tiger ... battering [her] body against the marble" (90). Still, as a final act of defiance, she sticks out her tongue at him once she is safely separated from him by the glass door and "rejoiced in his terrific rage" (93).

In this surprisingly bold and frank account Franklin demonstrates a keen awareness of the motives and practices of abusive men as well as the gender politics and cultural conventions that shape survivors' responses. Franklin especially understood the forces encouraging women to hide abuse. When Colin reappears after the assault "looking very attractive" and acting as if nothing had happened, the heroine stoically hides her rage and passively accepts her fate. Given her lack of economic resources and in light of cultural convention associated with the shame and stigma of abuse, she has few alternatives. So it is no surprise that after this brutal assault when the nurse's "bruised and blackened" body "would have furnished conclusive evidence to a coroner's jury", the heroine instead tells a story about a car accident to account for her injuries (103). As he demands her to fulfill the promise

---

18 Franklin, Pocket diary, 6 and 7 August 1914; S.M. Franklin, "The Menace of Great Armaments" *Life and Labor* (September, 1914): 260–263.

of marriage, she puts him off, but agrees to a later date, hoping, she explains, to go to "my precious Jim, confess what I had done and ask him to save me" (106).

Subverting White Slavery

" Red Cross Nurse", like the play "Virtue", reflects the "white slave" rhetoric actively circulating in Chicago at the time that was supported by social purity feminism and fuelled by Jane Addams' *A New Conscience and an Ancient Evil*.[19] The nurse, alone with no family or resources, is vulnerable to male predation. "It flashed upon me that I was in the hands of a criminal practiced and crafty, an amateur white slaver" declares the nurse, "and the horror of the thing crept down my spine" (59). However, the story is exceptional in its resistance to several central features of the white slave narrative.

Early in the story Franklin uses James Denvir's aunt to articulate the misogyny and self-centredness of men generally and Colin Maynard in particular. She foreshadows what will eventually transpire by digressing to comment on the problem of white slavery alongside her critique of her nephew. "This squealing against the white slave act [Mann Act]", she exclaims, "is a great barometer of the good American man" (11c). Although Franklin's story mirrors the vulnerability of impecunious women and the entitlement of men that provide the context for white slavery to occur, she subverts this discourse by portraying the heroine's self-possession and intentional sexual agency; her survival in the face of violence; and also by the disrupting traditional portrayals of abusers by casting the upper-class white male as the degenerate "white slaver".

First, although Franklin uses this story to illustrate men's power over women, the heroine is not the typical sexually innocent flower or chaste fallen heroine of traditional "white slavery" narratives. "Red Cross Nurse" startlingly refuses to silence female sexual agency, despite its disturbing content. The nurse is frank in expressing her sexual desire when she playfully asks James for permission for "one wild orgy of flirtation" to "*really* flirt, in the adult Eve way and not in in the kittenish way" (28). She is in "no hurry" for "matrimonial gags and chains" and does not want "to marry and be tame just yet" (10). She wants to avoid "settl[ing] down into the fell clutches of matrimony" (28). This bold request is presented in a playful, sexually teasing manner, to "James Esquire, two ends of a rogue and a liar" (28). He tells her "I leave it to your delicacy and your really precocious amount of good

---

19   Margit Stange, *Personal Property: Wives, White Slaves, and the Market in Women* (Baltimore: Johns Hopkins Press, 1998); Brian Donovan, *White Slave Crusades* (Urbana: University of Illinois Press, 2006).

sense to gage [sic] how far you had better go with this young man" (29). Given this latitude, the nurse replies to Colin's insistent requests with "a bubbling sense of mischief" (30). She is smitten by this handsome beau, whom she "craves" (38). In these initial encounters the nurse's sexual desire is delicately noted: "My enjoyment of [Colin] was purely, innocently, perhaps a little sensuously aesthetic, for beauty of any sort affects me visibly, immediately, and acutely" (17). This assertive New Woman is not only enamoured of his muscular body, but also his physical skills in driving and outdoor pursuits: "I looked with growing envy upon his splendid proportions used for nothing but play and dissipation" (16).

As the heroine is torn between desire for both suitors, she faces a central conundrum for rational mate selection: "I wanted them both and began to be torn by the thought of having to relinquish either" (37). In this declaration the nurse articulates her sexual choice. At the same time, as mentioned, throughout the narrative of Colin's brutal attack is a discourse of innocence and an absence of culpability. Franklin is keen to balance the nurse's lack of sophistication in these matters alongside this bold presentation of female sexual agency.

Second, it is especially when the attack occurs that the nurse resists the sentimental trope of the fallen woman who is either rescued or "redeemed" through madness, murder or suicide, or other forms of demise. In the case of "Red Cross Nurse" the protagonist refuses to cast herself as a victim. She fights back and refuses to be a slave, ultimately choosing her fate. "Perhaps, you prefer the company of slaves and harlots" she tells Colin, because they are "the only sort of creatures that would put up with you" (59, 54). The implication is that she is neither, will not put up with him, and will instead fight for her life. "I stood up breathing fire and unafraid of battle" (61), she exclaims, refusing to be beaten: "There was nothing to do but fight and fighting fall" (66). She bites him, regretting only that she "hadn't bitten harder" (60), jumps out of the car in several attempts at escape, and eventually manages to crawl away from him beyond the door of her apartment building. "You won't surrender?" inquires Colin, to which she replies: "Never while I have a breath in my body" (66). In addition to physical resistance, the heroine continually tries to outwit him through various forms of remonstration ranging from flattery and coquetry to protestation and tears. And eventually at the end she sticks out her tongue at him in final reproach. In this way the nurse refuses both fallen woman and victim tropes.

The heroine's survival also deviates from the debasement destinies of "white slave" narratives because the self-possessed heroine assertively makes the case that Colin's brutality and lack of control and self-restraint is a show of the weakness of men as a class and not merely a moral weakness of individual men. Men's misogyny leaves them weak in the face of women's independence. In this way it is actually her resistance to being the victim that empowers her and demoralises him: "I haven't a chance [with you]", exclaims Colin, "you make me feel about the size of a peanut" (70). It is precisely this diminishment and his subsequent feelings of inferiority, experienced as vulnerability, which spurs his rage. Alongside his feelings of inferiority is the vulnerability associated with the need for her: "I'd rather take you any way than not get you at all" (77). Although fearful, the nurse is repelled by his weakness, "delight[ed] in tormenting him thru this set of his unbridled emotions" (93). Through capturing his rage and therefore his vulnerability, the nurse claims her power and resists the victim trope of the meek and passive fallen woman. The nurse does not merely survive, however. "It is somewhat intoxicating to find that I had come off top in such an encounter" (93), she declares. This barely suppressed sadomasochistic element is unnerving to the present-day reader, reminding us again of Sybyl's relationship with Bobby Hoyne in *On Dearborn Street* as well as Stephen Garton's comment about Sybylla's bruises in *My Brilliant Career* as "a symbol of her victory, her medal proving that men are not invincible and invulnerable".[20] Given this logic that rage makes men relinquish power, the influence the nurse has over Colin might be understood as an equalising force. Ultimately, however, the differences between these narratives are salient. Here there is fear and revulsion associated with these serious attacks and there is no acceptance of violence beyond the exhilaration of survival. Indeed, her point is that women live every day with the consequences of male violence, which was normalised in the private sphere as it was also in the public spectre of war. Without their political and social emancipation in all spheres of life, women's lot was to suffer and endure male violence. There simply were no other alternatives for the nurse.

Third, although traditional white slave narratives played on class and racial distinctions, it is Colin Maynard, an upstanding member of white, upper-middle-class society who kidnaps the nurse, not a poor, working-class, immigrant or man of colour seeking financial gain. "Ah …" explains the nurse in remonstration against the prevailing myths of the men who enslave innocent white women, "if ever anyone had thru parentage the opportunity of being a gentleman it was Colin Maynard, and yet this is what he was! A woman beater and amateur white slaver … who nevertheless could walk among decent people with his head high with the assumption of superiority" (91). At a time when "racial" distinctions were made between what we now consider whites of various ethnicities, the nurse makes a point of describing Colin's golden hair, aquiline nose, and eyes "as blue as a china doll's" (17). She also points out his class differences in explaining that it "did not seem consistent that he represented the same species as the coal heavers and waiters and other vassals over whom he had dominion" (18). And even before the abuse begins, the nurse refuses to accept the case that he is a superior being

---

20 Garton, "Contesting Enslavement", 344.

in the evolutionary scheme of things and refers to his complexion as "the greatest joke of all", explaining that she could never take blond, blue-eyed people as "real in any case", but more like the dolls they resemble (21–22). Soon it is made clear that Colin, rather than presenting the eugenic solution, is demonstrating his biological inferiority. His "survival", for example, is "kept alive artificially" (19) through his gender and class privilege. Worse, as the relationship matures and Colin becomes violent, he is soon characterised as the most degenerate of all, "a cad of the white slaver type" (46).

In this way Franklin subverts traditional white slave narratives through an insistent feminist voice demonstrated through the nurse's sexual awakening, her terror and lessons learned at the hands of a man with class and race privilege, and her eventual survival. Concerned with issues of power and desire that plagued her interpersonal life, Franklin penned a protagonist in " Red Cross Nurse" who is hurt by masculine arrogance and an aggression mirrored in men's militarism, who recognises the fatal flaws in American manhood, and who survives her ordeal by making choices for herself that articulate her sexual agency. Reflecting the ideals and struggles of the urban New Woman, Franklin thus troubled the nature of American manhood in "Red Cross Nurse" by declaring (as feminists would continue to declare throughout the century and into the next) that masculinity not only impoverishes men as it enslaves women, but that different faces of masculinity, including those associated with militarism and war, provide varied although still problematic gender practices.

Conclusion

A Rush and a Swing

Miles Franklin's narrative about her little-understood American years often bemoaned being "sweated to obliteration by those reformers"[1] and trading the dreams of a "brilliant career" for the life of an "expatriate professional feminist".[2] Franklin's friend and biographer Marjorie Barnard also described this time between Franklin's early life in Australia and her later return to her homeland, as an "exile". "We know so little of Miles in those years", she wrote, noting that Franklin "never talked about her time in America or the later years during the war and in England. She could not be drawn out … It was as if, when she began to write again, all the years when she did not write ceased to be".[3] As I have emphasised in *Fallen Among Reformers*, such characterisations of Franklin's productivity are erroneous; despite the fact that almost all her Chicago writing remains unpublished, the expatriate period was ultimately formative rather than distractive. My goal has been to interrogate this "significant silence" and potentially reverse claims about "failures" by resurrecting these socially engaged Chicago manuscripts and making the case that they were produced because, and not in spite of, her fall among reformers.[4] These stories and plays are original and vital, and contain the confidently optimistic and spontaneously unrestrained exuberance of the New Woman tradition, which in my estimation is more innovative and compelling than the nostalgic novels of

---

1 Jill Roe, *Stella Miles Franklin: A Biography* (Sydney: Fourth Estate/Harper Collins, 2008), 189.
2 Susan Magarey, "*My Brilliant Career* and Feminism", *Australian Literary Studies* 20, no. 4 (2002): 389.
3 Marjorie Faith Barnard, *Miles Franklin* (New York: Twayne Publishers, 1967), 89.
4 Jill Roe, "The Significant Silence: Miles Franklin's Middle Years", *Meanjin Quarterly* 39, no. 1 (1980): 48–59; Roe, *Stella Miles Franklin*, 159.

her later years. Such spark is revealed in Franklin's note that Chicago was indeed invigorating. "Life goes with a rush and a swing over here", she declared. "Americans are simply adorable".[5]

I am not the first to make this claim about Franklin's literary productivity, nor to point out that it was enhanced by the maturity of her politics earned during the time in Chicago. Jill Roe suggests, for example, that these:

> American years were perhaps the most astonishing of Miles Franklin's life. She held down a demanding job in one of the most rackety cities of the world while in her own time writing compulsively, producing some three novels and at least two plays over the next four years.[6]

Similarly, Susan Pfisterer and Carolyn Pickett argue that the progressive development of her politics is most evident in the quality and scope of her plays written during this period. Roy Duncan also notes this in the introduction to *On Dearborn Street*, suggesting that Franklin's American writings show "a fuller zest and competence than do certain published works from before and after". Others, including Susan Bradley Smith, also echo these assessments in describing Franklin's expatriate work as "arguably the best and most productive of her personal and professional life".[7]

There is no doubt that Franklin spread her wings during these expatriate middle years in ways that expanded her horizons socially and intellectually and invigorated her feminist insights. Sometimes didactic, often pedantic, and invariably containing sometimes infuriating detail, the strength of this work rests in its distinct narrative authority earned from the sweat and pleasures of working and living among reformers. Essentially, Chicago functioned as her muse. Immersed in the exciting developments of the city's literary renaissance and consumed by the daily labours of progressive reform, Franklin wrote about her life. As Duncan suggests, she used "visibly authentic incidents from the actual world ... [to create] a legacy of little cameos which capture human attitudes at particular times".[8] These cameos provide a rare glimpse into her intellectual and emotional life during this period and illustrate the challenges and opportunities facing feminist writers like

---

5   Miles Franklin, letter to Eva O'Sullivan, 8 May 1912, ML MSS 544.
6   Roe, *Stella Miles Franklin*, 142.
7   Roy Duncan, "Introduction", *On Dearborn Street* (Large print/St Lucia: University of Queensland Press, 1987), iv; Susan Pfisterer and Carolyn Pickett, *Playing with Ideas: Australian Women Playwrights From the Suffragettes to the Sixties* (Sydney: Currency Press, 1999), 53; Susan Bradley Smith, "Miles Franklin's Dramatic Ambitions, or, Why Stella Really Came Home", *Antipodes*, (June 2007): 21.
8   Duncan, "Introduction", xvi.

Franklin who sought to critique and rewrite gender relations in the first decades of the twentieth century. Despite the most obvious challenge, Franklin's relative inability to publish these works, the beauty of this writing is that not only do these manuscripts reflect and rely on data from Franklin's actual world in "the windy city", but they also seek to transform that world.

My approach in reviving Franklin's little-known Chicago-era manuscripts has been to explore the ways they encompass broad political and aesthetic influences embedded in cultural patterns associated with the rise of US socialism, pacifism, social purity feminism, and suffrage. I have emphasised that this did not imply that Franklin was not exposed to these changes in turn-of-the-century Australia, and Sydney in particular, in the years prior to her departure, or that her New Woman writing was unique to the Chicago years. Nor do I ignore the fact that Australian New Woman writers like Ada Cambridge in *A Marked Man* or Frances Emily Russell's *Joyce Martindale* were also exploring the ways independent modern women were claiming masculine urban spaces and responding to the impulses of modernity. Franklin's political involvement among reformers is also not unique, as Angela Woollacott points out. Several prominent Australian women writers of this period (and she specifically mentions Christina Stead and Katherine Susannah Prichard as well as Franklin) engaged with political modernity.[9] Rather, my interest has focused on plotting the specific ways this Chicago period, the least-understood period in Franklin's life, exposed her to the chaos and creativity of modernity in this *particular* urban setting, complete with the promise and anxieties associated with independence, meaningful work, and opportunities for amusement and romance. Roe put it this way: what happened in Chicago "was not so much a reinvention of self as a natural development, since the optimistic Progressivist reform ethos that [Franklin] enthusiastically espoused flowed readily from the radical politics of New South Wales in which she had been reared".[10]

These Chicago manuscripts thus represent a continuation of Franklin's New Woman literary vision originating in *My Brilliant Career*, which sought to push against the limits of femininity imposed by society on women writers and their readers and to declare women's independence, distaste for marriage, the demand for economic and political equality, and the reform of manhood.[11] Chicago however, sharpened Franklin's politics as well as her wit, and provided experiences grounded in her work and social life that helped shape a literature about the

---

9   Angela Woollacott, *To Try Her Fortune in London: Australian Women, Colonialism, and Modernity* (New York: Oxford University Press, 2001), 214.
10 Roe, *Stella Miles Franklin*, 143.
11 Sally Ledger, *The New Woman: Fiction and Feminism at the* Fin de Siècle (College Station: Penn State University Press, 1999); Ann Ardis, *New Woman, New Novels: Feminism and Early Modernism* (New Brunswick, NJ: Rutgers University Press, 1990).

American New Woman. In this way I employ what Philip Mead calls a "locational literary history" centred on the socio-political and artistic context of Chicago at a moment when the city, and Franklin within it, were struggling with the opportunities and anxieties of modernity.[12] My point is that Franklin responded to the opportunities and met the challenges of these modern times of "turbulence, agitation, and panic" with gusto.[13] Her specific experiences among reformers and literary elites, as well as among working women and their families, not only galvanised her politics and precipitated an intellectual maturity, but also shaped her realist approach. This sought to represent the specific realities of modern life through the feminist lens of the independent American New Woman claiming her space in the city as well as in literature.

Alongside this localised history, it is also important to mark the ways Franklin's writing provides evidence for what Susan Pfisterer and Carolyn Pickett describe as "the depths of Franklin's internationalism".[14] She created literature across transnational spaces seemingly quite disparate, yet contexts sharing a similar ethos of embittered graceless toil as well as intrinsic beauty.[15] The extreme blistering heat of Australian summers, for example, oppress just as the intense cold of Midwestern US winters confounds and challenges. The "dog-eat-dog" spirit associated with Chicago's vociferous modernity is similarly paralleled in the unforgiving landscape of the harsh Australian bush, where only the strong survive, and then against great odds. Ultimately Franklin's exile and longing, and the somewhat permanent homesickness they triggered, helped shape her transcontinental literary career. This is invoked in *My Career Goes Bung*, "where the sea tracks lead to the WORLD".[16] However like Rosa Praed, Franklin reproduced her Australian origins "not simply as a setting but much more fundamentally as a source of [hybridised] aesthetic experience", spinning "yarns" within feminist stories,[17] and producing what Liz Conor calls the "peculiarly Australian aptitude for colloquialism".[18] Because these practices shaping Franklin's writing in various geographic locations necessarily represent a transnational literary history, it is important to note various

---

12 Philip Mead, "Nation, Literature, Location", in *The Cambridge History of Australian Literature*, ed. Peter Pierce (Melbourne: Cambridge University Press, 2009), 564.
13 Iveta Jusova, *The New Woman and the Empire* (Columbus: Ohio University Press, 2005), 1.
14 Pfisterer and Pickett, *Playing with Ideas*, 53.
15 Kerryn Higgs, "The Cosmopolitan Bushwoman", *Women's Review of Books* 27, no. 4 (July/August 2010), 10.
16 Quoted in Jill Roe, "The World of Miles Franklin", *Southerly* 54, no. 4 (1995): 85.
17 Andrew McCann, "Unknown Australia: Rosa Praed's Vanished Race", *Australian Literary Studies* 22, no. 1 (2005): 38.
18 Liz Conor, *The Spectacular Modern Woman: Feminine Visibility in the 1920s* (Bloomington: Indiana University Press, 2004), 44. See also, Julianne Lamond, "Stella vs. Miles: Women Writers and Literary Value in Australia", *Meanjin Quarterly* 70, no. 3 (2011).

engagements with specific processes of literary production within and between various locales, and which support the diversity and dynamism of the expatriate literature of the time.[19] Ultimately I hope this troubles the iconic and quintessentially nationalist figure we have come to accept.

Another important aspect of Franklin's transnational profile is her participation in transnational feminist networks that provided support, solidarity, and sustenance throughout these expatriate years.[20] Following contemporaries such as Charlotte Perkins Gilman, Franklin's literary responses to the plight of modern wage-earning women were "born from" a broader organised international women's and suffrage movement and intended for as broad an audience as possible. Underscoring the importance of transnational feminist networks, Franklin expressed feelings about her American years in a letter to Margery Currey (Dell) in 1950:

> I was going over my days in the USA and totting up what I had got out of it. The things through affection are the only ones that ever meant anything to me. I hadn't the gifts for acquisitiveness. Affection plus intelligence is the most delightful mixture of friendship and friendship the warmest most permanent thing in this existence, and I thought further that Editha [Phelps], you and Ethel [Mason] were my most beloved girlfriends. Editha was unique, Ethel was so lovely and soft – not an inharmonious or suffering note in her and you my dear well, we had such a congeniality in impishness, audacity of thought and in every way you are a delight to remember.[21]

Like much of life, memories are distilled down to that "warmest, most permanent thing", friendship, which sustained during her most vital years.[22] Almost twenty-seven years old when she arrived in the United States, Franklin would be thirty-six when she left. Roe put it this way: in Chicago her character was "broadening and mellowing, or at least having some of its intensities rubbed away 'in the maelstrom of Chicago life'. The imprint would be lifelong".[23]

This maelstrom might have mellowed Franklin, but she was still plagued by doubts and insecurities during this period, evidence of which has exacerbated the mysteries surrounding these expatriate years. Paul Giles confirms this in suggesting Franklin was "so assiduous about justifying her patriotic [Australian] credentials"

---

19 Robert Dixon and Veronica Kelly, *Impact of the Modern: Vernacular Modernities in Australia 1870s–1960s* (Sydney: Sydney University Press, 2008).
20 Kimberly Jensen and Erika Kuhlman, eds., *Women and Transnational Activism in Historical Context* (Dordrecht, Netherlands: Republic of Letters Press, 2010).
21 Quoted in Roe, *Stella Miles Franklin*, 190.
22 Quoted in Sylvia Martin, *Passionate Friends: Mary Fullerton. Mabel Singleton, and Miles Franklin* (London: Onlywomen Press, 2001).
23 Roe, *Stella Miles Franklin*, 143.

that she "repress[ed] her former American self" in order to avoid and denigrate "the road not chosen".[24] Certainly she went to great lengths in Chicago to maintain secrecy about her writing; practices which continued throughout her life. This desire for control and its compulsion for covertness is clear in a letter to Mary Fullerton in 1930, written when she was fifty years old: "I only wish for means to be a recluse and get away from everyone and what they say", she insisted, adding "[I] don't care if I'm never mentioned after my death. I don't want the scavengers and malicious muck-rakers romancing to show off their talents at my expense".[25]

This furtive manipulation of identity also signifies agency in its recognition of the novel and strategic nature of Franklin's pseudonyms. Pseudonyms destabilise truth claims and permit performative guises that disrupt fixed identities and elude authenticity (what Tricia Wang calls "an elastic self"), but they also are not without voice.[26] In other words, writing under assumed names contaminates identity; writing as a woman performing as a man allowed Franklin to expose the "normal" constitution of gender and subvert representations of authorship by providing suspicion about the referential accuracy of the signature.[27] Ultimately these practices of imposture are embedded in history, culture, and politics. Attending to them highlights the complexities of an era when cultural values were dramatically changing, when assuming a literary persona in areas still resistant to women's inclusion was tricky, and when various disguises might serve to relieve anxieties over public exposure and in the hopes of an unprejudiced reception.[28] And it is this compulsion for parody (revealing literary modes and their authority as performative and what we understand as "real life" to be constructed) that Barbara Schmidt-Haberkamp suggests was central to both Franklin's personal politics and her authorial stance.[29] "Life", wrote Franklin as Brent of Bin Bin, is "the most discursive and fragmentary experience".[30] And for Franklin that complex line

---

24 Paul Giles, *Antipodean America: Australasia and the Constitution of U.S. Literature* (New York: Oxford University Press, 2013), 332.
25 Miles Franklin, quoted in Martin, *Passionate Friends*, 9.
26 Tricia Wang, "The Elastic Self: Understanding Identity in Social Media", https://tinyurl.com/udbcsgw.
27 Anne Herrmann, *Queering the Moderns: Poses/Portraits/Performances* (New York: Palgrave, 2000), 166; Diana Fuss, *Essentially Speaking: Feminism, Nature and Difference* (New York: Routledge, 1989), xiii.
28 Valerie Kent, "Alias Miles Franklin", in *Gender, Politics, History and Fiction: Twentieth Century Australian Women's Novels*, ed. Carole Ferrier (St. Lucia: University of Queensland Press, 1985), 44–58. See also Robert J. Griffin, "Anonymity and Authorship", *New Literary History* 30, no. 4 (1999): 877–895.
29 Barbara Schmidt-Haberkamp, "Performing Gender and Genre in Miles Franklin's *My Career Goes Bung*", *Connotations* 9, no. 3 (1999/2000): 292.
30 Miles Franklin, quoted in Delys Bird, "Miles Franklin," *Australian Literature, 1788–1914*, ed. Selina Samuels (Detroit, MI: Gale, 2001), 126.

between life and fiction blurs when her "life" as the author becomes "the matter of fiction outside the novel even as it constitutes the subject matter of that novel".[31] Such strategies, as Brigitta Olubas explains, helped Franklin resist literary closure and maintain control: "she retains the last word over her own life, while suggesting that a last word is never really possible".[32]

A Net of Circumstance

In both her activism and her writing, Franklin confronted the issues of US modernity by negotiating the "net of circumstance", the gendered web of interconnected institutions (especially marriage and economics) and the systemic practices associated with them, which constrain women and construct their very being. It is fitting that her solution for revealing this web and breaking through it often relied on the yarn or personal tale with its interconnected wandering morality, the same term for a woven strand of fibres used in weaving or knitting, and not unlike the filaments of the net of circumstance itself. As *Fallen Among Reformers* attests, Franklin was a fictional polemicist whose literary goals during this period were always to explore and dramatise the effects of this web of institutions on women's lives, and to nudge a potential audience or reader towards transformation. This was a zealous quest. Writing in 1920, R. Brimley Johnson captured the energy that sustained this mission:

> The new woman, the female novelist of the twentieth century has abandoned the old realism. She does not accept *observed* revelation. She is seeking with passionate determination, for that Reality which is behind the material, the things that matter, Spiritual things, ultimate Truth.[33]

Such passionate determination to make sense of and break free from the net of circumstance is aptly demonstrated in Franklin's little-known realist novel with the same name, published in 1915. Captured in this web of inequities, the heroine of *The Net of Circumstance* laments her "perishing soul" that is left beating its wings against that very net.[34] The net holding women, including Franklin herself, which

---

31 Brigitta Olubas, "'Infinite Rehearsal' in the Work of Miles Franklin", *New Literature Review* 18 (1989): 38–9.
32 Olubas, "Infinite Rehearsal", 40.
33 R. Brimley Johnson, *Some Contemporary Novelists (Women)* (Leonard Parsons, 1920), xiv–xv.
34 Mr and Mrs Ogniblat L'Artsau (aka. Miles Franklin), *The Net of Circumstance* (London: Mills and Boon, 1915), 74. Subsequent references are to this edition and appear in parentheses in the text.

prevents their release and circumscribes all aspects of their lives, is constructed by and through the weaving together of all the themes of *Fallen Among Reformers*: work and the difficulties of economic survival; courtship, marriage, and the compulsory nature of domesticity; and men, to whom women must turn to cope with their economic burden, but who perpetuate the domesticity that further enslaves, dampening women's ambition, silencing their voices, and preventing their freedom. This is the tangled web where one gendered practice perpetuates another and that then feeds back into its original. *The Net of Circumstance* focuses specifically on this tangle, functioning as a staging ground for negotiations between requirements for women to conform to societal pressures and what Sandra Gilbert and Susan Gubar describe as the "unthinkable goal of mature freedom" by charting a heroine's journey as she attempts to break free.[35]

Described as a "too early flower of the springs of progress" (207), Constance Roberts, the thirty-something protagonist of *The Net of Circumstance*, is a classic New Woman heroine trying to cope with the vicissitudes of modern life. She is almost interchangeable with Sybyl Penelo, Joyce Frothingham, Maisie Pierce, or the anonymous nurse in being "advanced", intellectual, and sensitive, and in displaying the nervous disposition that invariably resulted from having to live amidst the conditions of modern life. And these conditions and the constraints they produce are also binding for all the spinsters who actually escape matrimony and its domestic enslavements in Franklin's stories and plays; the institution of marriage forms the primary structure of the net and shapes their lives whether they decry it or not. As Constance negotiates this tangled web of circumstance she mirrors Franklin herself, of course, who like this "too early flower", wrote to Rose Scott asking: "Do you suppose we are really ahead of our time, are we deluded fools or are we merely conceited?"[36]

Exhausted, underfed, and poorly paid as a stenographer, Constance lives in a hostel for working women, but is barely surviving the daily grind. For her there is just a "profitless, sapless existence, the bootless struggle for nothing but the maintenance of mere life and self-respect" (12). As Franklin was working on *The Net of Circumstance* in late 1911, she noted: "wrote a little on Net of C but went to bed tired and depressed".[37] It is no surprise then to read about Constance "toiling home, weary and dispirited, because life had afforded her nothing but futile drudgery ... [i]t was just flat and dreary and full of nothing but a struggle to earn bread and butter – very unappetizing bread and butter at that" (36, 207). Just as

---

35   Sandra M. Gilbert and Susan Gubar, *The Madwoman in the Attic: The Woman Writer and the Nineteenth-Century Literary Imagination* (New Haven, CT: Yale University Press, 1979), 339.
36   Roe, *Stella Miles Franklin*, 173-4.
37   Miles Franklin, Pocket diary, 21 December, 1911, ML MSS 364/2.

Conclusion

Franklin felt "as if life had become a deadly cul de sac and ... [wished] it were all over", so Constance declares, "I simply can't bear the thought of life again. Why should I continue living? My life is no service to others and is simply a terror to myself" (269).[38] Like other urban single women, both Constance and Franklin recognised the economic structures of the net of circumstance that discriminate through long hours, low pay, and poor working conditions, require participation in certain kinds of labour deemed appropriate for women in ways that constrain ambition and curb independence, and encourage sexual harassment. And it is during Constance's weary negotiation of the latter that we first meet her. On leaving the office and struggling against "convention and a gale in impractical garments", she confronts "the crude sporting instincts" of street harassment (4, 3).

Constance may be worn down by economic injustice but she resists her plight, declaring lines such as a woman "who speaks the inner truth has to be very brave – not only that, she has to be hard or she will die with the unpopularity and loneliness of telling the truth" (71). She also disdains domesticity and is cautious of matrimony. "As for marriage as a sphere of activity, a means of earning a livelihood", she declares,

> this was utterly revolting ... domesticity was not forced upon all men as a corollary of love and parenthood, regardless of whether they might or might not be suited to it. Life allowed them love and parenthood plus some useful field of activity in a business, profession or an art. Constance claimed the same right from life. (13–14)

Like all Franklin's New Woman heroines discussed in *Fallen Among Reformers*, here she is again, fully tangled in the net of circumstance, and fighting her way free. And her journey, like the others, is one that navigates between love and vocation, marriage and independence. For despite her disdain for matrimony and her quest for freedom, it provides a clear path out of at least one kind of drudgery, the daily grind. It is also the path expected by the romance template. Like Franklin's other stories, this negotiation proves tricky, and invariably unsatisfactory, but as Stephen Garton reminds us, the emotional confusion that results from this discord between modern content and traditional narrative strategies is understandable: "these were confusing times".[39]

Again, one solution for this almost-impossible choice between love and vocation is the New Man, a best bet for the emancipated modern woman. Enter Osborne Lewis, who "measures up higher than any man ... except those that

---

38 Franklin, Pocket diary, 22 November 1911.
39 Stephen Garton, "Contesting Enslavement: Marriage, Manhood and *My Brilliant Career*", *Australian Literary Studies* 20, no. 4 (2002): 347.

have been kept in a glass case" (118). Nonetheless, Osborne's motivations must be interrogated, because at base he was a "petted lion", whose dangers lay in the fact that he would be forgiven anything because women "were too ready to dance to [his] string" (45). The New Man's feminist politics privilege him because by contrast to the "ordinary" man, this "evolved" example of contemporary manhood expects women's immense gratitude. In other words, the danger of the New Man again lies in the fact that he is elevated without recognition of his entitlement. Just as Constance stands alongside Sybyl Penelo and the anonymous nurse, Osborne falls in line with Roswell Cavarley, and James Denvir.

As Franklin illuminates the social and economic vulnerabilities associated with the net of circumstance by offering critical reflections on work and matrimony, she transforms the romance plot with marriage as the narrative goal to marriage as the object of scrutiny. However she still employs courtship and the marriage plot – the source of her criticism – as the primary narrative strategy. Even though Constance wisely notes "the solution [about marriage] will probably lie in women ceasing to care so much and so stupidly" and instead lets "the lust of [creative work] fill her being", the novel ends as Constance meets "the radiant flood [of love]". Similar to *On Dearborn Street,* the obtuse and resigned, almost-happy ending is underscored by Constance's awareness of the web of circumstance shaping her choice, and her complicated bid for freedom that resides in the fact that Osborne had "no desire to fetter" (334, 339). Such deep ambivalence coinciding with plans to marry allowed Franklin to question traditional values without offending social mores or potential readers expecting marriage as the novel's finale. Again her somewhat reticent acquiescence announces its modernity by resisting moral consensus and a clear-cut resolution at the very same time that the more or less traditional ending provides readers with a sense of stability that contains the uncertainties of gender relations. Importantly, like almost all Franklin's New Woman writing, *The Net of Circumstance* employs a domestic feminism that encouraged readers to address publicly divisive aspects of modern life through the familiar containment of unsettled elements in the safe and familiar spaces of marriage and domesticity. It also provides, like so many of Franklin's other stories, a rhetoric of feeling or "impressionistic" realism, which focuses on the interiority of a character and the "registering of perceptions" to authorise women's experience.[40] It traces the New Woman's personal journey toward self-knowledge as someone worthy of both love and productive labour: "My mental backbone has returned", she exclaims (316).

The Net of Circumstance thus exemplifies a strategy present in almost all Franklin's New Woman writing where the narrative turns on the dissonance for

---

40   Lyn Pykett, *Engendering Fictions: The English Novel in the Early Twentieth Century* (London: Edward Arnold, 1995), 75.

the heroine between expectations for a conventional identity imposed on her by the systemic and interlocking web of institutional arrangements, and her own developing and changing experience of these practices. The novel of the modern woman therefore offers interiority and resistance to the conventional. However, although its content is subversive, the protest contained in this novel is declared in the earnest style of the all-knowing third-person omniscient narrator recognised by an early-twentieth-century literary establishment as both feminine and Victorian. Such narration is derided at best as "coy and irritating" and at worst as an embarrassing "lapse of artistry".[41] This renders *The Net of Circumstance* less innovative than *On Dearborn Street* or "Red Cross Nurse", and more in line with the more didactic and meandering "While Cupid Tarried", although somewhat more readable. Essentially *The Net of Circumstance* illustrates the hybridity and bridging characteristics of Franklin's New Woman writing that offers modern content through more traditional form.[42] As Talia Schaffer points out, the bridging function of this late-Victorian literary hybridity and its so-called "embarrassing and feminised" stories – and certainly all Franklin's New Woman writing would fall into this camp – was brought to bear in important and influential ways on both the gender politics it sought to address and a literary establishment women authors (sometimes unconsciously) were set to transform.[43] Recognising that temporal thresholds simultaneously disrupt and reinforce conceptual boundaries, Franklin's stories and plays from these years demonstrate the ways New Woman claims locked her into the new century as her sympathies caught her looking back towards both the sexual morality and the literary conventions of a previous generation.[44] In considering these transformations, Rita Felski also reminds us that the "Victorian image of genteel womanhood was not simply an outdated symbol to be swept away so that women could freely enter the modern world".[45] Operating as a palimpsest, this underscores the ways the past stays active in each contemporary present, and seemingly outdated practices of femininity exert powerful influences on later literary aesthetics.

---

41 Robyn R. Warhol, *Gendered Interventions: Narrative Discourse in the Victorian Novel* (New Brunswick, NJ: Rutgers University Press, 1989), vii.
42 Ann Heilmann and Margaret Beetham, eds., *New Women Hybridities: Femininity, Feminism, and International Consumer Culture 1880–1930* (New York: Routledge, 2004).
43 Talia Schaffer, "Writing a Public Self: Alice Meynell's 'Unstable Equilibrium'", in *Women's Experience of Modernity, 1875–1945*, ed. Ann L. Ardis and Leslie W. Lewis (Baltimore, MD: Johns Hopkins Press, 2003), 13.
44 Robert Newman, ed., *Centuries' Ends, Narrative Means* (Stanford: Stanford University Press, 1996), 1.
45 Rita Felski, "Afterword", in *Women's Experience of Modernity, 1875–1945,* ed. Ann L. Ardis and Leslie W. Lewis (Baltimore, MD: Johns Hopkins Press, 2003), 294.

As *Fallen Among Reformers* attests, such explorations of location and the different aesthetic practices they foster are well travelled by literary historians. Kathryn Holland, for example, privileges such cross-generational encounters and refers to them as "intertexts" where authors engage with preceding generations and reach across "political and aesthetic upheavals".[46] This reach necessarily helps the emergence and expression of what we now understand as modern literature at the same time that we recognise that the boundaries between the traditions along the cusp of the centuries are necessarily political projects themselves. Martin Hipsky makes this clear when he suggests that accessing feminist-inspired dreams for a mass readership through the familiar tradition of the romance narrative provides the case for "locating women romance writers on the cusp of late-Victorian and early modernist periods within the broader literary history of the modern period".[47] Similarly, in discussing the contributions of Australian writers to an emerging modernist literature, Anouk Lang specifically identifies Franklin as participating in "a shared project for many white modernists", quoting Laura Doyle and Laura Winkiel in their summation of this shared project as an exploration of "the non-normative phenomenology of disenfranchised experiences".[48] Critics such as Ann Ardis, Rita Kranidis, and Lyn Pykett as well as Jane Eldridge Miller certainly confirm this point, insisting that despite proselytising narrators and didactic prose, these New Woman "books of good intention" need to be reconfigured within literary histories as influential precedents for modern literature.[49] Franklin's Chicago protest writing was certainly motivated by good intentions, just as the hybridised literary strategies, which she and her contemporaries used, exerted pressure on traditional forms and conventions as they made their case for gender and economic justice. As emphasised throughout *Fallen Among Reformers*, however, this by no means infers Franklin as a modernist writer: a label she would have vehemently resisted, although I do like to think that Chicago's version of modernism in its Midwest geographical location, gritty opposition to the more dazzling coastal centres of literary innovation, and class-based modernist

---

46 Kathryn Holland, "Late Victorian and Feminist Intertexts: The Strachey Women in *A Room of One's Own* and *Three Guineas*", *Tulsa Studies in Women's Literature* 32 (2013): 75.
47 Martin Hipsky, *Modernism and the Women's Popular Romance in Britain, 1885–1925* (Athens: Ohio University Press, 2011), 6.
48 Anouk Lang, "Modernity in Practice: A Comparative View of the Cultural Dynamics of Modernist Literary Production in Australia and Canada", *Canadian Literature* 209 (2011): 61; Laura Doyle and Laura Winkiel, "Introduction: The Global Horizons of Modernism", in *Geomodernism: Race, Modernism, Modernity*, ed. Laura Doyle and Laura Winkiel (Bloomington: Indiana University Press, 2005), 13.
49 Sarah Grand (Frances McFall), *The Beth Book: Being a Study of the Life of Elizabeth Caldwell McClure, A Woman of Genius* (Introd. Elaine Showalter), (New York: Dial, 1980 [1897]), 460.

approaches originating from its industrial identity and midland realism, was potentially more palatable to her.[50]

Difference of View, Difference of Standard

A concern of *Fallen Among Reformers* has included tracing the ways the male literary establishment of early-twentieth-century US society redefined fiction on its own terms: a reconstruction in response to modernity and especially new gender arrangements as well as notions about the gender of fiction itself. This process rejected and denigrated both women and literary modes recognised as feminine. Virginia Woolf made this very plain, writing in 1929:

> [I]n both life and art the values of a woman are not the values of a man. Thus when a woman comes to write a novel, she will find that she is perpetually wishing to alter the established values – to make serious what appears insignificant to a man, and trivial what is to him important.[51]

New Woman writers were thus authors of change in a "double sense".[52] Writing during a period of perceived crisis and social instability, they documented the cultural shifts about which they were a key symbol, and also wrote to bring about further change in literature and society.

Franklin's conscious awareness of these politics and her attempt to articulate a feminine practice of writing are evident in much of this Chicago work, from Avis Gaylord's critique of the arts establishment in "The Survivors", the over-inflated egos of the writer Dayton Blanche in "Mrs Mulvaney's Moccasins" and academic James Denvir from " Red Cross Nurse", as well as in descriptions of the exceptional talent and constrained ambition of Sybyl Penelo of *On Dearborn Street*. Sybyl's work includes "copying, correcting, revising and re-arranging literary MSS" as well as ghost writing for famous, but mediocre male writers. When Sybyl's employer tells Roswell that "quite a bunch of society people claim credit for books and articles that would have been terrible only for Miss Penelo", noting one book in particular, he responds: "Ha! … [that author] was Swinbank Dummer Dummer-Jones. Many of us had suspected that Swinbank had either bribed the reviewers or retained some ghost" (26). This dialogue affirms the heroine's talent and the circumstances that

---

50 Liesl Olson, *Chicago Renaissance: Literature and Visual Art in the Midwest Metropolis* (New Haven, CT: Yale University Press, 2017); Carl Smith, *Chicago and the American Literary Imagination, 1880–1920* (Chicago: University of Chicago Press, 1984).
51 Virginia Woolf, *Collected Essays II* (London: Chatto and Windus, 1966 [1929]), 145–6.
52 Adrienne E. Gavin and Carolyn W. de la Oulton, *Writing Women of the Fin de Siècle: Authors of Change* (Basingstoke: Palgrave Macmillan, 2012), 2–3.

constrain her and privilege less exceptional male writers with fame and fortune. It also illustrates the ways – figuratively and literally – women perform unrecognised labour essential for men's success. It is also reminiscent of Franklin's estimation of Floyd Dell's literary fame, which she believed relied upon the insight and labour of his wife, Margery Currey Dell, an author in her own right.

In addition, it is *On Dearborn Street* where Franklin specifically acknowledges the denigration of sentimental fiction. In a preface titled "Note by Hero", the narrator defends "his" right to sentimentalism, which he associates with the American tradition. "Should I be accused of sentimentality", he declares, "then unabashed I claim the right to my national adjective", adding that he is "quite unabashed in diving into story-telling, which might, in this instance, more accurately be classified as tale-bearing".[53] In this preface Franklin makes the case for the effeminate emotionally engaged, rambling, and effusive yarn that was set in opposition to reticent and impersonal narratives transcending the local and particular. Ann Ardis and Laura Heffernan corroborate Franklin's insight in their discussion of modern literature's "rise" to aesthetic hegemony through a process of "remasculinization" that depended upon an estrangement from, and repression of, the popular and sentimental.[54]

However it is especially in *The Net of Circumstance* where the New Woman protagonist voices her disgust at a masculine literary establishment: "Women writers have always been condemned for failure", Constance declares. It is a "bulwark of logic to prove it [is] 'unnatural' for women to possess either talent or genius" (121). In this way, although men might incorporate the realist voice and employ the narrative authority of being a participant in the public world, women have to fight their way out of the romance genre.[55] Alongside her general critique of this literary establishment is Constance's ire at male authors and Osborne in particular, who is set up as God's gift to feminism, "confident that no man in the world understood the feminist movement so profoundly nor stood by it so gamely as himself" (44). Not only is his feminism pretentious and precarious,

---

53 Miles Franklin, *On Dearborn Street* (St Lucia: University of Queensland Press/Australian Large Print, 1987), 26, 1.
54 Ann Ardis, "Organizing Women: New Woman Writers, New Woman Readers, and Suffrage Feminism", in *Victorian Women Writers and the Woman Question*, ed. Nicola Diane Thompson (Cambridge: Cambridge University Press, 1999), 190; Laura Heffernan, "Reading Modernism's Cultural Field: Rebecca West's *The Strange Necessity* and the Aesthetic 'Systems of Relations'", *Tulsa Studies in Women's Literature* 27, no. 2 (2008): 309. See also Rita Felski, *The Gender of Modernity* (Cambridge, MA: Harvard University Press, 1995) and Bonnie Kime Scott, ed., *The Gender of Modernism: A Critical Anthology* (Bloomington: Indiana University Press, 1990).
55 Terry Lovell, *Consuming Fiction* (London: Verso, 1987); Gaye Tuchman and Nina Fortin, *Edging Women Out: Victorian Novelists, Publishers and Social Change* (New York: Routledge, 1989).

but also his literary talent. Armed with the confidence bestowed upon him by a patriarchal society that "found everything wide open to a man of his achievements", he "held success very high". His literary quest, however, was "to visualize the highly complex modern woman" (32), whom he imagined as English suffragettes "with their splendid rage and impatience … and the moral degradation that goes with it". Although Osborne "cherished" this vision "in his heart" and "worshipped her in his imagination" (31), the book he had written attempting "to explain the new woman" (30) was a failure, critiqued by the very feminists he hoped to explain. This assumption that a male author could speak for women "was like that of a comedian who has attempted serious drama, whose audience refuses to take him seriously, and if compelled to take him seriously refuses to take him at all". The irony of this literary reversal is not lost as the narrator adds, "[t]his sauce previously kept for literary geese set this gander talking" (32). Franklin thus points out that male authors have been confident in their ability to define women's lives and their assessments are accepted as objective and truthful. Women's claim to objectivity is more tentative; women artists cannot purport to understand something they have not experienced directly, and if they have, their portrayals are deemed subjective. This is Franklin's ire at masculinist presumptions and arrogance.

Franklin's critique is also lodged in the appropriation of the New Woman by male authors in the late-nineteenth and early-twentieth century, as evidenced, for example, by writers like H.G. Wells and Arnold Bennett, whom Franklin had read, and in the case of Arnold Bennett, someone she knew personally. Earlier authors such as George Gissing and George Meredith also appropriated the New Woman as a cultural product and were greeted relatively enthusiastically compared to the reception encountered by feminist New Woman authors of the period. Rita Kranidis writes about this appropriation of the New Woman, emphasising that male writers co-opted her "as if she were conclusively defined", working her into their stories "as a type of social problem". They tended not to be invested in her political significance and were not "motivated by any consideration other than their literary agendas".[56] In addition, as Elizabeth McLeod Walls points out, the reformist containment practices of domestic feminism specifically provided "ideological seeds" that were mimicked and appropriated by a male-dominated literary establishment.[57]

It is therefore no surprise when Osborne tries to make up for his failures by appropriating insights about the New Woman and using them for his own literary success. When he meets Constance again, he seizes on her to help capture "the

---

56 Rita S. Kranidis, *Subversive Discourse: The Cultural Production of Late-Victorian Novels* (New York: St Martin's Press, 1995), 108.
57 Elizabeth McLeod Walls, "'A Little Afraid of the Women of Today': The Victorian New Woman and the Rhetoric of British Modernism", *Rhetorical Review* 21, no. 3 (2002): 230, 235.

inner soul of a woman" (121), hopefully making up for the shortcomings of his earlier failed project in a new play he is writing. "Don't you think it would be good to find yourself thoroughly understood?" (70), he asks. He expounds that "the greatest of all art is sexless" and appears exceptionally indignant when Constance tells him that "men compelled female art to conform to male standards ... [and] simulate masculinity" (121). As she gives candid feedback on his writing, telling him he needs to let women tell their own story from their own point of view, he could "scarcely wait to thank her 'ere he sped away to work in the new and wonderful light that had fallen upon him" (124). This is the appropriation of her insight and vision, which he claims as his own. In addition, Constance is vocal about his privilege to work unhampered by material constraints and to usurp her limited and precious time off from the daily grind of her paid labour.

In this way Franklin's critique is directed not only against a masculine literary establishment and their arrogant presumption to speak for women despite their lack of narrative authority, but also against male novelists who are unhampered by femininity. The following quote represents Franklin's deeply felt observation evident throughout her Chicago writing that the conventions of literature allow and reward men for speaking for women while women authors themselves are constrained from speaking for themselves. Inherent in this observation are the material realities of living and working under these conditions, something Franklin keenly felt from her own experience:

> [Constance] had endured long weeks of cod-fish and hash, and would be compelled to endure many more, squeezed in a box of a room in which the sun never shone and in a dirty, crowded, questionable part of the city, so that she could afford this slight respite from mere unbrightened bread winning. What right had he to squander any of her precious, hard-won idleness in furnishing him a model to depict more truly the heart of woman ... Why was he a successful writer with all the fullness and glory of life cast in a banquet before him, and she on the outside ... Why, if not because women had always to give, and give, and give? They had to pour forth from the very finest fibres of soul and brain in sympathy, unswerving loyalty, inspiration; they had to be ever on the alert to please and encourage in a way that was very wearing. And what could they take – the leavings of life? (72–73)

Franklin's resolution of this story, however, is optimistic because Osborne recognises his appropriation and remedies it through public recognition of Constance's joint authorship at the opening night of the play when he also provides her with half of the royalties and earnings from the production. These behaviours result in the attentions of the New Woman and a tentative, almost-engagement is secured. The domestic happy ending is retrieved at the last minute, the hope for American manhood once more promised, and a potential romance-loving readership assuaged.

Vera Brittain was on the same page as Franklin when she made the case that "subversive doctrines" were best shared "through the medium of light dissertations upon innocent-looking domestic topics".[58] Franklin's subversive political agenda, with its expansive desires and emancipatory vision for gender and economic justice, was channelled into a domestic feminism that declared itself light-hearted but contained within these stories and plays serious strategies for personal and social transformation through feminist education and consciousness-raising. Franklin was thus able to convey literature's political commitment by embodying the social and material conditions of modernity in the lives of her characters, showing how they might break free from the net of circumstance and maximise their self-advancement and self-protection. Through the personal journeys of protagonists and their confrontations with the inequities of modern life, as well as their dreams for self-empowerment, Franklin challenged realism's promise of providing a direct equivalent of life and helped destabilise a masculinist literary establishment. Such effort, what Molly Youngkin declares as "the realistic method in its best expression", produced bold representations of women's agency for both the New Woman and the New Man.[59] From the perspective of Franklin's potential readers and audience, representations of new feminist-inspired material realities like economic self-sufficiency within matrimony or self-empowered spinsterhood, which might be argued for in purely academic or intellectual ways, were instead combined with more pleasurable and accessible romantic fantasies of companionate relationships built on trust and respect that promised women freedom.

Although the twin motivations of unsettling femininity and pleasing a feminine audience schooled in the romance tradition created difficulties and resulted in sometimes awkward prose and unsatisfactory endings in particular, Franklin rose to the occasion as a literary strategist, employing whatever techniques were at hand to assert literary authority, and make the case for women's freedom.[60] These techniques, amply shared by her New Woman contemporaries, have been described as a key aspect of the genre's "fluid politics" that witnessed and responded to the "exhilarating drama of the old yielding to the new".[61] It was this process that

---

58 Vera Brittain, quoted in Ann Heilmann, *New Woman Strategies: Sarah Grand, Olive Schreiner, Mona Caird* (Manchester: Manchester University Press, 2004), 16.
59 Molly Youngkin, *Feminist Realism at the* Fin de Siècle: *The Influence of the Late-Victorian Woman's Press on the Development of the Novel* (Columbus: The Ohio State University Press, 2007), 136.
60 Rachel Blau DuPlessis, *Writing Beyond the Ending* (Bloomington: Indiana University Press, 1985), 1–19.
61 Jane Eldridge Miller, *Rebel Women: Feminism, Modernism and the Edwardian Novel* (London: Virago, 1984), 202.

encapsulated Franklin as a somewhat precarious writer positioned between the centuries, facing the social conditions of modernity in this boisterous city and advocating for women's freedom, yet straddling different cultural conceptions of what that might mean. It was also the process that energised her desire "to reinvent herself as a modern writer". "So great was the stimulus of time and place", adds Roe, "she very nearly succeeded".[62]

---

62   Roe, *Stella Miles Franklin*, 173, 43

Works Cited

Addams, Jane. *Twenty Years at Hull House*. New York: Macmillan, 1910.
--. *A New Conscience and An Ancient Evil*. New York: Macmillan, 1912.
Aliaga-Buchenau, Ana-Isabel. *The "Dangerous" Potential of Reading: Readers and the Negotiation of Power in Nineteenth-Century Narratives*. New York: Routledge, 2004.
Allen, Judith. "Our Deeply Degraded Sex" and "The Animal in Men": Rose Scott, Feminism and Sexuality, 1890-1925", *Australian Feminist Studies* 7-8 (1988): 64-91.
--. *Rose Scott: Vision and Revision in Feminism*. Oxford: Oxford University Press, 1994.
--. *The Feminism of Charlotte Perkins Gilman: Sexualities, Histories, Progressivism*. Chicago: University of Chicago Press, 2009.
Amalgamated Clothing Workers of America (ACWA), Research Department. *The Clothing Workers of Chicago, 1910-1922*. Chicago: The Chicago Joint Board, ACWA, 1922.
Amsterdam, Susan. "The National Women's Trade Union League", *Social Service Review* 56, no. 2 (1982): 259-72.
"Another Chicago Waiters' Strike". *New York Times*, 9 July 1903, 12.
Ardis, Ann. *New Woman, New Novels: Feminism and Early Modernism*. New Brunswick: Rutgers University Press, 1990.
--. "Organizing Women: New Woman Writers, New Woman Readers, and Suffrage Feminism". In *Victorian Women Writers and the Woman Question*, edited by Nicola Diane Thompson. Cambridge: Cambridge University Press, 1999.
Auerbach, Nina. *Woman and the Demon: The Life of a Victorian Myth*. Cambridge, MA: Harvard University Press, 1982.
Ault, Phillip H. and Edwin Emery. *Reporting the News*. New York: Dodd, Mead and Co., 1959.
Bacchi, Carol L. "The 'Woman Question in South Australia". In *The Flinders History of South Australia: Social History*, edited by E. Richards. Adelaide: Wakefield Press, 1986, 403-32.
Bae, Youngsoo. *Labor in Retreat: Class and Community Among Men's Garment Workers of America*. Albany: State University of New York Press, 2001.
Bannister, Robert. *Social Darwinism: Science and Myth in Anglo-American Thought*. Philadelphia, PA: Temple University Press, 1989.
Barnard, Marjorie. *Miles Franklin*. New York: Twayne Publishers, 1967.
Baylen, J. O. "The 'New Journalism' in Late Victorian Britain". *Australian Journal of Politics and History* 18 (December 1972): 367-85.
Bederman, Gail. *Manliness and Civilization: A Cultural History of Gender and Race in the US, 1880-1914*. Chicago: University of Chicago Press, 1995.

Margaret Bettison and Jill Roe, "Miles Franklin's Topical Writings: A Listing", *Australian Literary Studies* 20, no. 1 (2001): 94–105.

Beer, Gillian. *The Romance*. London: Routledge and Kegan Paul, 1970.

Bennett, Susan. "Theatre History, Historiography and Women's Dramatic Writing". In *Women, Theatre and Performance: New Histories, New Historiographies*, edited by Maggie B. Gale and Vivian Gardner. Manchester: Manchester University Press, 2000, 46–59.

Bennett, Tony. "The Politics of 'The Popular' and Popular Culture". In *Popular Culture and Social Relations*, edited by Tony Bennett, Colin Mercer, and Janet Woollacott, Philadelphia, PA: Open University Press, 1986. 1–21.

Bird, Delys. "Miles Franklin". In *Australian Literature, 1788–1914*, edited by Selina Samuels. Detroit, MI: Gale, 2001. 113–130.

Birns, Nicholas. *Contemporary Australian Literature: A World Not Yet Dead*. Sydney: Sydney University Press, 2015.

Blake, Kathleen. *Love and the Woman Question in Victorian Literature: The Art of Self-Postponement*. Sussex: Harvester, 1983.

Bland, Lucy. *Banishing the Beast: Sexuality and the Early Feminists*. New York: New Press, 1995.

Bland, Lucy and Laura Doan. *Sexology Uncensored: The Documents of Sexual Science*. Chicago: University of Chicago Press, 1998.

Blood, Melanie N. "Theatre in Settlement Houses: Hull-House Players, Neighborhood Playhouse, and Karamu Theatre". *Theatre History Studies* 16 (1996): 4–69.

Brandes, Stuart D. *American Welfare Capitalism, 1880–1940*. Chicago: University of Chicago Press, 1976.

Bode, Katherine and Robert Dixon, eds. *Resourceful Reading: The New Empiricism, eResearch and Australian Literary Culture*. Sydney: Sydney University Press, 2009.

Bourke, Joanna. *Dismembering the Male: Britain, Male Bodies and the Great War*. Chicago: University of Chicago Press, 1996.

Breckinridge, Sophonisba P. "Concerning the Garment Workers' Strike (Chicago): Report of the Sub-Committee to the Citizens' Committee", History of Women, microfilm, no. 8605. New Haven, CT: Research Publications, 1977 (1910).

Brownfoot, Janice N. "Vida Jane Goldstein", *Australian Dictionary of Biography*, http://adb.anu.edu.au/biography/goldstein-vida-jane-6418.

Brunton, Paul. *Miles Franklin: A Brilliant Career?* Sydney: State Library of New South Wales, March 2004.

Brunton, Paul, ed., *The Diaries of Miles Franklin*. Crows Nest: State Library of New South Wales, 2004.

Bulmer, Martin. *The Chicago School of Sociology: Institutionalization, Diversity, and the Rise of Sociological Research*. Chicago: University of Chicago Press, 1984.

Cappetti, Carla. *Writing Chicago: Modernism, Ethnography, and the Novel*. New York: Columbia University Press, 1993.

Carnes, Michael. *Meanings for Manhood: Constructions of Masculinity in Victorian America*. Chicago: University of Chicago, 1990.

Case, Sue-Ellen. *Feminism and Theatre*. New York: Methuen, 1988.

Ceplair, Larry. *Charlotte Perkins Gilman: A Nonfiction Reader*. New York: Columbia University Press, 1991.

Chansky, Dorothy. *Composing Ourselves: The Little Theatre Movement and the American Audience*. Carbondale: Southern Illinois University Press, 2004.

"Chicago at the Front: A Condensed History of the Garment Workers' Strike". *Life and Labor*, January 1911, 4–13.

Chicago Vice Commission, "The Social Evil in Chicago: A Study of Existing Conditions with Recommendations by the Vice Commission of Chicago: A Municipal Body Appointed by the

Works Cited

Mayor and the City Council of the City of Chicago, and Submitted as its Report to the Mayor and City Council of Chicago, 1911."

"Chicago Waiters' Demands". *New York Times*, 17 April 1893, 2.

Christiansen, Richard. "Theater Companies." In *The Encyclopedia of Chicago*, edited by James R. Grossman, Ann D. Keating, and Janice L. Reiff. Chicago: University of Chicago Press, 2004, 817–18.

––. *A Theater of Our Own: A History and Memoir of 1001 Nights in Chicago*. Evanston, IL: Northwestern University Press, 2006.

Christie, Jane Johnstone. *The Advance of Woman from the Earliest Times to the Present*. Philadelphia, PA: J. B. Lippincott, 1912.

Chugerman, Samuel. *Lester F. Ward: The American Aristotle*. Durham, NC: Duke University Press, 1939.

Clark, Suzanne. *Sentimental Modernism: Women Writers and the Revolution of the Word*. Bloomington: University of Indiana Press, 1991.

"Clubwomen Lead Chicago Strike Riot". *New York Times*, 2 November 1910, 1.

Coleman, Verna. *Her Unknown Brilliant Career: Miles Franklin in America*. Sydney: Angus & Robertson, 1981.

Coles, Nicholas and Janet Zandy. *American Working-Class Literature: An Anthology*. New York: Oxford University Press, 2007.

Connelly, Mark, T. *The Response to Prostitution in the Progressive Era*. Chapel Hill: University of North Carolina Press, 1980.

Conor, Liz. *The Spectacular Modern Woman: Feminine Visibility in the 1920s*. Bloomington: Indiana University Press, 2004.

Cooper, Katherine and Emma Short, eds. *The Female Figure in Contemporary Historical Fiction*. London: Palgrave, 2012.

Crittenden, Ann. *The Price of Motherhood*. New York: Henry Holt, 2001.

Crotty, Martin. *Making the Australian Male: Middle-Class Masculinity, 1870–1925*. Melbourne: Melbourne University Press, 2001.

Dale, Leigh. "'Only Scratch the Surface': Reading Franklin's *Cockatoos*". *Southerly* 67, no. 1–2 (2007): 337–90.

Dalziell, Tanya. "Colonial Displacements: Another Look at *My Brilliant Career*". *ARIEL* 35, no. 3–4 (2004): 39–57.

––. *Settler Romances and the Australian Girl*. Perth: University of Western Australia Press, 2004.

––. "No Place for a Book? Fiction in Australia to 1890". In *The Cambridge History of Australian Literature*, edited by Peter Pierce. Melbourne: Cambridge University Press, 2009. 93–117.

Davis, Allen F. "The Women's Trade Union League: Origins and Organization." *Labor History* 5, no. 1 (1964): 3–17.

Davis, Jill. "The New Woman and the New Life". In *The New Woman and Her Sisters: Feminism and Theatre, 1850–1914*, edited by Vivien Gardner and Susan Rutherford. Hemel Hempstead: Harvester Wheatsheaf, 1992, 17–36.

Dawson, Graham. *Soldier Heroes: British Adventure, Empire and the Imagining of Masculinities*. Routledge, 1994.

Dell, Floyd. *Women as World Builders: Studies in Modern Feminism*. Chicago: Forbes, 1913.

––. *Homecoming: An Autobiography*. New York: Farrar and Rinehart, 1933.

D'Emilio, John, and Estelle B. Freedman. *Intimate Matters: A History of Sexuality in America*. New York: Harper, 1988.

Digby-Junger, Richard. *The Journalist as Reformer: Henry Demarest Lloyd and Wealth Against Commonwealth*. Westport, CT: Greenwood Press, 1996.

"Dinner Gifts for Strikers". *Chicago Daily Tribune*, 25 November 1910, 2.

Dixon, Ella Hepworth. "Why Women Are Ceasing to Marry." *Humanitarian* 14 (1899): 391–96.

Dixon, Robert. "The New Woman and the Coming Man". In *Debutante Nation: Feminism Contests the 1890s*, edited by Susan Magarey, Sue Rowley, Susan Sheridan. St. Leonards, NSW: Allen & Unwin, 1993, 163–74.

--. "Home or Away? The Trope of Place in Australian Literary Criticism and Literary History". *Westerly* 54, no. 1 (2009): 12–17.

Dixon, Robert and Veronica Kelly. *Impact of the Modern: Vernacular Modernities in Australia 1870s–1960s*. Sydney: Sydney University Press, 2008.

Dixon, Robert and Brigid Rooney, eds. *Scenes of Reading: Is Australian Literature a World Literature?* Melbourne: Australian Scholarly Publishing, 2013.

Doan, Laura, L. ed. *Old Maids to Radical Spinsters: Unmarried Women in the Twentieth-Century Novel*. Urbana, IL: University of Chicago Press, 1991.

Dolan, Jill. *The Feminist Spectator as Critic*. Ann Arbor: Michigan University Press, 1988.

Donovan, Brian. *White Slave Crusades*. Urbana: University of Illinois Press, 2006.

Doyle, Laura and Laura Winkiel. "Introduction: The Global Horizons of Modernism". In *Geomodernism: Race, Modernism, Modernity*, edited by Laura Doyle and Laura Winkiel. Bloomington: Indiana University Press, 2005. 1–16.

Dreier, Mary. Margaret Dreier Robins, *Her Life, Letters and Work*. New York: Island Press Cooperative, 1950.

Duffy, Daniel. "Feminist Discourse in Popular Drama of the Early- and Mid-Victorian Era". In *Feminist Readings of Popular Victorian Texts*, edited by Emma Liggins and Daniel Duffy. Aldershot, UK: Ashgate, 2001, 126–46.

Dukore, Bernard F. *Maurice Browne and the Chicago Little Theatre*. Urbana: University of Illinois, 1957.

Duncan, Roy. "Introduction". In *On Dearborn Street*, by Miles Franklin. St Lucia: University of Queensland Press/Australian Large Print, 1981, iii–xvii.

DuPlessis, Rachel Blau. *Writing Beyond the Ending: Narrative Strengths of Twentieth-Century Women Writers*. Bloomington: Indiana University Press, 1985.

Dvorak, Robert. "The Chicago Garment Workers". *The International Socialist Review* 11, no. 6 (1910): 353–59.

Eagleton, Mary. "Gender and Genre". In *Re-Reading the Short Story*, edited by Clare Hanson. New York: St Martin's Press, 1989. 55–68.

Eagleton, Terry. *Literary Theory*. Oxford: Blackwell, 1983.

Edwards, P.D. "Sensation Novels". In *Victorian Britain: An Encyclopedia*, edited by Sally Mitchell. London: Garland, 1988 703–4.

Eltis, Sos. "The Fallen Woman in Edwardian Feminist Drama: Suffrage, Sex and the Single Girl", *English Literature in Transition, 1880–1920* 50, no. 1 (2007): 27–49.

"The End of the Struggle: the Chicago Garment Workers' Strike". *Life and Labor,* March 1911, 88–89.

Faderman, Lillian. *Surpassing the Love of Men: Romantic Friendships and Love between Women from the Renaissance to the Present*. New York: Harper Collins, 1998.

Feffer, Andrew. *The Chicago Pragmatists and American Progressivism*. Ithaca, NY: Cornell University Press, 1993.

Fell Alison. "Gendering the War Story", *Journal of War and Culture Studies* 1, no. 1 (2007): 53–58;

Felski, Rita. *The Gender of Modernity*. Cambridge, MA: Harvard University Press, 1995.

--. "Afterword". In *Women's Experience of Modernity, 1875–1945*, edited by Ann L. Ardis and Leslie W. Lewis. Baltimore, MD: Johns Hopkins Press, 2003, 290–99.

--. "Context Stinks". *New Literary History* 42, no. 4 (2011): 573–91.

Ferrier, Carole, ed. *Gender, Politics, History: Twentieth Century Australian Women's Novels*. St Lucia: University of Queensland Press, 1985.

Ferres, Kay, ed. *The Time to Write: Australian Women Writers 1890–1930*. Penguin: Melbourne, 1993.

Ferrill, Harriet. "Some Side Lights on the Strike of the Garment Workers", *Chicago Daily Tribune*, 13 November 1910, 3.

Works Cited

"Fetes for Strikers' Young", *Chicago Daily Tribune*, 24 December 1910, 4.
Fitzsimmons, Linda and Vivien Gardner, eds. *New Women Plays*. London: Methuen, 1991.
Flanagan, Maureen. *Seeing With their Hearts: Chicago Women and the Vision of the Good City, 1871-1933*. Princeton, NJ: Princeton University Press, 2002.
Flexner, Eleanor. *Century of Struggle: The Woman's Rights Movement in the United States*. New York: Atheneum, 1974.
Foner, Philip S. and Ronald Lewis. *The Black Worker: A Documentary History From Colonial Times to the Present, vol. 1: The Black Worker to 1859*. Philadelphia, PA: Temple University Press, 1978.
Francis, Mark and Michael Taylor, eds. *Herbert Spencer: Legacies*. Abingdon, Oxon: Routledge, 2015.
Franklin, Miles. "The Survivors", 1908, ML MSS 445/25/1.
- -. "Uncle Robert's Wedding Present", 1908, ML MSS 445/21.
- -. "Teaching Him", n.d., circa. 1909, ML MSS 445/22.
- -. *Some Everyday Folk and Dawn*. Edinburgh: Blackwood, 1909.
- -. "When Cupid Tarried", n.d. circa. 1909, ML MSS 445/18.
- -. "The Love Machine", n.d. circa. 1909, ML MSS 445/2.
- -. "Mrs. Mulvaney's Moccasins", n.d. circa. 1911, ML MSS 445/22.
- -. [Grandpa Griddle] "The Illogical Sex", *Life and Labor*, September 1911, 287–288.
- -. "Aunt Sophie Smashes a Triangle", n.d. circa. 1913, ML MSS 445/25/2
- -. "The Waiter Speaks", n.d. circa. 1913, ML MSS 6035/14.
- -. "Aunt Toby's Party: How I Queered a Queer's Party", n.d. circa. 1913, ML MSS 445/22.
- -. "When Bobby 'Got' Religion", 1914, ML MSS 445/21.
- -. "Red Cross Nurse and Armored Chauffeur", 1914, ML MSS 445/3
- -. "A Business Emergency" [Mr. and Mrs.Ogniblat L'Artsau], n.d. circa. 1915, ML MSS 364/58.
- -. "Virtue" [Mr. and Mrs. Ogniblat L'Artsau], n.d. circa. 1915, ML MSS 445/28/6
- -. [Mr. and Mrs. Ogniblat L'Artsau]. *The Net of Circumstance*. London: Mills and Boon, 1915.
- -. "Sam Price from Chicago", n.d., circa. 1921, ML MSS 445/17.
- -. [Brent of Bin Bin]. *Back to Bool Bool: A Ramiparous Novel with Several Prominent Characters and a Hantle of Others Disposed as the Atolls of Oceania's Archipelagoes*. Edinburgh: Blackwood, 1931.
- -. *My Career Goes Bung: Purporting to Be the Autobiography of Sybylla Penelope Melvyn*. Melbourne: Georgian House, 1946.
- -. *Cockatoos: A Story of Youth and Exodists*. Sydney: Angus & Robertson, 1954.
- -. *Laughter, Not for a Cage: Notes on Australian Writing, with Biographical Emphasis on the Struggles, Function, and Achievements of the Novel in Three Half-Centuries*. Sydney: Angus & Robertson, 1956.
- -. *My Brilliant Career*. Sydney: Angus & Robertson, 1979 [1901].
- -. *The End of My Career*. New York: St. Martin's Press, 1981.
- -. *On Dearborn Street*. St Lucia: University of Queensland Press/Australian Large Print, 1987.
Franklin, S. M. "The Women Delegates", *Life and Labor*, August 1912, 234–36.
- -. "Walter Burley Griffin, Winner of the Federal Capital Prize", *Daily Telegraph* (Sydney), 3 August 1912, 15.
- -. "Women to March on the Coliseum", *The World*, 25 August 1912.
- -. "The Women Delegates", *Life and Labor*, August 1912, 234–36.
- -. "Henry Demarest Lloyd", *Life and Labor*, September 1912, 275–76.
- -. "Elizabeth Maloney and the High-Calling of the Waitress, *Life and Labor*, February 1913, 36–40.
- -. "When We Have Time to Read: My Little Sister", *Life and Labor*, March 1913, 83–84.
- -. "Women and War: Chicago's Little Theatre", *Life and Labor*, March 1913, 87.
- -. "Suffragette Militancy". *Life and Labor*, April 1913, 128.
- -. "When We Have Time to Read: Way Stations". *Life and Labor,* June 1913, 181–82.
- -. "When We Have Time to Read: V.V.'s Eyes", *Life and Labor*, October 1913, 364–66.
- -. "Mrs Pankhurst in the United States". *Life and Labor*, December 1913, 364–66.

--. "Agnes Nestor of the Glove Workers: A Leader in the Women's Movement". *Life and Labor*, December 1913, 370-74.

--. "The Menace of Great Armaments", *Life and Labor*, September, 1914, 260-63.

Franklin, S.M. and Alice Henry. "Why 50,000 Refused to Sew". *The Englishwoman* 10 (June 1911): 297-308.

Freeman, Ruth and Patricia Klaus. "Blessed or not? The New Spinster in England and the United States in the Late-Nineteenth and Early-Twentieth Centuries". *Journal of Family History* 9, no. 4 (1984): 394-414.

"From Near and Far: Drama League of America", *Life and Labor*, March/April 1911, 93.

Fuss, Diana. *Essentially Speaking: Feminism, Nature and Difference*. New York: Routledge, 1989.

Gale, Maggie B. and Vivien Gardner, eds. *Women, Theatre and Performance: New Histories, New Historiographies*. Manchester: Manchester University Press, 2000.

Gardner, Susan. "My Brilliant Career: Portrait of the Artist as a Wild Colonial Girl". In *Gender, Politics and Fictions: Twentieth Century Australian Women's Novels*, edited by Carole Ferrier. St Lucia: University of Queensland Press, 1985. 22-43.

Gardner, Vivien G. and Susan R. Rutherford. *The New Woman and Her Sisters: Feminism and Theatre, 1850-1914*. Ann Arbor: University of Michigan Press, 1992.

Garton, Stephen. "Contesting Enslavement: Marriage, Manhood and *My Brilliant Career*", *Australian Literary Studies* 20, no. 4 (2002): 336-49.

Gavin, Adrienne E. and Carolyn W. de la Oulton, eds. *Writing Women of the Fin de Siècle: Authors of Change*, Basingstoke: Palgrave Macmillan, 2012.

Gilbert, Sandra M. and Susan Gubar. *The Madwoman in the Attic: The Woman Writer and the Nineteenth-Century Literary Imagination*. New Haven, CT: Yale University Press, 1979.

Giles, Paul. *Antipodean America: Australasia and the Constitution of U.S. Literature*. Oxford: Oxford University Press, 2013.

Gilman, Charlotte Perkins. *The Home: Its Work and Influence*. New York: McClure, Philips & Co, 1993 [1903].

--. *Women and Economics; A Study of the Economic Relation Between Men and Women as a Factor in Social Evolution*. Boston: Small, Maynard & Co, 1910 [1898].

"The Girls' Own Stories". *Life and Labor*, February 1911, 51-52.

Glenn, Susan A. *Daughters of the Shetl: Life and Labor in the Immigrant Generation*. Ithaca, NY: Cornell University Press, 1990.

Grand, Sarah (Frances McFall). *The Beth Book: Being a Study of the Life of Elizabeth Caldwell McClure, A Woman of Genius*. New York: Dial, 1980 [1897].

Green, Laura. "'I Recognize Myself in Her': Identification with the Reader in George Eliot's The Mill on the Floss and Simone de Beauvoir's Memoirs of a Dutiful Daughter", *Tulsa Studies in Women's Literature* 24, no. 1 (2005): 57-79.

Greiner, Donald J. *Adultery in the American Novel: Updike, James, Henry, 1843-1916*. Columbia: University of South Carolina Press, 1987.

Griffin, Robert J. "Anonymity and Authorship". *New Literary History* 30, no. 4 (1999): 877-95.

Grimshaw, Patricia. "Bessie Harrison Lee and the Fight for Voluntary Motherhood". In *Double Time: Women in Victoria -150 Years*, edited by Marilyn Lake and Farley Kelly. Melbourne: Penguin, 1985. 139-47.

Hall, Leslie A. "Hauling Down the Double Standard: Feminism, Social Purity and Sexual Science in Late Nineteenth-Century Britain". *Gender and History* 16, no. 1 (2004): 36-56.

--. *Sex, Gender and Social Change in Britain Since 1880*. New York: Palgrave Macmillan, 2013.

Hamilton, Cicely. *Marriage as a Trade*. Detroit: Singing Tree Press, 1971 [1909].

Hampton, Mark. *Visions of the Press in Britain, 1850-1950*. Urbana: University of Illinois Press, 2004.

Hanson, Clare. "'Things Out of Words': Towards a Poetics of Short Fiction". In *Re-Reading the Short Story*, edited by Clare Hanson. New York: St Martin's Press, 1989. 22-33.

Hanson, Clare, ed. *Re-Reading the Short Story*. New York: St Martin's Press, 1989.

Works Cited

Hansord, Kate. "Symbolism and the Antipodes: The Fallen Woman in Caroline Leakey's *Lyra Australis, or Attempts to Sing in a Strange World*". *Australian Literary Studies* 30, no. 3 (2015): 121–33.
Harding, G. L. "Feminism and the Propagandist Drama", *The Freewoman*, 14 December 1911, 76–78.
Hart, John. *Floyd Dell*. New York: Twayne Publishing, 1971.
Hawkins, Mike. *Social Darwinism in European and American Thought, 1860–1945*. New York: Cambridge University Press, 1997.
Hedley, Jocelyn. "The Unpublished Plays of Miles Franklin". Master's Thesis, School of English, Media and Performing Arts, University of New South Wales (Sydney), 2007.
Heffernan, Laura. "Reading Modernism's Cultural Field: Rebecca West's The Strange Necessity and the Aesthetic, "Systems of Relations", *Tulsa Studies in Women's Literature* 27, no. 2 (2008): 309.
Heilmann, Ann. *The Late-Victorian Marriage Question, vol. 1: Marriage and Motherhood*. New York: Routledge, 1998.
--. *New Woman Fiction: Women Writing First-Wave Feminism*. New York: St Martin's Press, 2000.
--. *New Woman Strategies: Sarah Grand, Olive Schreiner, Mona Caird*. Manchester: Manchester University Press, 2004.
Heilmann, Ann, ed. *Feminist Forerunners: New Womanism and Feminism in the Early Twentieth Century*. London: Pandora, 2003.
Heilmann, Ann and Margaret Beetham, eds. *New Women Hybridities: Femininity, Feminism and International Consumer Culture*. New York: Routledge, 2004.
Henderson, Ian. "Gender, Genre, and Sybylla's Performative Identity in Miles Franklin's *My Brilliant Career*", *Australian Literary Studies* 18, no. 2 (1997): 165–73.
--. "The Body of an Australian Girl", in *Feminism and the Body: Interdisciplinary Perspectives*, edited by Catherine Kevin. Newcastle: Cambridge Scholars, 2009, 116–33.
Henry, Alice. *Trade Union Woman*. New York: D. Appleton and Co., 1915.
--. *Women and the Labor Movement*. New York: George H. Doran, 1923.
Henry, Alice and S.M. Franklin. "Suffragists Annoyed", *Daily Telegraph* (Sydney), 6 November 1912, 15.
Higgs, Kerryn. "The Cosmopolitan Bushwoman". *Women's Review of Books* 27, no. 4 (July/August 2010): 10–12.
Hipsky, Martin. *Modernism and the Women's Popular Romance in Britain, 1885–1925*. Athens: Ohio University Press, 2011.
"Holding the Fort: The Chicago Garment Workers' Strike", *Life and Labor*, February 1911, 48–50.
Holdsworth, Annie E. *A Garden of Spinsters*. Leipzig: Tauchnitz, 1904.
Holland, Kathryn. "Late Victorian and Feminist Intertexts: The Strachey Women in *A Room of One's Own* and *Three Guineas*". *Tulsa Studies in Women's Literature* 32 (2013): 75–98.
Holmes, Katie. "Spinster Indispensable: Feminists, Single Women and the Critique of Marriage, 1890–1920". *Australian Historical Studies* 29, no. 110 (1998): 68–90.
Howlett, Caroline. "Femininity Slashed: Suffragette Militancy, Modernism and Gender". In *Modernist Sexualities*, edited by Hugh Stevens and Caroline Howlett. Manchester: Manchester University Press, 2000. 72–91.
Hughes, Winifred. *The Maniac in the Cellar: Sensation Novels of the 1860s*. Princeton, NJ: Princeton University Press, 1980.
Hyman, Colette A. "Labor Organizing and Female Institution-Building: The Chicago Women's Trade Union League, 1904–1924". In *Women, Work and Protest: A Century of US Women's Labor History*, edited by Ruth Milkman. Boston: Routledge and Kegan Paul, 1985. 22–41.
Jackson, Shannon. *Lines of Activity: Performance, Historiography, Hull-House Domesticity*. Ann Arbor: University of Michigan Press, 2000.
Jeffreys, Sheila. *The Spinster and Her Enemies: Feminism and Sexuality, 1880–1930*. London: Pandora, 1985.
Jenkins, Alice and Juliet John, eds. *Rereading Victorian Fiction*. New York: Palgrave, 2000.

Jensen, Kimberly and Erika Kuhlmans, eds. *Women and Transnational Activism in Historical Context*. Dordrecht, Netherlands: Republic of Letters Press, 2010.

Johnson, Michael. *The New Journalism: The Underground Press, the Artists of Nonfiction, and Changes in the Established Media*. Lawrence: University of Kansas Press, 1971.

Johnson, R. Brimley. *Some Contemporary Novelists (Women)*. London: Leonard Parsons, 1920.

Josephson, Matthew. *Union House, Union Bar: The History of the Hotel and Restaurant Employees' and Bartenders' International Union, AFL-CIO*. New York: Random House, 1956.

Jusova, Iveta. *The New Woman and the Empire*. Columbus: Ohio State University Press, 2005.

Katz, Susan L. "Singleness of Heart: Spinsterhood in Victorian Culture". PhD dissertation, Columbia University, 1988.

Kelly, Katherine E. ed. *Modern Drama by Women, 1880s–1930s: An International Anthology*. London: Routledge, 1996.

Kent, Valerie. "Alias Miles Franklin". In *Gender, Politics, History: Twentieth Century Australian Women's Novels*, edited by Carole Ferrier. St Lucia: University of Queensland Press, 1985. 44–58.

Kessler-Harris, Alice. *Out to Work: A History of Wage-Earning Women in the United States*. New York: Oxford University Press, 1982.

--. *Gendering Labor History*. Urbana: University of Illinois Press, 2007.

Kimmel, Michael. *Manhood in America: A Cultural History*. New York: Free Press, 1996.

Kirkby, Diane. "Miles Franklin on Dearborn Street, 1906–15". *Australian Literary Studies* 10, no. 3 (1982): 344–57.

Kirkpatrick, Peter. "Dulcie Deamer and the Bohemian Body". In *Wallflowers and Witches: Women and Culture in Australia, 1910–1945*, edited by Maryanne Dever. St Lucia: University of Queensland Press, 1994.

Knowles, Sandra. "'Oh, for Some Refuge – for Myself – to Be Myself': The Search for Gender Neutrality in the Diaries of Miles Franklin", *Australian Feminist Studies* 25, no. 63 (2010): 63–77.

Kranidis, Rita S. *Subversive Discourse: The Cultural Production of Late Victorian Feminist Novels*. New York: St Martin's Press, 1995.

--. *The Victorian Spinster and Colonial Emigration*. New York: St Martin's Press, 1999.

Krueger, Kate. "Evelyn Sharp's Working Women and the Dilemma of the Urban Romance", *Women Writing* 19, no. 4 (2012): 563–83.

Krueger, Kate, ed. *British Writers and the Short Story, 1850–1930: Reclaiming Social Space*. New York: Palgrave Macmillan, 2014.

Lacey, Candida Ann. "Striking Fictions: Women Writers and the Making of a Proletarian Realism". *Women's Studies International Forum* 9, no. 4 (1986): 373–84.

Lake, Marilyn. "Sexuality and Feminism: Some Notes on their Australian History", *Lilith* 7 (1991): 33–5.

--. "Between Old Worlds and New: Feminist Citizenship, Nation, and Race, and the Destabilisation of Identity". In *Suffrage and Beyond: International Feminist Perspectives*, edited by Caroline Daley and Melanie Nolan. New York: New York University Press, 1994.

__. *Getting Equal: The History of Australian Feminism*. St Leonards, NSW: Allen & Unwin, 1999.

Lake, Marilyn and Henry Reynolds. *Drawing the Colour Line: White Men's Countries and the International Challenge of Racial Equality*. Cambridge: Cambridge University Press, 2008.

Laite, Julia A. "The Association for Moral and Social Hygiene: Abolitionism and Prostitution Law in Britain (1915-1959)". *Women's History Review* 17, no. 2 (2008): 207–223.

Lamond, Julianne. "Stella vs. Miles: Women Writers and Literary Value". *Meanjin Quarterly* 70, no. 3 (2011). https://meanjin.com.au/essays/stella-vs-miles-women-writers-and-literary-value-in-australia/

Lang, Anouk, "Modernity in Practice: A Comparative View of the Cultural Dynamics of Modernist Literary Production in Australia and Canada", *Canadian Literature* 209 (2011): 48–65.

Langbauer, Laurie. *Women and Romance: The Consolidation of the English Novel*. Ithaca, NY: Cornell University Press, 1990.

Works Cited

Leckie, Barbara. *Culture and Adultery: The Novel, the Newspaper, the Law, 1857–1914*. Philadelphia: University of Pennsylvania Press, 2015.
Ledger, Sally. "The New Woman and the Crisis of Victorianism". In *Cultural Politics at the Fin de Siècle*, edited by Sally Ledger and Scott McCracken. Cambridge: Cambridge University Press, 1995, 22–45.
––. *The New Woman: Fiction and Feminism at the Fin de Siècle*. College Station: Penn State University Press, 1999.
Lee, Janet. "Miles Franklin on American Manhood and White Slavery: The Case of 'Red Cross Nurse'". *Australian Literary Studies* 23, no. 1 (2007): 36–48.
––. "Miles Franklin and 'The Survivors'". *Australian Literary Studies* 26, no. 1 (2011): 83–93.
––. "'The Waiter Speaks': Stella Miles Franklin and the Chicago Garment Workers' Strike". *Women Studies International Forum* 34 (2011): 290–301.
––. "'Marriage Among the 'Murkans': Miles Franklin's Marriage Problem Stories". *Australian Feminist Studies* 26, no. 70 (2011): 469–483.
––. "'Aunt Sophie Smashes a Triangle': Stella Miles Franklin and the 1913 Adultery Narratives". *Journal of Australian Studies* 37, no. 2 (2013): 225–42.
––. "The Chicago Spinsters: Stella Miles Franklin and the New Woman Response to Marriage Inequality". *Women's Studies International Forum* 44 (May–June 2014): 1–9.
––. "How Miles Franklin Queered a Queer's Party". *Hecate: An Interdisciplinary Journal of Women's Liberation* 39, no. 1/2 (2014): 64–71.
––. "'Living in Sin': Money and Morals in 'Virtue', a Play by Stella Miles Franklin". *Australian Literary Studies* 31, no. 5 (2016): 1–12.
––. "'Early Flower Meets Petted Lion': The New Woman and the Pro-Feminist Man in Miles Franklin's 'Lost' Novel, The Net of Circumstance", *Women: A Cultural Review* 28, no. 3 (2017): 193–216.
Liggins, Emma. "Writing Against the 'Husband-Fiend': Syphilis and Male Sexual Vice in the New Woman Novel", *Women's Writing* 7, no. 2 (2000):175–95.
––. "Introduction: 'New' Female Sexualities, 1870–1930", *Critical Survey* 15, no. 3 (2003): 1–4.
––. "Prostitution and Social Purity in the 1880s and 1890s", *Critical Survey* 15, no. 3 (2003): 39–55.
––. "Having a Good Time Single?" In *Writing Women of the Fin de Siècle: Authors of Change*, edited by Adrienne E. and Carolyn W. de la Oulton. Basingstoke: Palgrave Macmillan, 2012, 98–110.
––. "The 'Modern Spinster's Lot' and Female Sexuality in Ella Hepworth Dixon's *One Doubtful Hour*", *Women's Writing* 19, no. 1 (2012): 5–22.
Liggins, Emma, ed. *Odd Women? Spinsters, Lesbians and Widows in British Women's Fiction, 1850s–1930s*. Manchester: Manchester University Press, 2014.
Liggins, Emma and Daniel D. Duffy. *Feminist Readings of Victorian Popular Texts: Divergent Femininities*. Brookfield, VT: Ashgate, 2001.
Liggins, Emma, Andrew Maunder and Ruth Robbins, *The British Short Story*. New York: Palgrave, 2011.
"Lights and Shadows in Christmas Eve Incidents". *Chicago Daily Tribune*, 25 December 1910, 4.
Lindberg, Richard. *Chicago by Gaslight: A History of Chicago's Netherworld, 1880–1920*. Chicago: Academy Chicago Publishers, 1996.
Link, Arthur S. and Richard L. McCormick. *Progressivism*. Arlington Heights, IL: Harlan, Davidson, 1983.
Demarest Lloyd to Miles Franklin, 24 and 30 September 1914, ML MSS 364/12.
Lovell, Terry. "Consuming Fiction". In *The New Man, Masculinity and Marriage in the Victorian Novel*, ed. Tanya MacDonald. New York: Routledge, 2016.
Mackinnon, Alison. *Love and Freedom: Professional Women and the Reshaping of Personal Life*. Cambridge: Cambridge University Press, 1997.
Macieski, Robert. "Life and Labor". *History Workshop Journal* 22, no. 1 (1986): 173–77.

Magarey, Susan. "History, Cultural Studies, and Another Look at First-Wave Feminism in Australia", *Australian Literary Studies* 106 (1996): 96–110.

--. *Passions of First-Wave Feminists*. Sydney: University of New South Wales Press, 2001.

--. "My Brilliant Career and Feminism". *Australian Literary Studies* 20, no. 4 (2002): 389–98.

Magarey, Susan, Sue Rowley, and Susan Sheridan, eds, *Debutante Nation: Feminism Contests the 1890s*. St Leonards, NSW: Allen & Unwin, 1993.

Martin, Susan K. "Relative Correspondence: Franklin's *My Brilliant Career* and the Influence of Nineteenth-Century Australian Women's Writings". In *The Time to Write: Australian Women Writers, 1890–1930*, edited by Kay Ferres. London: Penguin Books, 1993.

Martin, Sylvia. *Passionate Friends: Mary Fullerton. Mabel Singleton, and Miles Franklin*. London: Onlywomen Press, 2001.

Mason, Ethel, and S.M. Franklin. "Low Wages and Vice – Are They Related? Chicago Testimony". *Life and Labor*, April 1913, 108–11.

Mayne, Judith. *Cinema and Spectatorship*. New York: Routledge, 1993.

McCann, Andrew. "Unknown Australia: Rosa Praed's Vanished Race". *Australian Literary Studies* 22, no. 1 (2005): 37–51.

McCreesh, Carolyn Daniel. *Women in the Campaign to Organize Garment Workers, 1880–1917*. New York: Garland, 1985.

McInherny, Francis. "Miles Franklin, *My Brilliant Career* and the Female Tradition", *Australian Literary Studies* 9 (1980): 275–85.

Mead, Philip. "Nation, Literature, Location". In *The Cambridge History of Australian Literature*, edited by Peter Pierce. Melbourne: Cambridge University Press, 2009. 549–67.

Mencken, Henry Louis. "The Literary Capital of the United States". In *On American Books*, edited by Francis Hackett. New York: W.B. Huebsch, 1920.

Meyer, Jessica. *Men of War: Masculinity and the First World War in Britain*. New York: Palgrave Macmillan, 2009.

Miller, Jane E. *Rebel Women: Feminism, Modernism and the Edwardian Novel*. London: Virago, 1994.

Mizruchi, Susan L. "Becoming Multicultural: Culture, Economy, and the Novel". In *Cambridge History of American Literature*, vol.3: Prose Writing, 1860–1992, edited by Sacvan Bercovitch. New York: Cambridge University Press, 2005. 413–740.

Modjeski, Drusilla. *Exiles at Home: Australian Women Writers, 1925–1945*. Sydney: Angus & Robertson, 1981.

Morrison, Fiona. *Christina Stead and the Matter of America*. Sydney: Sydney University Press, 2019.

Mrozek, Donald J. "The Habit of Victory: the American Military and the Cult of Manliness", In *Manliness and Morality: Middle-class Masculinity in Britain and America, 1800–1940*, edited by J.A. Mangan and James Walvin. New York: St Martin's Press, 1987. 220–241.

National Women's Trade Union League (NWTUL). "Some Facts Regarding Unorganized Working Women in the Sweated Industries". *History of Women*, no. 8623, microfilm. New Haven, CT: Research Publications, 1977 [1914].

Nead, Lynda. *Myths of Sexuality: Representations of Women in Victorian Britain*. Oxford: Basil Blackwell, 1988.

Nekola, Charlotte and Paula Rabinowitz, eds. *Writing Red: An Anthology of American Women Writers, 1930–1940*. New York: Feminist Press at the City University of New York, 1987.

Newey, Kate. "Women's Playwriting and the Popular Theatre in the Late-Victorian Era, 1870–1900". In *Feminist Readings of Popular Victorian Texts*, edited by Emma Liggins and Daniel Duffy. Aldershot, UK: Ashgate, 2001. 147–67.

Newlin, Keith. *American Plays of the New Woman*. Chicago: Ivan R. Dee, 2000.

Oldfield, Sybil. "From Rachel's Aunts to Miss La Trobe: Spinsters in the Fiction of Virginia Woolf". In *Old Maids to Radical Spinsters: Unmarried Women in the Twentieth-Century Novel*, edited by Laura L. Doan. Urbana, IL: University of Chicago Press, 1991. 85–103.

Works Cited

Olson, Liesl. *Chicago Renaissance: Literature and Visual Art in the Midwest Metropolis*. New Haven, CT: Yale University Press, 2017.

Olubas, Brigitta. "'Infinite Rehearsal' in the Work of Miles Franklin". *New Literature Review* 18 (1989): 39–47.

Ouida, "The New Woman", *North American Review* 158 [1894]: 610–19.

Overton, Bill. *Fictions of Female Adultery, 1684–1890: Theories and Circumtexts*. New York: Palgrave Macmillan, 2002.

Parkins, Wendy. "Moving Dangerously; Mobility and the Modern Woman". *Tulsa Studies in Women's Literature* 20, no. 1 (2001): 77–92.

Paris, Michael. *Warrior Nation*. London: Reaktion Books, 2000.

Passet, Joanne. *Sex Radicals and the Quest for Women's Equality*. Chicago: University of Illinois Press, 2003

Pastorello, Karen. *A Power Among Them: Bessie Abramowitz Hillman and the Making of the Amalgamated Clothing Workers of America*. Urbana: University of Illinois Press, 2008.

Patterson, Martha H. *The American New Woman Revisited*. New Brunswick, NJ: Rutgers University Press, 2008.

Payne, Elizabeth A. *Reform, Labor, and Feminism: Margaret Dreier Robins and the NWTUL*. Urbana: University of Illinois Press, 1988.

Peiss, Kathy. *Cheap Amusements: Working Women and Leisure in Turn-of-the-Century New York*. Philadelphia: Temple University Press, 1986.

Pfisterer, Susan, ed. *Tremendous Worlds: Australian Women's Drama 1890–1960*. Sydney: Currency Press, 1999.

Pfisterer, Susan and Carolyn Pickett. *Playing with Ideas: Australian Women Playwrights From the Suffragettes to the Sixties*. Sydney: Currency Press, 1999.

Pinkerton, Jan and Randolph H. Hudson, eds. *Encyclopedia of the Chicago Literary Renaissance*. New York: Fact on File Inc., 2004.

Postlewait, Thomas. "From Melodrama to Realism: The Suspect History of American Drama". In *Melodrama: The Cultural Emergence of Genre*, edited by Michael Hays and Anastasia Nikolopoulou. London: Macmillan, 1996.

Prime, Leonie N. "The New Woman and the Australian Girl". MPhil thesis, University of Western Australia, 1998.

Pykett, Lyn. "Writing Around Modernism: May Sinclair and Rebecca West". In *Outside Modernism: In Pursuit of the English Novel, 1900–1930*, edited by Lynne Hapgood and Nancy L. Paxton. New York: St Martin's Press, 2000. 103–122.

--. *The "Improper" Feminine: The Women's Sensation Novel and the New Womanv Writing*. London: Routledge, 1992.

--. *Engendering Fictions: The English Novel in the Early Twentieth Century*. London: Edward Arnold, 1995.

Rich, Charlotte J. *Transcending the New Woman: Multiethnic Narratives in the Progressive Era*. Columbia: University of Missouri Press, 2009.

Richardson, Angelique. *Love and Eugenics in the Late Nineteenth Century*. Oxford: Oxford University Press, 2003.

--. "Introduction", in *Women Who Did: Stories by Men and Women*, edited by Angelique Richardson. London: Penguin, 2002.

Richardson, Angelique, and Chris Willis, eds. *The New Woman in Fiction and in Fact: Fin-de-Siècle Feminisms*. New York: Palgrave, 2001.

Robins, Margaret Dreier. "More About Pearl Buttons". *Life and Labor* (December 1911), 377–79.

Robinson, Paul. *The Modernization of Sex: Havelock Ellis, Alfred Kinsey, William Masters, and Virginia Johnson*. New York: Harper & Row, 1976.

Roe, Jill. "The Significant Silence: Miles Franklin's Middle Years". *Meanjin Quarterly* 39, no. 1 (1980): 48–59.

--. "Introduction." *Everyday Folks and Dawn*. London: Virago, 1986.
--. *My Congenials: Miles Franklin and Friends in Letters, vol. 1: 1879–1938*. Sydney: Angus & Robertson, 1993.
--. "The World of Miles Franklin". *Southerly* 54, no. 4 (1995): 84–94.
--. *Stella Miles Franklin: A Biography*. Sydney: Fourth Estate/Harper Collins, 2008.
--. "Miles Franklin's Record". *Australian*, 13 August 2012, 13.
Roe, Jill and Margaret Bettison, eds. *A Gregarious Culture: Topical Writings of Miles Franklin*. St Lucia: University of Queensland Press, 2001.
Rosen, Ruth. *The Lost Sisterhood: Prostitution in America, 1900–1918*. Baltimore, MD: Johns Hopkins Press, 1982.
Rosenthal, Naomi Braun. *Spinster Tales and Womanly Possibilities*. Albany: State University of New York Press, 2002.
Ross, Jack. *The Socialist Party of America: A Complete History*. Lincoln, NE: Potomac Books, 2015.
Satter, Beryl. *Each Mind a Kingdom: American Women, Sexual Purity and the New Thought Movement, 1875–1920*. Berkeley: University of California Press, 2001.
Scates, Bruce. "*My Brilliant Career* and Radicalism." *Australian Literary Studies* 20, no. 4 (2002): 370–78.
Schaffer, Talia. "Writing a Public Self: Alice Meynell's 'Unstable Equilibrium'". In *Women's Experience of Modernity, 1875–1945*, edited by Ann L. Ardis and Leslie W. Lewis. Baltimore, MD: Johns Hopkins Press, 2003. 13–30.
Schmidt-Haberkamp, Barbara. "Performing Gender and Genre in Miles Franklin's *My Career Goes Bung*". *Connotations* 9, no. 3 (1999/2000): 289–95.
Schroeder, Patricia. *The Feminist Possibilities of Dramatic Realism*. Madison, WI: Farleigh Dickinson Press, 1996.
Scott, Bonnie Kime, ed., *The Gender of Modernism: A Critical Anthology*. Bloomington: Indiana University Press, 1990
Scott, Clifford H. *Lester Frank Ward*. Boston: Twayne Publishing, 1976.
Searles, Patricia and Janet Mickish. "'A Thoroughbred Girl': Images of Female Gender Role in Turn-of-the-Century Mass Media". *Women's Studies* 3 (1984): 261–81.
"See Pictures; Forget Strike". *Chicago Daily Tribune*, 17 November 1910, 3.
Shaw, Valerie. *The Short Story: A Critical Introduction*. London: Longman, 1983.
Shepherd-Barr, Kirsten E. "'It Was Ugly': The Maternal Instinct on State at the Fin de Siècle". *Women: A Cultural Review* 23, no. 2 (2012): 216–34.
Sheridan, Susan. "'Temper, Romantic; Bias, Offensively Feminine': Australian Women Writers and Literary Nationalism". *Kunapipi* 7, no. 2–3 (1985): 49–58.
--. "Louisa Lawson, Miles Franklin, and Feminist Writing, 1888–1901". *Australian Feminist Studies* 7, no. 8 (1988): 29–47.
--. *Along the Faultlines: Sex, Race and Nation in Australian Women's Writing 1880s–1930s*. St Leonards, NSW: Allen & Unwin, Sydney, 1995.
--. "*My Brilliant Career*: The Career of a Career". *Australian Literary Studies* 20, no. 4 (2002): 330–35.
Simons, Judy and Kate Fullbrook, eds. *Writing: A Woman's Business: Women, Writing and the Marketplace*. Manchester: Manchester University Press, 1998.
Sklar, Katherine Kish. *Florence Kelley and the Nation's Work*. New Haven, CT: Yale University Press, 1995.
Smith, A.A. "Organising Women Workers in America". *Vote*, 16 September 1911, 256–58.
Smith, Alys Pearsall. "A Reply from the Daughters, II". *Nineteenth Century* 35 (1894): 446–50.
Smith, Carl. *Chicago and the American Literary Imagination, 1880–1920*. Chicago: University of Chicago Press, 1984.
Smith, Susan Bradley. "Miles Franklin's Dramatic Ambitions, or, Why Stella Really Came Home". *Antipodes* (June 2007): 16–21.

Works Cited

Smith, Michelle J. "The 'Australian Girl' and the Domestic Ideal in Colonial Women's Fiction". In *Domestic Fiction in Colonial Australia and New Zealand*, edited by Tamara Wagner. London: Routledge, 2016.

Smith-Rosenberg, Carroll. *Disorderly Conduct: Visions of Gender in Victorian America*. New York: Oxford University Press, 1985.

Spence, Mary Lee. "They Also Serve Who Wait". *The Western Historical Quarterly* 14 (1983): 5–28

Stange, Margit. *Personal Property: Wives, White Slaves, and the Market in Women*. Baltimore: Johns Hopkins Press, 1998.

Stebner, Eleanor. *The Women of Hull House: A Study in Spirituality, Vocation, and Friendship*. Albany: State University of New York Press Press, 1997.

Stowell, Sheila. *A Stage of Their Own: Feminist Playwrights of the Suffrage Era*. Manchester: Manchester University Press, 1992.

––. "Rehabilitating Realism", *Journal of Dramatic Theory and Criticism* 6, no. 2 (1992): 81–88.

Summers, Ann. *Damned Whores and God's Police: The Colonization of Women in Australia*. London: Allen Lane, 1975.

Swiney, Frances. *The Mystery of the Circle and the Cross, or the Interpretation of Sex*. London: Open Road, 1908.

Sykes, Gillian E. "The New Woman in the New World: Fin de Siècle Writing and Feminism in Australia". PhD thesis, University of Sydney, 2002.

Tanner, Tony. *Adultery in the Novel: Contract and Transgression*. Baltimore, MD: Johns Hopkins Press, 1979.

Tasker, Meg. "Francis Adams: Realism and Sensation in the 1880s". *Australian Literary Studies* 30, no. 3 (2015), 79–95.

"Tell Suffering of the Strikers". *Chicago Daily Tribune*, 12 December 1910, 6.

Tisdale, Julie. "Venereal Disease and the Policing of the Amateur in Melbourne During World War I". *Lilith* 9 (1996): 35–50.

Tosh, John. *A Man's Place: Masculinity and the Middle-Class Home in Victorian England*. New Haven, CT: Yale University Press, 1995.

Tuchman, Gaye and Nina Fortin. *Edging Women Out: Victorian Novelists, Publishers, and Social Change*. New York: Routledge, 1989.

Vicinus, Martha. *The Industrial Muse: A Study of British Working-Class Literature*. London: Croon Helm, 1974.

––. *Independent Women: Work and Community for Single Women, 1850–1920*. Chicago: University of Chicago Press, 1985.

Wagner, Tamara S. *Domestic Fiction in Colonial Australia and New Zealand*. New York: Routledge, 2004.

Walls, Elizabeth McLeod. "'A Little Afraid of the Women of Today': The Victorian New Woman and the Rhetoric of British Modernism". *Rhetorical Review* 21, no. 3 (2002): 229–46.

Wandor, Michelene. "The Impact of Feminism on the Theatre". *Feminist Review* 18 (1984): 76–92.

Wang, Tricia. "The Elastic Self: Understanding Identity in Social Media". *Tricia Wang*, 26 January 2014. https://www.triciawang.com/updates/2014/1/26/new-talk-the-elastic-self-understanding-identity-in-social-m.html.

Ward, Lester. *Pure Sociology*. New York: Macmillan, 1903.

––. *Dynamic Sociology* [1883]. New York: Johnson, 1968.

Warhol, Robyn R. "Toward a Theory of the Engaging Narrator: Earnest Intervention in Gaskell, Stowe, and Eliot", *PMLA* 101 (1986): 811–18.

Warhol, Robyn R. *Gendered Interventions: Narrative Discourse in the Victorian Novel*. New Brunswick, NJ: Rutgers University Press, 1989.

Watkins, Susan Cotts. "Spinsters", *Journal of Family History* 9, no. 4 (1984): 310–25.

Webby, Elizabeth. "Miles Franklin Revealed in Her Letters", *Sydney Morning Herald* ("Spectrum" section), 2 October 1993, 11.

--. "Reading *My Brilliant Career*". *Australian Literary Studies* 20 (2002): 350–58.
--. "Introduction", *My Brilliant Career and My Career Goes Bung* [1901, 1946]. Sydney: Harper Collins, 2004.
Weiler, Sue N. "Walkout: The Chicago Men's Garment Workers' Strike, 1910–1911". *Chicago History* 8, no. 4 (1979): 238–49.
Welter, Barbara. "The Cult of True Womanhood, 1820–1960", *American Quarterly* 18, no. 2 (1966): 151–74.
White, Kevin. *The First Sexual Revolution: The Emergence of Male Heterosexuality in Modern America*. New York: New York University Press, 1993.
--. *Sexual Liberation or Sexual License? The American Revolt Against Victorianism*. Chicago: Ivan R. Dee, 2000.
Whitehead, Kay. "The Spinster Teacher in Australia from the 1870s to the 1960s", *History of Education Review* 36, no. 1 (2007): 1–17.
Willis, Chris. "'Heaven Defend Me from Political or Highly Educated Women!': Packaging the New Woman for Mass Consumption". In *The New Woman in Fiction and in Fact: Fin-de-Siècle Feminisms*, edited by Angelique Richardson and Chris Willis. New York, Palgrave, 2001. 53–65.
Women's Trade Union League (WTUL) of Chicago. "Official Report of the Strike Committee, Chicago Garment Workers' Strike, October 29, 1910–February 18, 1911". *History of Women*, no. 7161, microfilm. New Haven, CT: Research Publications, 1977 [1911].
Woolf, Virginia. *A Room of One's Own*. New York: Harcourt Brace Jovanovich, 1963 [1929].
--. *Collected Essays II*. London: Chatto & Windus, 1966 [1929].
Woollacott, Angela. *To Try Her Fortune in London: Australian Women, Colonialism, and Modernity*. Oxford: Oxford University Press, 2001.
Yeo, Eileen Janes, ed. *Radical Femininity: Women's Self-Representations in the Public Sphere*. Manchester: Manchester University Press, 1998.
Young, Marguerite. *Harp Song for a Radical: The Life and Times of Eugene Victor Debs*. New York: Alfred Knopf, 1999.
Youngkin, Molly. *Feminist Realism at the Fin de Siècle: The Influence of the Late-Victorian Woman's Press on the Development of the Novel*. Columbus: Ohio State University Press, 2007.

Index

Abbott, Edith 14
Abbott, Grace 14, 50
Addams, Jane 9, 127
   A New Conscience and an Ancient Evil 27, 128, 147
adultery 26, 28, 119–125, 133
agency 2, 35, 38, 42, 86, 93, 111, 124, 156
   sexual 6, 23, 28, 47, 83–86, 87, 93, 96, 97, 105, 126, 135, 137, 147
Allied Militant Suffragette Association 45
Anderson, Margaret 16
   Little Review 16
Anderson, Sherwood 15
Ardis, Ann 162, 164
Austen, Jane 75
"Australian Girl" 5–6
Australian women's movement 7, 68

Barnard, Marjorie 31, 151
Beer, Gillian 68
Bennett, Arnold 53, 165
Bennett, Tony 70
betrayal 138, 143
bildungsroman 86, 137, 139
Bird, Delys 11
Birns, Nicholas 12
Blackwood (publisher) 7, 24
Blackwoods Magazine 69
Book Lover (magazine) 9, 24, 71
Breckinridge, Sophonisba 14
Bridle, Edwin 8, 10
Brittain, Vera 167
Brooke, Emma
   A Superfluous Woman 95

Browne, Maurice *see* Little Theatre movement
Brunton, Paul 88
Bulletin, The (newspaper) 4, 102

Cambridge, Ada 5
   A Marked Man 153
   Sisters 68
capitalism 12, 15, 16, 38, 40
Catt, Carrie Chapman 8
Chicago Federation of Labor 59
Chicago Garment Workers' Strike 17, 21, 51, 53
Christie, Jane Johnston
   The Advance of Woman 67
class 20, 25, 38, 43, 61, 62, 75, 102, 139–140, 149
   inequality 4, 18, 35, 38, 41
   privilege 80, 140
   relations 15, 59, 149
   struggle 40
Coleman, Verna 35, 44, 70
colonialism 5, 8
compassion 80, 110
Cosmopolitan (magazine) 69
Couvreur, Jessie Catherine 5
   A Fiery Ideal 68
Cupid 24, 106, 107, 111–112, 114
Currey, Margery *see* Dell, Margery Currey
Cusack, Dymphna 11
   Come in Spinner 11

Daily Telegraph (newspaper) 8
Dark, Eleanor
   Timeless Land, The 11
Darwin, Charles 41–42
darwinism, social 35, 41–42

Dawn, The (magazine) 7, 69
Dell, Floyd 16, 28, 131, 164
Dell, Margery Currey 28, 69, 155, 164
Devanney, Jean 11
Dixon, Ella Hepworth 104
   One Doubtful Hour and Other Sidelights on the Feminine Temperament 69
Dixon, Robert 31
Doyle, Laura 162
Dreier, Mary 17, 60
Dreier Robins, Margaret *see* Robins, Margaret Dreier
Duncan, Roy 152
Dunne, Mary Chavelita
   Keynotes 69

education, women's access to 9, 19, 28, 61, 103, 109, 113
Egerton, George *see* Dunne, Mary Chavelita
Ellis, Edith Havelock 131
Ellis, Henry Havelock 130, 132
equality 16, 47, 83, 84, 153
  in marriage 7
  political 7, 153

Felski, Rita 161
femininity 6, 19, 20, 45, 79, 88, 93, 99, 104, 109, 113, 161
  performative 75, 89, 106
feminism 7, 8, 9, 71, 80, 85, 93, 123, 133, 155, 167; *see also* social purity feminism
  critique of policies 12, 141
  domestic 47, 76, 105, 160, 165, 167
  drama 2, 17, 29, 36, 47–48, 133
  protagonists 7, 23, 86, 92, 107, 133, 134, 142
  sentimentality 2, 6
  spinsters and 24, 115
Findlater, Mary and Jane
  Crossriggs 105
Ford, Ford Madox 121
Forster, E.M.
  Where Angels Fear to Tread 105
Franklin, Stella Miles
  as a feminist 2, 3, 4, 8–8, 15, 69, 89, 137, 151
  Brent of Bin Bin (pseudonym) 11, 156
  in London 11, 15, 29, 120
  Ogniblat L'Artsau, Mr and Mrs (pseudonym) 22, 29, 72, 120
  Vernacular (pseudonym) 8
Franklin, Stella Miles (works)

A Business Emergency 22, 29, 72, 73, 76–78, 119–125, 134
All That Swagger 11
Back to Bool Bool 11
Bring the Monkey 11
Cockatoos 1, 7, 11
Gentlemen at Gyang Gyang 11
Illogical Sex, The 21, 67, 80
Mrs Mulvaney's Moccasins 21, 67, 71, 73, 75, 79, 163
My Brilliant Career 1–6, 15, 25, 30, 68, 70, 83, 91–93, 141, 153
Net of Circumstance, The 30, 157–161, 164
Old Blastus of Bandicoot 11
On Dearborn Street 23, 83–87, 91, 92, 94, 97, 98, 101, 106, 152, 163
Pioneers on Parade 11
Prelude to Waking 11
Red Cross Nurse and Armored Chauffeur 29, 137–139, 141, 147, 150, 163
Sam Price from Chicago 11, 126
Some Everyday Folk and Dawn 7, 68
Survivors, The 16, 35, 37–38, 40, 45–46, 48, 163
Teaching Him 21, 67, 71, 73–75, 77
Ten Creeks Run 11
Uncle Robert's Wedding Present 24, 101, 106, 110, 114
Up the Country 11
Waiter Speaks, The 53–54, 56, 59–63
When Bobby 'Got' Religion 23, 92
When Cupid Tarried 24, 101, 106, 109, 111, 114

Garity, Geraldine 45
garment workers 49–55, 58, 59, 61, 63; *see also* Chicago Garment Workers' Strike
Garton, Stephen 2, 83, 141, 149, 159
Gaunt, Mary 5
gender 5, 16, 19, 87, 93, 130, 134, 163
  justice 16, 18, 101, 162, 167
  literary representations of 5
  politics 4, 25, 89, 137, 146, 161
  poverty and 17, 35
  relations 13, 35, 67, 81, 153, 160
  roles 19, 30, 45, 78, 80, 86, 135
Gilbert, Sandra 158
Gilman, Charlotte Perkins 14, 42, 69, 73–74, 110, 122
  The Home: Its Work and Influence 73, 122
  Women and Economics 69

Index

Gissing, George 165
Goldman, Emma 14
Goldstein, Vida 7
Goulburn Evening Penny Post 4
Grand, Sarah 19, 21
  Emotional Moments 69
Gubar, Susan 158

Hamilton, Cicely 67, 76, 98
  Marriage as a Trade 67
Hanson, Clare 70
Hardy, Thomas
  Jude the Obscure 96
Heffernan, Laura 164
Henry, Alice 9, 17, 58
Hipsky, Martin 162
Holdsworth, Annie E.
  A Garden of Spinsters 105
Holland, Kathryn 162
Holmes, Katie 103
housekeeping trade 67, 78, 108
Hull House 9, 13, 16, 36, 53

Immigrants' Protective League 14
independent women 20, 24, 24, 77–80, 103, 153–154
  and paid work 113
  economics and 67, 68, 68, 78, 120
  eschewing marriage 101, 103
  feminist journey towards 6, 24
  protagonists 73, 75, 84, 86, 159
Industrial Workers of the World 40, 61
infidelity *see* adultery

James, Henry
  The Golden Bowl 121
Jeffreys, Sheila 103, 132
journalism 7, 14, 18, 51–53, 55, 57

Kennedy, Charles Rann 123
Kirkpatrick, Peter 130
Kranidis, Rita 162, 165

Ladies Home Journal, The 113
Lang, Anouk 3, 162
Lawson, Henry 5
Lawson, Louisa 7, 22, 68
Ledger, Sally 89
Liggins, Emma 95
Little Theatre movement 16, 16, 53

Lloyd, Demarest 10, 23, 29, 88, 90, 91, 98, 141, 143
Lloyd, Henry Demarest 9, 52
Lloyd, William (Bill) Bross 9, 10, 29, 89, 98, 121, 129
Lothian (publisher) 24
Laughter, Not for a Cage 3, 11

Magarey, Susan 2, 6
Maloney, Elizabeth 14, 18
Mann Act (1910) 127, 147
marriage 13, 19–26, 67–69, 72–73, 75–78, 80–81, 103–106, 122, 130, 159–160
  as a transaction 68, 71, 75, 112, 124
  critique of 6, 21, 22, 67, 68, 72, 113, 133
  economics of 67, 68, 71, 76, 80, 124
  in literature 20
  love and 105, 106, 114, 139
  politics of 108
  reform 24, 71, 73, 77
  rejection of 19, 77, 80, 94, 101, 112, 115, 153
  trapped in a 28, 102
masculinity 13, 140, 141, 144, 150
  changing nature of 26, 134
  failure of 25, 150
  toxic 137, 141
Mayor, F.M.
  Third Miss Symons, The 105
McDowell, Mary 14
Meredith, George 165
Michaelis, Karin
  The Dangerous Age 94
militarism 94, 139, 146, 150
Miller, Jane Eldridge 3, 104, 108, 162
modernism 3, 15, 162
modernity 3–5, 15, 19, 36, 106, 107, 140, 153–154, 163
  U.S. modernity 3, 15, 26, 140, 157
Mudie, Ian 11

National Women's Trade Union League 1, 9–17, 30, 38, 39, 39, 43; *see also* Women's Trade Union League (WTUL)
  Life and Labor (magazine) 1, 10, 17–18, 43, 51–53, 72
nationalism 3–6, 11
Nestor, Agnes 14
'New Man' 13, 23–26, 47, 85, 88, 99, 142–144, 159

'New Woman' 1–7, 16–26, 30, 35, 37, 45, 52, 69, 71, 72, 75–77, 81, 83–89, 95, 101, 104–106, 119, 148, 153–154, 160–162, 165

Olubas, Brigitta 157
O'Reilly, Leonora 14
O'Sullivan, Mary Kenney 14

Peiss, Kathy 128
Pfisterer, Susan 8, 36, 38, 152, 154
picket lines 14, 57, 59
Pickett, Carolyn 8, 36, 38, 152, 154
Pischel, Emma 10
Pischel, Fred 22, 23, 90, 143
Praed, Rosa Campbell 5, 68
   An Australian Heroine 5
   The Bond of Wedlock 68
Prichard, Katharine Susannah
   Coonardoo 11
protest 61–63
protest play 16, 35, 38, 46, 47–48, 53, 126
Pykett, Lyn 30, 53, 135, 162

race 26–27, 102
Robins, Elizabeth 53
Robins, Margaret Dreier 10, 16, 21, 24, 50, 59–61
Roe, Jill 15–16, 18, 28, 30, 36, 52, 83–84, 95, 114, 131, 143, 152, 153, 155

Sandburg, Carl 15
Schaffer, Talia 161
Schmidt-Haberkamp, Barbara 156
Schneiderman, Rose 14
Scott, Rose 7–8, 22, 69, 95, 158
sexism 4, 26, 46, 89, 134
sexual agency *see* agency
sexuality 68, 89, 93, 96
Shaw, Anna Howard 74
Shaw, George Bernard 105
Shepherd-Barr, Kirsten 113
Smith, Alys Pearsall 84
Smith, Henry Justin 52
Smith, Susan Bradley 152
social darwinism *see* darwinism, social
social purity feminism 23, 26, 26, 28, 85, 96, 112, 119, 120, 130, 135, 145, 153; *see also* feminism

Spence, Catherine Helen 20
   Clara Morison 5
Spencer, Herbert 41–43
Stead, Christina 12, 153
strikes 13–15, 17, 21, 49–51, 54–60, 63
suffrage 7–8, 13, 21, 28, 35, 59, 61, 107, 115, 120
   campaigns 108, 111, 120
   drama 53
   suffragettes 45, 80
Swiney, Frances 120
Sydney Morning Herald 8, 21

Tasma *see* Couvreur, Jessie Catherine
Thurston, Katherine Cecil 96
transnationalism 3, 8, 12, 72, 123, 154–155
Turner, Ethel
   Seven Little Australians 5

Union Labor Advocate 14
University of Chicago 14, 39
urbanism 13, 15, 19–21, 25, 35, 38, 127, 153

Victorian literature 2, 3, 45, 107, 161
Victorian society 5, 46, 81, 130, 161–162
Vote, The (magazine) 7, 55, 59

Walls, Elizabeth McLeod 76, 165
Wang, Tricia 156
Webby, Elizabeth 12, 31
Wells, H.G. 165
   Ann Veronica 71
   Time Machine, The 106
Whelan, Carrie 8
white slavery 29, 127, 137, 147–150
Willis, Chris 71
Winkiel, Laura 162
Woman's Voice (magazine) 7
Women Writers' Suffrage League 67
Women's International League for Peace and Freedom 14
Women's Political Education League 7
Women's Trade Union League (WTUL) 17, 17, 18, 50, 50, 58–61; *see also* National Women's Trade Union League
World War I 11, 94, 102, 137

Yellow Book 69

www.ingramcontent.com/pod-product-compliance
Lightning Source LLC
Chambersburg PA
CBHW081826230426
43668CB00017B/2390